STARPOWER!

From all sides the mob surged forward en masse and pandemonium broke loose. People began shoving and pushing to reach Lana. At one point, a woman reached out and grabbed one of Lana's pearl and diamond earrings, Lana yelping in pain as the fan tried to pull it from her pierced ear.

Their progress measured in inches, the police managed to get Lana to the limousine and were about to shut the door when she yelled, "Wait! Where's Taylor?"

I could hear her, but that's all I could do. I was still several paces away, trying vainly to push my way through the surging humanity. I called out to her, and the policeman who had come to the dressing room turned in my direction, reached through the crush of people and grabbed the lapel of my tuxedo. With one strong movement, the officer pulled me through the jungle and forced me unceremoniously onto the floor of the limousine. I didn't mind; when I heard the door slam I knew I was safe.

A motorcycle _____ _____ _____ _____ nied the car as it c _____ _____ _____ nore fanatic memb _____ _____ the windows and _____ _____ had not had this much _____ _____ e, and actually enjoyed being mobbed in won _____ devoted New York City. For me, it was a frightening experience, one I'll never forget. But, as I'd learned, being Lana Turner's personal manager, confidant, and lover, it was just one of the hazards of the job.

escort, sirens blasting, accompan...
swept through the crowd, whose pres...
cars had their noses pressed to...
were calling Lana's name. Lan...
a substitution for quite some consid...
...red attempt of...

ALWAYS, LANA

**Taylor Pero
and
Jeff Rovin**

BANTAM BOOKS
TORONTO · NEW YORK · LONDON · SYDNEY

PUBLISHER'S NOTE

Lana Turner is one of Hollywood's legends, who, despite her seven notorious marriages and widely publicized romances with many of the movies' leading men, has recently avoided the public eye. Little has been written about her.

Taylor Pero was Miss Turner's private secretary and personal manager for ten years. He worked with her, travelled with her, partied with her, and he loved her. This book is not a Lana Turner biography. This is Taylor Pero's own story of his life with Lana Turner—the fascinating, often exasperating, but always lovely woman as he knew her.

ALWAYS, LANA
A Bantam Book / November 1982

ISBN 0-553-20805-5

Published simultaneously in the United States and Canada

Bantam Books are published by Bantam Books, Inc. Its trademark, consisting of the words "Bantam Books" and the portrayal of a rooster, is Registered in U.S. Patent and Trademark Office and in other countries. Marca Registrada. Bantam Books, Inc., 666 Fifth Avenue, New York, New York 10103.

Throughout the long and arduous times that it has taken to bring this book into reality, there has been one person—above all others—who gave the support, confidence and reassurance so necessary to me. He has guided me through a confusing maze of technicalities; always with unerring good judgment and unflappable sense of humor. His contributions have been enormous. I am pleased to dedicate this book to Alan Feldstein, my friend and manager......
and to his wife, Lisa, who introduced us in the first place.

ALWAYS, LANA

"No matter who you're with or what you're doing, the audience is looking at you. That's star quality."

Kirk Douglas in *The Bad and the Beautiful*

"Lana is one of our truly lovely ladies and is even starting to become a cult. But she hasn't got a job. Everybody wants an autographed picture. But where's the part...where's the play...where's the something for her?"

Debbie Reynolds in a recent interview

Prologue

There was simmering fury in the air.

For over an hour, director Vincente Minnelli had been bustling about, attending to countless little adjustments on the prop automobile he would be using to shoot the last scene needed to complete *The Bad and the Beautiful*. During that long hour of niggling preparation, Minnelli kept turning to his star and muttering, "Just one more minute, Lana." With rising impatience, the reigning queen of MGM stood to one side, trying not to scream at him or at anyone else even remotely connected with this indignity.

Though *The Bad and the Beautiful* would go on to win five Oscars and earn a fistful of money, neither the director nor the legendary Lana Turner was thinking beyond this final shot.

Lana was annoyed, first and foremost, because she'd had to interrupt a long-anticipated vacation in Mexico to do this one lousy shot—and for a film she thought she had finished three months before. It hadn't been easy rounding up Helen Young, her hairdresser, or Del Armstrong, her makeup man, both of whom had other commitments. It proved equally difficult to recreate exactly the face and hairdo she had worn months before.

Now, apart from the inconvenience, Minnelli was keeping her waiting. Since she had expected to be called at any moment, Lana hadn't bothered to return to the comfort of her bungalow or to her sumptuous dressing room—a portable apartment that was moved from stage to stage and, behind its fence, comprised a half acre of private terrain. Though Lana's feet hurt, she couldn't even sit down for fear of wrinkling her freshly pressed white evening gown.

Yet, surpassing the delay and her physical discomfort was the fact that Minnelli hadn't even bothered to discuss the scene with her! He seemed more concerned with the car, a preoccupation that angered Lana, distracting her from the few facts she'd been told about the scene: that it followed the one in which her character, having been rejected by Kirk Douglas, ran crying from his Beverly Hills mansion, threw herself into her car, and drove away. Lana couldn't understand why they were extending the scene at all, for she knew it played well as it was. But Minnelli wasn't satisfied, and now she was supposed to do *something*—though the director hadn't told her *what!*

Finally, Minnelli deigned to walk over to Lana. His thick lips constantly puckered as his mind whirled. "Lana," he said at last, "I think we can shoot it now."

The actress looked as though she would slap him. "Shoot *what?* What do you want me to *do?*"

Minnelli looked at Lana for a long moment, pursing and unpursing his lips. "Well, my dear . . . I'm not quite sure. Why don't you just get in the car and let's see what happens."

Lana simply couldn't believe what she'd heard. Vincente Minnelli, one of the movie industry's most esteemed directors, was asking her to play a scene with no direction. It was unheard of, and not only was Lana angry, she felt betrayed. Minnelli knew that she was an actress who relied heavily on her directors, and she was hurt by this careless, unsympathetic brush-off. She could feel that hurt rising within her as she walked numbly to the automobile mock-up that had been specially built for this scene.

The set was designed in such a way that crew members stationed at either corner of a raised platform could tilt and rock the car in any direction Lana might turn the steering wheel. As it was supposed to be a rainy night, another crew member was stationed with a hose in front of the windshield. This man was right in Lana's line of vision, which made concentration all the more difficult.

Minnelli positioned himself in his director's chair, just to the right of the camera. He leaned forward, studying Lana. "Now dear . . . just let us know when you're ready."

Lana took a deep breath, trying to calm herself. She

closed her eyes for a moment as she sought to recapture the emotion she had felt playing actress Georgia Lorrison, who had been betrayed by her conniving producer-lover. Lana thought to herself, *All right, Herr Director. You want a scene, I'll give you a scene!*

Nodding silently, Lana indicated to Minnelli that she was ready. Everyone on the Culver City sound stage froze in their tracks, even before the assistant director called for quiet on the set. Vincente Minnelli puckered his lips one last time, then softly said, "Action."

Drawing upon the pain and frustration that Minnelli had whipped up inside her, Lana pretended to gun the automobile at reckless speeds through the stormy night. She began to weep, and as the tension within her was released, the sobs built to the verge of hysteria. Water cascaded over the windows, and the automobile was turned, tilted, and rocked as Lana spun the wheel. At one point she reacted frantically when the special effects man used lights to create the impression that an oncoming vehicle, horn blaring, had narrowly missed hitting her. Lana allowed her emotions to build even higher until she emitted a full-voiced scream, throwing her head back and draping her arms over the steering wheel. She remained in that position for a long time, wracked by unrelenting, heart-wrenching sobs, her head down, her blond hair falling in her face, the stream of tears ruining her meticulously made-up face.

After an unusually long silence, the crew applauded. Vincente Minnelli smiled. "Cut," he said softly. "Print that . . . that's a wrap."

An hour of unwitting preparation, and in just one take Lana Turner had played the most memorable scene of her career, indeed one of the most stunning and disquieting sequences in film history. There are few other actresses who could have done as well playing an emotionally taut movie queen.

Twenty-three years later, an eager audience of over two thousand people was jammed to the rafters in New York City's Town Hall theatre. It was Sunday night, April 13, 1975, and they had come for a one-night-only retrospective of Lana Turner's film career billed as "A Tribute to Lana Turner, In Person and on the Screen." After nearly two hours of film clips, the famous car sequence was screened. Lana's sobs echoed through the packed hall, and following the spine-tingling automobile scene, the giant movie screen went blank. The audience exploded into generous applause for the classic excerpts they had just seen.

The stage was empty now, save for a spotlight focused on its rear left corner. The applause had begun to wane after a minute when a delicate female hand with perfectly mani-cured pink nails appeared and then dramatically swept the heavy curtain aside. Lana Turner stepped into the spotlight, and in unison, the audience rose to give her a standing ovation.

Lana stood for a moment, bathed in that stark spotlight, drinking in the waves of love and affection pouring onto the stage. The cheers, the shouts, the whistles, the clapping, the sheer adulation went on as though it would never stop. Lana stood before them as if she were a goddess, wearing an outfit designed just for the occasion, a floor-length white satin gown that accentuated her still-perfect figure. Over the gown she wore a matching white satin jacket with long, loose sleeves made of beige chiffon and heavily beaded with crystals. Her earrings were matching pearls, each hanging from a slender length of diamonds, and on her left hand she wore a magnifi-cent, thirty-five carat marquise diamond. No movie star ever looked more glamorous. Few could.

Lana walked closer to her audience, almost overcome with the joy she was feeling; it was difficult to believe that only hours earlier she had asked me, "Do you really think anybody will show up?"

She had her answer.

Lana had not disappointed her audience, that was the half of it. There she was, looking just as stunning in person as she had on the big screen. She hadn't grown old and fat like so many of her contemporaries, and many who saw her would no doubt wonder how it was possible. The answer, simply put, is that for Lana Turner, the options were unthinkable.

After the lengthy adoration died down and the countless photographers who always doted over Lana had retired, Lana sat gracefully in one of the two thick-cushioned, white rococo chairs that occupied center stage. In the other sat noted publicist John Springer, who conducted an interview that spanned four decades of his guest's dazzling career. Never given to impromptu speaking, Lana admitted being nervous, though she soon had the crowd laughing and applauding her natural wit and sense of humor. ("To this day," she said innocently, "I don't know who created that title, 'The Sweater Girl.' I had never been accustomed to any parts of my anatomy being so important. I finally got rid of mine . . . I mean the title.")

The interview, originally scheduled to run forty-five minutes, lasted twice that long, due to the number of questions. As it finally drew to a close, I made my way backstage to the lounge that was Lana's dressing room for the evening. I had been with her long enough to know that she would want a drink immediately, so I fixed her a vodka and tonic. A few minutes later she entered the stark, yellow room, radiant and glowing, escorted by John and two uniformed policemen. The officers advised us to get her out of the theater as quickly as possible, due to the throng of celebrity seekers gathering outside the theater to get an even closer look at the living embodiment of all that is glorious and anathema in Hollywood.

John had a few quick words of congratulations for Lana, then he left us alone so that I could help her into an ensemble she had brought to wear to the private party being given in her honor by John Bowab, the director of two of her recent stage plays.

Never willing to leave before she is absolutely ready, Lana took time to freshen her makeup while she enjoyed her drink. All the while, New York's finest were holding a restless mob at bay just outside the stage door. Beyond the exit was a long alleyway through which we would have to pass to reach our limousine, which itself was already surrounded by several dozen people.

Eventually, one of the policemen came around to tell us that if we didn't leave right away, they would have to let some of the officers go on to assignments in other parts of the city. Lana took one last sip, slipped into her white mink coat, and was escorted to the car by a phalanx of six policemen, who formed a flying wedge around her for protection. I found myself trailing behind, unable to keep up with the group due to stragglers who broke through the ranks and pushed me back as they tried to reach Lana. Finally, from all sides the mob surged forward and pandemonium broke loose. People began shoving and pushing to reach Lana and, in so doing, pushed me even further from her side. At one point a woman reached out and grabbed one of Lana's pearl and diamond earrings. Lana yelped in pain as the fan tried to pull it from her pierced ear.

Their progress measured in inches, the police managed to get Lana to the limousine and were about to shut the door when she yelled, "Wait! Where's Taylor?"

I could hear her, but that's all I could do. I was still several paces away, trying vainly to push my way through the surging crowd. I called out to her, and the policeman who had come to the dressing room turned in my direction. Recognizing who I was, he reached through the crush of people and grabbed the lapel of my tuxedo. With one strong movement, the officer pulled me through the jungle of arms and torsos and forced me unceremoniously onto the floor of the limousine. I didn't mind; when I heard the door slam, I knew I was safe.

A motorcycle escort, sirens blasting, accompanied the car as it crept through the crowd, whose more fanatic members were staring in the windows and calling Lana's name. Lana had not received this much attention for quite some time, and she actually enjoyed being mobbed in wonderful, devoted New York City. For me, it was a frightening experience, one I'll never forget. But as I'd learned being Lana Turner's personal manager, confidant, and lover, it was just one of the hazards of the job.

I first met Lana in 1969. I had been at a cocktail party where I was introduced to Jack Freeman, who was Lana's makeup man. The hazy nature of these parties is such that, without realizing it, I'd been introduced to Jack several times before. This time we stopped to chat.

During the course of conversation, I mentioned that I'd just spent three-and-a-half years touring the world with Johnny Mathis, as a singer-dancer in his small backup group called Our Young Generation. I'd also handled Johnny's public relations while we were on the road, writing press releases about his activities and sending them back for distribution to his Sunset Boulevard offices.

Jack mentioned that, oddly enough, Lana happened to be looking for someone with public relations experience and a knowledge of the entertainment industry. She had a young man who was presently employed as her secretary, but he wasn't working out. He had flubbed a few minor assignments, then muddled a big one by failing to tell Lana that she was expected to work one day on her soon-to-debut television series "The Survivors." When the phone rang at nine o'clock in the morning, the assistant director wanted to know where she was. Lana replied that she was not working that day, whereupon she was informed that, to the contrary, they were all waiting for her on the set.

Embarrassed to the extreme, Lana sprang from bed. She put in a call for the limousine and was driven to the Universal Studio lot, where she was ready for filming after the lunch break. By day's end she was actively looking for someone to replace her secretary. She disliked firing anyone, preferring to stick with someone who was imperfect but familiar. But this person had screwed up grievously.

Though Jack wasn't empowered to act as Lana's solicitor, he very seriously broached the subject of my going to work for her. I responded by laughing. Not only had I resolved to rest for about a decade after the grueling tours I'd put in with Johnny Mathis, but the thought of working for a legend seemed unreal. I'd been introduced to dozens of celebrities through Johnny, from Princess Grace to the king and queen of Thailand, from Ed Sullivan to Shirley Bassey. I was awed and impressed by most of them, but at the same time content just to *meet* them, not to know them as *intimates*. I've never been big on clay feet, and part of the fascination we *all* hold for celebrities is their mystique. To see someone every day, as I had Johnny, I had had to labor hard to reinforce that mystique rather than to enjoy it. Besides, I wanted to establish a career of my own. The reason I had left Johnny's troupe was to become a singer on my own. I had recently cut a record that earned very little money but promising reviews; if I lost even that minimal momentum, it would be difficult to recover. Add to this, a broken marriage and a teenage daughter.

Then there was this matter of my prospective boss. She was beautiful, an observation that didn't exactly put me in the genius class, and she had made a fair share of classic films, including *The Postman Always Rings Twice* and *Madame X*. I had heard many things about Lana Turner. The very mention of her name conjured up all kinds of recollections, from her legendary discovery at a malt shop to the scandal of a lover being murdered in her home.

I didn't want to work for Lana Turner, that was for sure. However, here was an opportunity to meet a notoriously famous lady. Since one doesn't get an invitation like that every day, I told Jack to try and arrange an interview. If nothing else, it would be a great story to tell at parties.

More than a week passed before Lana found time in her busy agenda to see me. I was in my little apartment in Studio City, watching "The Mike Douglas Show," on which the film critic Rex Reed was a guest. I almost fell off the sofa when Reed began discussing his latest assignment, the fulfillment of a lifelong dream: he was flying from Philadelphia to Hollywood to interview his all-time favorite movie star, Lana Turner. Mike Douglas seemed impressed, as was the audience, and I must confess feeling a wave of self-importance. There were these noted personalities talking about Lana Turner, and here *I* was waiting for a call to come and meet her. I knew then that my singing career was going into hibernation.

Jack called later that day and said that Lana would be home over the weekend, would I drop by on Sunday afternoon? I dutifully recorded her address and kept myself humble by reflecting that none of the cocktail parties I attended was ever in so swanky a location as the peak of Mulholland Drive.

Naturally, I was quite nervous when Sunday arrived. I wanted to make a good impression, not just for the sake of the job but for sheer vanity. It was August, and, although Los Angeles was suffering a heat wave, I put on a tie and sport jacket—after first buffing up my modest Ford convertible. I didn't want to chance someone looking out a window and seeing a filthy car pulling up to the house.

At the time Lana was living on a summit just off the intersection of Mulholland and Coldwater Canyon. Charlton Heston was a neighbor, living atop another hill in a sprawling complex decorated with artifacts from his epic films *Ben-Hur* and *El Cid*. On a quiet day you could actually hear the soundtrack from *Ben-Hur* riding the still air. As Heston once said, "If you made as much money from that film as I did, you'd damn well want to be reminded of it, too." As I drove up tortuous Coldwater Canyon from the valley side—envying those who had to approach the summit from Beverly Hills—I began wondering not only what Miss Turner would be like but what the *house* would be like. I arrived at a formidable house spread all over the hillside. However, I couldn't tell anything else about it since there wasn't a single window. So much for my clean car. I pulled up beside a new, black Cadillac Eldorado parked in the spacious carport and looking very impressive indeed. A small fountain gurgled into a shallow fish pond to the left of the driveway, set well back from the street between slender white marble columns that supported the overhanging roof of the house.

Trying to be nonchalant and charming as I rang the doorbell, I probably looked more like Woody Allen than Cary Grant. I heard the bell chime deep within the house, and after what seemed hours, the white door was opened by a tall, athletic-looking man. He was dressed in white tennis shorts, a white tennis shirt, a white sun hat, and very dark glasses. I later learned that he didn't play tennis. But he did have a very sonorous speaking voice, and I knew this must be Lana's husband, Ronald Dante, a man Jack had told me little about, though Dante, like his wife, was a frequent subject of cocktail-party tattle.

The six-foot, three-inch man in white introduced himself as "Doctor" Dante, though he was neither a physician nor a Ph.D., just as he wasn't a tennis player—or even a good husband as I quickly discovered. However, "doctor" was what he wanted, so Dr. Dante it was. His actual profession was nightclub magician and hypnotist, and although I never saw him perform, Lana admitted to me long after their marriage breakup that his act *was* good.

Dr. Dante grasped my shoulder and ushered me through a white marble foyer into what was one of the largest living rooms I'd ever seen. In fact, it was second only to the living room in the Topanga Canyon home of producer-actor John Houseman; that one was a full half acre with a built-in swimming pool. The walls of Lana's home were white and covered with dozens of oil paintings done primarily in reds, oranges, and greens. The carpeting was white shag beneath an array of handsome sofas, a bumper-pool table in the bar area, and, at a remote end of the room, a white, baby-grand piano on which a silver-framed photograph of the Lady of the

House was prominently displayed. Beyond it hung the framed
document issued by the Academy of Motion Picture Arts and
Sciences citing Miss Turner for her Best Actress of the Year
nomination as Constance MacKenzie in *Peyton Place*. There
was a fireplace faced in white marble and, in contrast to the
blank street-side of the house, the inside consisted of floor-to-
ceiling windows that looked out on the canyon below and
across the pool and rows of cypress trees, an arboreal regi-
ment that surrounded the hilltop and guarded the privacy of
its occupants. Altogether it was a stunning place, though far
from overpowering, due to the good taste of its appointments.

Dr. Dante was making small inquiries about my background as we stood near an open sliding-glass door that led
directly to the pool. We had been talking for a very short
time when I heard a faint brush of bare feet on the carpet, the
stirring of fabric. I turned and saw Lana approaching, her
right hand extended in a gesture of welcome.

I remember that moment clearly, perhaps more so than
any other in our decade-long relationship. I was struck, at
once, by how tiny she was. When you're accustomed to
seeing someone forty feet tall on the screen, you expect that
they will at least be taller than you are in real life. However,
her size did nothing to diminish the breathtaking *presence* of
the woman.

The hot August breeze was blowing toward her, rustling
her sleeveless, floor-length muumuu, which was colored in
delicate shades of blue and violet. She wore very little
makeup, just lipstick and some eyebrow pencil, and her smile
was wide and sensuous. She came forward, and because of
her graceful carriage and the way her extended hand hovered
lightly before her, she seemed to reach me a few paces before
she did, as if to touch me and reassure me. There was
nothing to fear. We were just two human beings who were
going to sit down and talk.

Sure.

Near the open glass door was a white table with four
large, leather-cushioned chairs. After we had exchanged the
usual hellos and nice-to-meet-yous, my hostess indicated that
we should sit. Lana asked more than once if I wouldn't be
more comfortable taking off my jacket and loosening my tie,
but I deferred. Both garments were helping to hold me

together. She sat directly across from me, and the light reflected by the pool revealed one of the most beautiful complexions I have ever seen. Lana was pale but healthy looking, and there was something about her skin that made you want to reach out and touch it. It was a tactile rather than erotic allure; I can only describe it as having the attraction of a fresh rose petal.

I was offered something to drink, though I declined. Lana had a glass of juice, though subsequent experience taught me that she rarely drank *anything* that wasn't laced with alcohol. The portrait that first day was still utterly idealized.

It's interesting to note that Dr. Dante stayed with us for the duration of my visit. None of the questions had to do with his work or private life, and his questions were for the most part irrelevant. Even more distracting was that he refused to take off those dark sunglasses. It's terribly difficult to be charming when you look someone in the eyes to answer a question and all you can see is your own reflection.

The interview lasted two and one-half hours, a pleasant enough chat in which Lana asked about my experience and, in general terms, about my personal habits, then explained in detail what the job entailed. As our talk drew to a close, Lana said she would call me one way or the other within a few days. In response, I was surprised to find myself saying that I would very much *like* to work for her. She was a seductive, gracious, charming lady, very much in command but quite feminine and almost childlike in her enjoyment of our far-reaching conversation. A salary was briefly discussed, and although it was not as much as I had been making with Johnny Mathis, I found myself really *wanting* to be hired. By this time it was more than ego; it was a vague but very real desire to be around this woman. After determining that my evenings and weekends would be my own, leaving me free to sing at whatever clubs or fairs would have me, I was convinced that the job really *did* seem ideal. But I was naive in other ways as well.

As I rose to leave, Lana asked me something I found rather peculiar. Clapping her hands once, she said, "OK, now for the *big* question."

I thought she was going to ask which of her movies was

my favorite. I had seen about half of them and was going to answer, diplomatically, that I was equally fond of *The Bad and the Beautiful* and *Peyton Place*.

"Tell me," she urged, "when is your birthday?"

I stared at her for a moment, disarmed by the girlish question. "February ninth," I answered.

Lana threw back her head and trembled with laughter. "I knew it! Mine is February eighth, and my mother's is February twelfth." My blank stare compelled her to add, "We're all Aquarians!" So we were. Apart from our astrological compatibility, that fact enabled us all to conveniently steep together in hot water.

Lana subsequently told me that she had never bothered to interview anyone else for the job. She had made up her mind then and there that I was the person for her. I was honored but not surprised, the interview having been the most relaxed of my life. It was certainly more pleasant than when I auditioned for Johnny Mathis; then I had to belt out "There Is Nothin' Like a Dame" while I was wearing a suit and tie, staring at myself in a mirror that hung behind Mathis in his office.

The instant I reached my apartment, I called Jack. Before he could ask me how the meeting had gone, I blurted out a question that had been troubling me for hours. "Just tell me, Jack. Who makes the decisions in that household, Lana or Dr. Dante?"

Without hesitation Jack replied, "Lana does."

"Good," I said, sighing, "because I like her a lot, and I think she liked me. But I got very bad vibes from her husband."

—"Don't worry about him," Jack assured me. "Lana runs her own career, and the truth is no one does that sort of thing better. That's one reason why she's still working while Hayworth, Lamarr, and all the others who were big in the forties aren't."

I thanked Jack again, and he said he hoped he'd be seeing me soon in a professional capacity.

Lana wasn't able to call for several days. When she did, it was in the evening, and I was out. A friend of mine who was visiting Los Angeles took the call. It practically did him in. I got in quite late that night, but my guest shot right up from a dead sleep and gushed, in one breathless sentence,

"Lana Turner called right here on *this* phone, and I talked to her, and she wants you to come to *work* for her, for Pete's sake, and she was real nice and started to choke on something while we were talking, so I told her to get a glass of water and—and my God, Taylor, you've got the job!"

I called Lana the following day, and she was once again very sweet. "Well," she asked, "have you given some thought about coming to work for me?" My answer was affirmative. "Fine," she replied. "Let's start on Monday. Just come to the main gate at Universal Studios, and I'll have left word with the guard that you are expected. He'll direct you to my dressing room and show you where to park."

I knew, then, that I wasn't the most worldly guy in Southern California. The job would hold a few surprises, I suspected. But I'd been in and around the entertainment industry long enough to have picked up a core of knowledge and a veneer of sophistication. What I didn't know, I knew I could bluff until I got a handle on it.

Looking back, I'm astounded how badly I'd misjudged what I didn't know, not about the business but about people. I was about to go through the looking glass into sick, joyous, twisted, wealthy, lying, exploitative Wonderland—a world very few people have ever seen firsthand and, frankly, wouldn't want to for very long. Little did I know that this seemingly superficial job would envelop my life and soul over the next ten years. If I could go back in time, I might have done a number of things instead of becoming an emotionally burned-out man of thirty-seven scrabbling about to rediscover his own identity.

Yes, there would be first-class trips to Europe, lavish Hollywood parties and gala events, limousines, celebrities, feasts, and caviar. There would also be tragedy and responsibilities almost beyond comprehension. I handled it all by developing a passion for scotch—which, toward the end, was something I couldn't live without to blot out the madness of what was going on around me.

Taylor Pero was about to take a ten-year trip in limbo. He ceased to exist as a sentient, independent creature. Henceforth, when he was awake and when he slept, when he was with people or alone, his life was, always, Lana.

Chapter One

It was either very late at night or very early in the morning when Lana and I got into one of our "drink-talk" sessions. It was not unusual at such times, when exhaustion and liquor made our inhibitions crumble, for us to confess various things that we had done of a sexual nature.

As always when we got into one of these marathons, we were at Lana's bar. She inevitably sat on one of the upholstered barstools while I sat behind the bar and continually replenished our drinks. Somehow the subject of virginity came up, and Lana went on to reveal who, as she put it, "got my cherry." I was surprised to learn that sex goddess Lana Turner was well into her teens before she gave herself to a man, and only then with one whom she felt sure she was in love. Her name had already been linked with his in the Hollywood gossip tabloids, and when not enhancing his reputation as a ladies' man, Gregson Bautzer was an up-and-coming Hollywood attorney to boot. Today, in his early sixties, he is still well-known in both capacities.

Lana's love for Bautzer was deeply felt, to say the least. There were, no doubt, a staggering number of young men around Lana who fantasized about bedding this young girl, a girl who even by Hollywood's standards was one of nature's finest creations. Only the strong hold that Lana's mother then had upon her kept that from happening.

Mildred Turner not only wasn't a "Hollywood mother" in the sense of pushing her daughter into the spotlight or into the bed of some influential producer, but for as long as she was able, she struggled to keep Lana's values sane and earthbound. Not that Lana hadn't had one harsh dose of reality after another; not that it wasn't, in fact, her miserable childhood that drove her toward hedonism as an adult.

Julia Jean "Judy" Turner was born in 1921 in Wallace, Idaho, the only child of Virgil and Mildred Turner. Virgil was a hearty, good-natured man who had been employed as an insurance salesman, miner, and bootlegger among other professions. He was also an avid gambler. Forced by hard times to move his family frequently in search of work, Virgil finally settled them in San Francisco. There, he found a job as a dockworker and continued to try to supplement his income by gambling. Then, on December 15, 1930, after winning heavily in a crap game, Virgil Turner was clubbed over the head and robbed. He died in that alley beside the *Chronicle* newspaper building, and his killer was never found. One of the men who had been at the game later told police, "He'd been so happy because now he could buy his daughter a bicycle for Christmas."

Mildred could not afford to spend much time mourning. She went to work in a beauty salon while the nine-year-old Judy was sent to live with friends of the family in Modesto. Unfortunately, Judy was badly treated by these "friends." She was made to answer for the failings of their own daughter and beaten frequently with a switch. Mildred discovered the abuse by accident when she visited her daughter one day. She asked her to remove her garments so that she could inspect their condition. Seeing the welts and bruises, Mildred hastily gathered up Judy and her few possessions.

Living together in San Francisco, the mother and daughter were frequently near starvation; many times they survived only through the charity of the woman who owned the beauty shop where Mildred worked. Judy was nonetheless forced to attend classes rather than go to work, enrolling in a Catholic school—where, ironically, she entertained thoughts of becoming a nun. However, before Judy could realize her ambition, Mildred developed a chest condition due to the damp, blustery climate of San Francisco. The Turners were forced to move to the more clement environment of Los Angeles. There, Mildred was able to get a job at another beauty parlor. As for Judy, she was registered at Hollywood High.

Hollywood has many, many legends, most of which are apocryphal, created by studio publicity departments or enthusiastic press agents. Yet, the most famous legend of all, the archetypal Cinderella story, happens to be absolutely true. In January of 1936, the fifteen-year-old Judy skipped a typing class and went to the Top Hat Malt Shop on Sunset Boulevard—not Schwab's, which has long claimed credit but was, in fact, too many miles away for Lana to have patronized. There, at what is now the site of a Texaco service station, the pert and quite beautiful teenager frequently used her lunch money to purchase a Coke. While she sat at the counter on this particular day, Judy was spotted by one Billy Wilkerson, publisher of the trade newspaper *The Hollywood Reporter*. The industry powerbroker presented his card to Judy and, smiling, asked, "How would you like to be in pictures?" Even in 1936 that line was old hat, and Judy politely declined. But the publisher was persevering, and he asked the girl to bring her mother up to his office for a chat.

When Judy told Mildred what had happened, the woman was disbelieving—but not so foolish as to deny Wilkerson the benefit of the doubt. She went right out and thumbed through a copy of *The Hollywood Reporter*, checking Wilkerson's card against the paper's masthead. Everything seemed in order, so she phoned the publisher's office and, in a state of mild shock, set up an appointment. Wilkerson, a man in love with Hollywood and its stars, sent them to see talent agent Henry Willson. In short order, Willson managed to land Judy a part as an extra in *A Star is Born*, for which she was paid twenty-five dollars. However, the picture's producer, David O. Selznick, whose instincts were usually right-on, was not sufficiently impressed with Willson's find to offer her a contract. Nor was RKO, which wouldn't even give her work as an extra, or Twentieth Century-Fox. Finally, Willson took Judy to see producer-director Mervyn LeRoy at Warner Brothers. LeRoy happened to be searching for an innocent young woman with a sexy walk for a film he was about to make. Seeing the baby-faced Judy come trembling through the door, he ceased interviewing starlets and hired her on the spot. Her salary was fifty dollars per week—five times more than her mother was earning at the salon.

Judy's second screen appearance was considerably more important than the first, not only in terms of duration but for its impact. She was dressed in a tight-fitting sweater and equally tight skirt in a film appropriately titled *They Won't*

Forget. In her few brief scenes before being murdered, Judy was an unqualified sensation. Literally overnight she became the one-and-only Sweater Girl. For Judy's part, she was astounded by the publicity she received, though not quite so astounded as when she and her mother had first attended a screening of the film. Judy never realized that her breasts bounced quite so much as she walked, movements that had been accentuated onscreen by the rhythmic musical accompaniment provided by composer Adolph Deutsch. Lana later told me, "We were very embarrassed, and we both slid low—and I mean *low*—in our seats. I'd never been so completely self-conscious about a part of my anatomy, and I just wanted to *die*."

Judy recovered sufficiently to allow Mervyn LeRoy to continue helping her along the road to stardom. One of the first orders of business was a name change from Judy to something fittingly celestial. As Lana recalls, "We literally started down the alphabet. We got to the Ls. A *Louise* I am not. The whole office was terribly quiet, everyone thinking. Then I opened my dear, unknowledgeable mouth and said, 'Well, what about *Lana*?' Mr. LeRoy looked at me and said, 'How would you spell it?' I said, 'I don't know. L-A-N-A . . . simple!' He went walking around the office saying, 'Lana . . . Lana Turner. *Lana*. That's it!'" LeRoy claims he named her after a girl he had known named Donna.

Lana's salary was boosted by fifty percent, and her mother quit her job. After wading through a series of unimportant Warner productions and proving that she could hold an audience, her fee tripled. At this point LeRoy moved over to MGM, where, shortly thereafter, Jean Harlow died and left the studio without a sex symbol. They found one in Lana; as author Irving Wallace would later observe, Lana had what Harlow had, only twice as much. Still under LeRoy's wing, Lana appeared in *Love Finds Andy Hardy* as a promiscuous young schoolgirl. For $1,250.00 per week she was assigned similar roles for a while, finally working her way up to more prestigious MGM productions like *Dr. Jekyll and Mr. Hyde* with Spencer Tracy and *Honky Tonk* starring Clark Gable. Tutored by experience and not by MGM drama coach Lillian Burns, Lana became a solid actress. But it was her own natural beauty and command of the camera that made her a movie star, and by 1945 her salary was $4,500 for five days' work. Hollywood proved quite a cornucopia for someone who hadn't owned a bicycle as a child.

There is no overstating the impact that Lana Turner has had on the motion picture industry. Almost from the start, this exquisite woman was ranked in the pantheon of Hollywood immortals. What is considerably *less* well-known or understood is the impact that Hollywood has had on Lana Turner. Despite the careful guidance of her mother, Lana was a young woman who found herself in an industry that not only spun romantic fantasies on the screen but also helped its participants to live them. Professionally, it remains a business where the better the faker, be it actor or special effects technician, the more they're paid; a giddy playground where children are not encouraged to grow up. In this earlier era of the studio system, when actors were given seven- to ten-year contracts that guaranteed films tailored to them and a regular flow of work, the moguls all but wiped their stars' noses. When Lana became pregnant by her first husband, a hospital stay and an abortion were easily arranged. When she was overworked, MGM organized a cruise and sent along a companion. Legal, fiscal, creature, and even social problems were lifted from the shoulders of the stars—as long as they pulled in the box-office coin. It's no wonder that when Lana left MGM after back-to-back flops in the mid-fifties, she was like a landlubber cast asea. She recovered, not because she was a worldly or astute businesswoman, but because she is a survivor.

Since the studios wanted their stars to be content, Lana, like many of her peers, accepted amusement and shunned responsibility. It's no surprise that the fondest recollections she has from her MGM days are not the noteworthy achievements in her profession but the fun she had. Practical jokes pulled by Clark Gable to relieve Lana of beginner's nerves. Playing opposite Vincent Price in *The Three Musketeers,* she as the evil Lady de Winter, he as the corrupt Cardinal Richelieu, each in their scenes together trying to act more evil than the other as they schemed against the crown, arching their eyebrows higher and higher until neither star could keep a straight face. People raised in this environment of plenty, of happy endings, expect real life to be no less

perfect. Obviously this is not the case, even under a studio's
protection, and in Lana's case everything that could go wrong
did.

That night, during our mammoth drink-talk session,
Lana told me with more than a hint of ire not only that she
was deflowered by Greg Bautzer but how he drove her into
marrying her first husband. It is interesting to speculate if
Bautzer *had* married Lana, whether six other husbands would
have followed the first.

Lana wanted to belong to Bautzer, and she wanted him
to be hers. For his part, Bautzer loved Lana. He even got
into a fistfight over her with a rival suitor at the roller derby.
But his manly defense of Lana's honor was not enough. He
saw other women, and it infuriated Lana when his name was
linked with those of rival stars or starlets in the gossip
columns.

As it happened, Lana had just completed her eleventh
film, *Dancing Co-ed*, made in 1939 and co-starring popular
bandleader Artie Shaw. Having been stood up by a date,
Shaw called Lana on the off chance that she might like to go
for a drive. The timing was perfect. Bautzer himself was out
with another woman, and Lana, furious, decided to use Shaw
to flaunt her social and sexual independence. Heedless of her
mother's warning about rebounding into the arms of another
man, she accepted her co-star's invitation.

Lana admits now that she knew Shaw was all wrong for
her. But, being Lana, she was unable to do something in a
small way. She had begun their relationship by telling off her
co-star at the onset of filming, chastising him for his self-
centered behavior on the set. Rather than being put off, Shaw
was impressed by her forthrightness—he himself had recently
declared his fans to be "morons"—and on that first date they
kept one another on their toes. Shortly thereafter, Lana and
the twice-wed Shaw decided to throw courtship to the wind
and get married. The proposal, if one can call it that, consisted
of Lana saying, "I want a man who has the brains to be
satisfied with only me," an oblique reference to Bautzer,
which exacted an agreement from Shaw. They flew at once to
Las Vegas to solemnize the agreement.

After three days Lana knew that the marriage to Shaw
was over, although it took her four months to file for divorce,
since she was busy making movies. They were not antago-

nists: the couple simply hadn't anything in common. Lana
typified the up-and-coming glamour generation in love with
the glitter and night life of Hollywood, while Shaw detested
everything about the town. What is most notable about her
brief marriage to Shaw is that Lana said she tried smoking
marijuana for the first and only time. Today she is loath to be
around the weed, though at the time she was trying, she
explained, to be more like her husband and his musician
friends who smoked it all the time, years before it became
fashionable. Looking back, Lana laughed that even then, at
eighteen years of age, she was ahead of her time. She said
that smoking pot did nothing for her other than to stir up a
ravenous appetite that caused her to fly to the kitchen and
open every can she could get her hands on. Today, while
Lana knows next to nothing about preparing a decent meal,
she proudly refers to herself as "the greatest can opener in
the world."

Lana followed her divorce by romancing then-coast
guardsman Victor Mature, whom she met at the Club Mocambo.
Mature was with Betty Grable when he was smitten by Lana;
Betty very understandingly provided him with her phone
number. Mature, as well as Buddy Rich, Tony Martin, and
Tommy Dorsey came and went in quick succession. Contrary
to speculation, Lana had *not* discovered promiscuity; the
many stories about her alleged sexual excesses were simply
unschooled interpretations of why Lana changed escorts so
frequently. Typical is one story I'd heard about Lana, that
during lunch breaks on any given film she would select one of
the crew members for a brief tryst. The truth is that Lana is
so concerned about her makeup, hair, and costumes, not to
mention learning her dialogue for the coming scenes, that she
seldom has time for a meal, let alone sex. Rather, Lana had
discovered the joys of being able to rely on men for companionship and support, a feeling she'd not enjoyed since the
tragic death of her father. There *was* an element of spontanei-
ty on occasion; she told me about waking up in bed in Mexico
one morning, with a world-famous matador at her side, his
household staff peeking through the partially opened door
and admiring her long blond hair; she also told me about
having a romance with a restauranteur in Acapulco, a much-
married man with many children. Lana freely admits dating
in excess of one hundred and fifty men over the years. But

with each man it was never a *casual* fling. The rapid turnover is attributable to the influence of Hollywood itself, hectic daily schedules and the ever-present party scene—with its attendant temptations—hardly being conducive to lasting relationships. Certainly not in the case of Lana Turner, whose idea of romance was inherently Byronic: flaming but brief.

Husband number two was Stephen Crane, who was married to Lana by the same Las Vegas judge responsible for uniting Lana with Artie Shaw. "This time," Lana admonished as they stood before him, "make sure the knot stays tied for keeps." Crane was the father of Lana's only child, daughter Cheryl Christine, born July 25, 1943. Lana had had three miscarriages before Cheryl was born, and at the time it was doubtful whether even this baby would live. Lana's blood is Rh negative, Cheryl's Rh positive; the mother's rejection of her baby's blood left the newborn dangerously anemic and in need of a complete transfusion. For three days Lana lay in her hospital room, not having been able to hold her own infant yet suffering the cries of babies being brought to other mothers. But the blood transfusion was successful—so much so that in years to come, during periods of trial and harsh disagreement, Lana said that she would often look at Cheryl and wonder, *Just whose venomous blood is flowing in your veins?*

Lana married Crane on July 17, 1942, and when he was one of the many young men drafted to help the Allied cause, she used her considerable influence to make certain that he was not sent into active duty overseas. She also had his regulation uniforms custom-tailored and made sure that he was in every way well provided for. Though this may seem an untoward indulgence on the part of the army, stars of Lana's stature contributed to the USO and to war bond rallies, which meant that very little was unavailable to them— even while the rest of the nation was growing victory gardens and rationing food.

After the war, Crane opened a restaurant in Beverly Hills, which Lana had helped to finance. Thereafter, almost nightly, she would go to the Luau on Rodeo Drive. Thanks to Lana's patronage, the restaurant became a celebrity hangout and a major tourist attraction, and it enjoyed an excellent reputation for decades. The Luau was finally torn down in 1980 to make way for an office building. Right up until the end, however, it remained one of Lana's favorite places for business meetings and interviews. On those nights that we didn't go there for dinner, I would call and order food sent over to Lana's home.

Lana talked very little about her marriage to Crane. Other than the fact that he was the father of her child, she appeared to have little interest in him. There was nothing vitriolic about their life together; like Lana and Shaw, they simply had nothing in common. The most sensational aspect about their year together was Lana's learning that their marriage had never been legal in the eyes of the law. It seems that Crane had been married before and had divorced his first wife in Juarez, Mexico. Unfortunately, the Mexican divorce was not recognized in the United States. Lana quickly arranged to have her marriage annulled, through none other than her attorney Greg Bautzer. Shortly thereafter, she discovered that she was pregnant and, employing cloak-and-dagger tactics that would have astounded even the OSS, MGM had Crane's first divorce quickly sanctified by the California courts, and Lana quietly remarried him—only, she said, so that her unborn child would have a legal name. Lana stayed married at the studio's insistence, but only long enough so that she could file for divorce without seeming to have used Crane merely as a sire the second time around.

Following her divorce from Crane, Lana made headlines by dating a succession of celebrities, such as Rory Calhoun, John Hodiak, Peter Lawford, Ricardo Montalban, Turkish star Turhan Bey—to whom she was briefly engaged—Tyrone Power, and Howard Hughes.

Hughes was easily the most colorful of these figures, and Lana told me that, contrary to rumor, he was never dirty and did not have body odor, despite the fact that he always seemingly wore the same pair of black pants, white shirt with no tie, and white tennis shoes. He was a very quiet and likable man, but he did not exactly overwhelm Lana with the force of his personality. Three years later, after piling his test plane into a residential area of Beverly Hills and sustaining injuries that would plague him for the rest of his life, Hughes became the recluse who confounded us all. Back then, he was boyishly eccentric rather than enigmatic.

However, Hughes did manage to befuddle Lana in one respect. Lana has a habit of keeping people waiting, and not

even Howard Hughes was spared. Yet in this case, the
power-exercise backfired. Lana, Mildred, and baby Cheryl
were all sharing a large house in Bel-Air, and one night Lana
came downstairs to find Hughes sitting half dressed, talking
to her mother in his slow and deliberate manner. The millionaire had apparently discovered a tear in the back of his
rather worn black pants, and Mildred had told him to go into
the powder room, take them off, and wrap a towel around his
extremely thin waist while she mended the slacks. He did as
he was told, and he so obviously enjoyed the company of the
thirty-eight-year-old Mildred that, ever after, Lana wondered
which of them he had really come to see.

Though Lana and Howard Hughes were engaged for
exactly eight hours once, the betrothal beginning and ending
impulsively on a cross-country flight, I don't believe there
was ever anything of a serious nature between them. Although Lana maintains that she *never* went on dates arranged
by MGM for publicity purposes unless she genuinely liked
her prospective escort, she was smart enough to recognize
the value of being seen and photographed with this international magnate. The reason nothing *could* have developed
between them is that whatever Howard Hughes may have
been, he was not a romantic. For Lana, romance is as
necessary as the air she breathes. That's one reason she fell in
love with so many movie stars. It was actually a fannish
infatuation: she'd see them on the screen, make up her mind
to date them, then inevitably be disappointed in the genuine
article. She compensates for these letdowns by infusing romance into everything else she does. From the time she
awakens in the afternoon, there is soft music playing throughout her home, and she dresses in the fashion of fairy-tale
royalty. For me, this ambience she so diligently maintained
was one of the pleasanter aspects of my long stay in Wonderland.

Having said this, I must hasten to add that from my
observation Lana *does* love to flirt. It's an unparalleled attention-
getter, and she has mastered the science. I have seen her
come on to men half her age, and after a while, not only were
these men anxious to go to bed with her but they were almost
in a frenzy of lust. Many of these men were lured as far as her
bedroom door, only to find it closed ever so softly in their
faces. For Lana, the hunt was infinitely more rewarding than
the kill. And when she *did* get her man, the sensuality of that

hunt was instantly replaced with soft lights and the cozy embrace of romance.

Of all the amorous encounters Lana has had, she admits that the thirty-three-year-old Tyrone Power was the one man she adored above all others, husband or beau—and the one man who would never be hers. They were the most publicized couple of 1947, and without a doubt the handsomest. Lana told me that Power embodied everything she had ever wanted in a mate. And, a rarity in her relationships, he had achieved the zenith of success and was not trying to use her.

Apart from the obvious attraction of his perfect good looks, dark hair, and piercing brown eyes, Lana described Power as a man of great sensitivity. He was very well educated, something that Lana probably respected due to her own rather limited formal education. Though he was still married to his first wife, Annabella, Lana fully expected Power to leave that already shaky union and marry her. It wasn't to be.

Lana's relationship with Power had its ups and horrible downs, its moments of humor and great tragedy. Pertaining to the former, Lana tells one very funny story about the time she was shooting a picture in the comfort of the MGM lot while Power was struggling in the wilds of Mexico filming the epic swashbuckler *Captain from Castile*. On impulse, Lana decided to take advantage of a two-day break in her shooting schedule to fly down and surprise her lover. She managed to do just that, but when it came time to return to the United States, bad weather prevented any flights from leaving Mexico for several days. This meant a loss to MGM of thousands of dollars per day, and Lana was terrified when she finally returned to Culver City. She very vividly describes how she crept onto the sound stage, which was empty and very dark with just a worklight glowing in its cavernous center. She inched her way inside, calling softly, "Hello? Anybody here?" Suddenly, all the lights flared on, and there stood the entire cast and crew of the film, wearing sombreros, clicking castanets, and clenching roses between their teeth. Lana turned bright red, although, as ever, the precocious girl was forgiven her indiscretion.

Lana is not a person who lives in the past, and only once during this night of very personal confession did the years seem to disappear. One evening, after many drinks she alluded to the fact that she had become pregnant by Power.

He was still working on *Captain from Castile* when she informed him that she thought she was going to have his child. I sensed Lana reliving the hurt she had felt as she recounted his terse response to the news. His voice, she said, was clear and flat as he told her, "Get rid of it." After finishing one of the finest movies of her career, *The Postman Always Rings Twice*, the studio arranged a two-month "vacation" to South America. The trip was well-timed to comply with Power's blunt instructions. Just how well powerful MGM kept a lid on the true nature of the visit is revealed in a quote from the fan magazine *Movie Stars Parade* of June, 1946, which described Lana's travel plans thusly:

It was strictly a spree. There were no theatre appearances, no publicity chores for her new film, nor any of the semiofficial business which many stars take on when they visit South of the Border. There was not even a studio representative with her, only her longtime friend, writer Sara Hamilton.

As deeply in love as she was with Power, Lana was frustrated by his procrastination in obtaining a divorce. She was also not one to sit home alone evenings pining away. She was fond of the nightclub circuit, and despite the rigors of filming long hours at MGM, she managed to go out dancing and partying almost every night. That had *always* been her way, even when she was just starting out; club owners would look the other way when she or any of the young stars would order a cocktail before they were twenty-one years old. The only rule was that they hide their drinks or cigarettes under the table if a photographer came by. The stars complied, not only to keep the owners out of trouble but to keep the studios happy by showing the public that Hollywood wasn't really a den of corruption. However, if it frustrated Lana that Power was mired in a marriage to someone else, it angered him no less to learn that Lana was dating other men. The proverbial last straw from Power's point of view was Frank Sinatra, whom Lana dated more than once to try and jar Power into expediting his divorce. She was clearly taking a calculated risk working on Power's jealousy, and much to Lana's public humiliation, her gamble did not pay off. Enraged by the way Sinatra had been flaunted in his face, Power began seeing a beautiful young actress named Linda Christian. The two had been introduced by Power's friend, actress Brenda Joyce, and he escorted the ex-protégée of Errol Flynn to the most chic night spots in Hollywood. Shortly thereafter, Power was divorced and married Linda Christian. Lana was thoroughly devastated, though she still cherishes Power and her memories of the times they shared.

As an interesting sidelight to this romance, twenty years later I took a call from a young girl who introduced herself as Romina Power Carrisi, the daughter of Tyrone Power and Linda Christian. Romina explained that she was trying to put together a book about her father. Although the book was intended for publication, she admitted that writing it was really a means for her to find out more about a man who had died when she was seven years old. I told Romina that I would tell Miss Turner of her call but that, in the meantime, she should write a short note outlining just what she wanted. The call, after all, could have been a ruse by either a reporter or a fan, many of whom have tried outrageous ways of getting personal introductions or interviews. The note arrived a few days later, and it was authentic. It was a dear little letter, one that concluded with "warmest saluti from the sunny side of Italy." Lana read Romina's letter very carefully, then asked me to contact her. Lana explained that, unfortunately, she was leaving town and would not be back for quite some time. I suspected, then as now, that Lana had decided she did not want to meet the girl who could have been her child by Tyrone Power.

Lana had to do something to show Power that she could live without him—and live well. The result was her third marital entanglement, this time with millionaire tin-plate heir Henry J. "Bob" Topping. Lana told me that the thrice-wed Topping knew that she was not in love with him, but he offered Lana financial security for herself and Cheryl. Lana made a great deal of money, of course, but she also spent a great deal. Even more disconcerting was that for the first time in a decade, Lana was briefly suspended by MGM for dating a succession of married men and creating an immoral image that did not meld with what film czar Louis B. Mayer expected from his stars. Topping was a buffer against the whims of the studio and her own free-spending ways. To sweeten the pot, he showered Lana with diamonds and other expensive jewels. On the "first

date" I had with Lana, she wore a diamond bracelet valued at
forty-eight thousand dollars, just one of the many gifts from
Topping.

Lana described Topping as a fun-loving man, a gentle
person of whom she grew to be genuinely fond but for whom
she never had any real passion. Like his brother Dan, who
married ice skating champion and movie star Sonja Henie—
whose fabled jewelry collection was acquired largely through
the Topping fortune—Bob Topping certainly treated his wife
to a lavish life-style.

The Topping family owned a country estate called Round
Hill, located in rural Connecticut. Round Hill was a beautiful, brick, Tudor-style mansion with forty-three rooms, nes-
tled atop a gently sloping hill surrounded by acres of beautiful gardens, a swimming pool, and tennis courts. Lana has an
album of photographs showing the estate being built in the
early 1920s with the help of horse-drawn wagons, which had
to drag the necessary materials through miles of unpaved
roads and up the hill.

To reach Round Hill from Los Angeles was itself a study
in typical Topping extravagance. Railroads were still a popular
mode of transportation, and Bob Topping had his own private
railroad car. Prior to departure, Lana would order the servants to stock the Pullman with everything that she, her
husband, her mother, and Cheryl and her nanny would need
for the five-day ride across the United States. There was a
very expensive shop on Rodeo Drive called Jewel Park that
specialized in lingerie and lounging robes for those who could
afford them. Lana and her mother reveled in buying flowing
chiffon robes for their cross-country trips. Once aboard the
train, they would avoid streetwear until they reached their
destination. While in transit, the family would while away the
hours playing with Cheryl, enjoying the finest food and drink,
reading, and playing gin rummy—a game at which Lana
excels. She and I always had a deck of cards on hand for our
own trips together.

Round Hill holds many fond recollections for Lana. She
genuinely cared for all the members of the Topping family,
and it was my impression that, given her own impoverished
childhood, Round Hill was like a fantasy come true. Apart
from security, the loving, generous Bob Topping represented
the father figure she craved; in his sister, Lana found the

sister she had always wanted. It was idyllic, made even more so when Topping bought Lana a yacht, which they kept in the South of France. They named the vessel *Snuffy* after their favorite comic strip character Snuffy Smith, and they spent many happy days both on board the yacht and on the beach at St. Tropez. Years later, after moving Lana into her high-rise condominium in Century City, I came across a set of solid silver dinnerware. Each piece was emblazoned with the word *Snuffy,* and I felt as if I were viewing Charles Foster Kane's sled, Rosebud, a corpse never fully intended to be buried.

Bob and Lana made their permanent home on three and one-half acres in Beverly Hills, property that Lana had bought prior to their marriage. There was more than enough room for the family to live, and since Topping favored Italian food, there was also a chef on hand to prepare his favorite dishes. Lana, for her part, had acquired a taste for French cuisine and hired a personal chef for *her*self.

This period of personal revelry was one of professional inactivity for Lana, so she indulged herself in every way. Her clothes began to get a little snug, and zippers were difficult to close; Lana blamed the cleaners and bought new garments. In time, she was forced to face the truth: she was overweight. Still, Lana dutifully avoided the bathroom scale until she had signed to do a film. By then she was shocked to discover that she was now carrying 140 pounds on her five foot, three-and-one-half-inch frame. She went at once to her doctor, who advised her to dismiss the French chef. Then he put her on a strict diet that, Lana confided, was absolute hell—not only because it limited her intake of solids but because Lana was restricted to just one shot glass of liquor per day. It was a ration she would take hours to finish, nursing it, savoring it, knowing that it was all she could have until the following day.

Lana does not deny that she was unbearable to be near while peeling off the pounds. But through near starvation and her stubborn Dutch willpower, she managed to get down to her normal 106 pounds. From that experience, Lana vowed never again to be overweight. With determination rivaled only by Scarlett O'Hara, she has doggedly kept that promise. I always found it amusing when women would corral me at this or that social function and ask for Lana's secret of keeping her beautiful figure. The answer is easy, I'd tell them. Lana only samples everything that's put in front of her. Without

exception, restaurant owners who don't know Lana come to
the table and nervously inquire if something is wrong with
the food. Lana, who has ordered whatever she felt like
tasting, always smiles graciously and explains, "The food is
wonderful. It's just that there's so *much* of it, and I have a
very tiny tummy." We would always take the leftovers home,
where Lana would pick at it over the next day or two. What
with the proliferation of diet books on the bestseller lists,
more than once I suggested to Lana that she pen one of her
own. She never took that thought seriously, remarking, "Who'd
buy a book with just two words in it: self-control?"

Marriage, as an institution, seems to lull many of us into
very necessary routines from which we seek diversion and
amusement. In Lana's case it was food. In my own case it was
travel, followed by divorce. In the case of Bob Topping it was
gambling. As a result of his bad luck, Topping began to drink
to excess and changed from a man of calm and humor into a
frustrated boozer. Almost overnight he became abusive,
explained Lana, rude to her mother, and neglectful of Cheryl.
To make matters worse, the Topping fortune simultaneously
took a nose dive because Sonja Henie practically cleaned
them out in a divorce settlement. It fell to Lana to support
the family in the manner to which they had become accustomed, and she often told me about the day she had to face
the fact that yet another marriage was over. Lana was seated,
she said, at the bar, where a large stack of checks awaited her
signature. Her mother was sitting across from her, elbows on
the bar, chin perched in her open palms, her expression one
of resignation as she watched her daughter signing the checks.
As Lana took note of each one she was endorsing, she
remarked to Mildred, "I see a lot of money going out but
very little coming in."

It had been a rhetorical observation, though it provided
an entrée for what Mildred had recognized long before. With
typical bluntness the woman replied, "Let's face it, you just
can't afford to keep a millionaire."

Lana did one of those classic, comic strip double takes.
She hadn't viewed the change in their relationship quite that
way, but her mother was right. Her husband had dropped the
financial ball, and she had unselfishly picked it up and run
with it—beyond duty, and now beyond good sense. Characteristically, Lana immediately saw the humor of her folly. She

threw her head back and laughed. "You're right! By God, mother, you are *right!*" Within minutes, Lana had contacted her attorney and told him to initiate divorce proceedings.

Lana had married Bob Topping on April 26, 1948, and divorced him on December 16, 1952. It had been her longest marriage to date and the happiest until the end. Lana did not fare as well as Sonja Henie in parting from a Topping.

Alexander "Lex" Barker was the only professional actor that Lana ever married. He had established a career as an action star by playing Tarzan in five films, distinguishing himself admirably after being chosen from nearly two thousand applicants to follow Johnny Weissmuller in the role.

The thirty-four-year-old, six-foot, four-inch Barker had been married twice before, to Constance Thurlow in 1948 and to Arlene Dahl in 1951. He had five children from these couplings. The strikingly handsome Barker met his future wife at a party held in honor of singer Johnny Ray. They saw a great deal of each other in Europe, where they both arranged to shoot their next films, and were married in Turin, Italy, on September 8, 1953. Upon their return to the United States, Barker moved into the Beverly Hills estate, and Cheryl soon found herself with a flock of stepbrothers and stepsisters. Lana, who loves children of any age, took to mothering her inherited brood whenever they came to stay with their father. She claims to have purchased the first Volkswagen bus ever seen on the streets of Southern California so that she could pick up all the kids after school and take them to an amusement park at the corner of Beverly Boulevard and La Cienega, just east of Beverly Hills. "Kids were hanging out of every window and sticking their heads through the sun roof," she remembers—kids who usually included Liza Minnelli, since Judy Garland was the Barkers' next-door neighbor and Cheryl and Liza were best of friends. Cheryl often told me how she and Liza would meet on their garage roofs to escape their respective nannies and Liza would frequently ask, "Do you wanna see my mother's new act?" Whereupon Liza would perform for Cheryl. They were both preteens at the time. Cheryl and Liza remain close today, though their life-styles are worlds apart. Lana took great pleasure in being able to provide these children with the innocent pleasures that she had been denied.

Lana felt that she had found happiness at last, enjoying

not only the children but Lex himself. Though there was no question that she was a bigger star than he, Lana was very careful not to let that get in the way of their relationship. She would earnestly solicit his opinion in matters of script and character, and she kept a lower public profile than usual. Fortunately, Barker was secure in his own abilities, and though he was ambitious, he was never envious of Lana. He had, in fact, completed his final Tarzan film and had made a successful segue into westerns, confident that he could shed his jungle image and become a leading man.

The couple was divorced on July 22, 1957. Immediately thereafter, Barker was offered a film in Europe; he went overseas and stayed to become a popular international star. He later remarried, dividing his time among homes in Geneva, Barcelona, and Rome, and his fifty-foot yacht. When he died of a massive heart attack on the streets of New York nearly twenty years later, he had been negotiating a return to the mainstream of Hollywood filmmaking. When Lana heard of his death, she said to me, "What took him so long?"

One of the curiosities about Lana's marriages and affairs is that, for the most part, she has tended to pursue men who were professionally or financially beneath her. Tyrone Power and Howard Hughes are the obvious exceptions, though it's telling that she landed neither man. Her men were like grown-up dolls, dressed and wheeled about, with mommy calling the shots. That's Lana, the selfish child. The playful girl. The domineering woman. However, Lana was one thing more: endangered.

Of all the lovers of Lana Turner, there is one whose name will forever be linked with hers. The two of them made front-page headlines the world over and, though I was still a teenager at the time, I remember consuming all the lurid and sensational details as they unfolded.

The brief, official record on Johnny Stompanato reads as follows: born 1925, Woodstock, Illinois; graduate of Kemper Military School, Booneville, Missouri, 1943. Attended Notre Dame University and served in the U.S. Marine Corps 1944–1947. Divorced three times, with a son, John III, presently in his twenties.

Lana met Johnny Stompanato shortly after her divorce from Barker. Lana was in a state of confusion and depression, and

Stompanato seemed the perfect man to whom to turn for affection. Tall, olive-skinned, and ruggedly handsome, with thick, wavy black hair, he was fun loving and enjoyed a romantic reputation among the ladies of Hollywood's elite inner circle.

Stompanato was the owner of a Los Angeles gift shop, though he had spent most of his time while in Southern California serving as a bodyguard for the infamous mobster Mickey Cohen. With the collapse of Cohen's underworld empire, Stompanato was more or less on his own, though he retained close ties with his former colleagues. Stompanato called Lana shortly after her divorce, smooth-talking her into a date and obliquely referring to his formidable physical endowments as a cure for what was ailing her. Undoubtedly his charm and the promise of companionship meant far more to Lana than his legendary equipment.

The two fell passionately in love with one another, though Lana always kept one eye on her image, rarely allowing herself to be photographed with this man who had six arrests to his credit. At this time in her career, Lana was scheduled to go to England to shoot *Another Time, Another Place*. It was an important film for her. In December of 1957, audiences had made *Peyton Place* the top-grossing picture of the year, but her next film, *The Lady Takes a Flyer*, took a nose dive. *Another Time, Another Place* could accurately have been titled *Another Soap Opera*, a commercial property that Lana wanted very much to turn into a superhit. Sadly, the film would end up as just the opposite, although it did launch the career of the striking young actor whom she had personally selected to play opposite her, Sean Connery.

By the time Lana left England late in 1957, she had known Johnny Stompanato some four months. Fearful of the men Lana might meet in England, Johnny borrowed plane fare from Mickey Cohen and flew to Europe in express disregard for Lana's instructions. As much as she loved Stompanato, she felt that his presence would distract her from the very intense job at hand. Besides, she had brought Cheryl with her and wanted to use whatever free time she could wangle to tour the United Kingdom with her daughter.

But Stompanato came, and it's not surprising that *more* than Lana's worst fears were realized. In deference to the fourteen-year-old Cheryl, Lana rented a separate house for her lover in a fashionable district of London, although he rarely made use of it: certainly never during the day, when he was at the studio from the instant Lana arrived until she left at night. Lana found it difficult to concentrate with this would-be Svengali lurking in an environment that was otherwise professional and under her control. Worse, at night they would argue in her hotel suite, making it all the more difficult for her to concentrate on work the next day. Nor was it long before Stompanato's pervasive jealousy bubbled to the surface, though his first intrusion along these lines was also his last. In no way pleased with how chummy Sean Connery was getting with Lana offcamera, he pulled a pistol on the actor and threatened to use it if the Scotsman didn't keep his hands to himself. Connery, whom I have met and found earnestly friendly and ever a gentleman with *all* of his co-stars, promptly hauled off and dropped his antagonist. Stompanato didn't strike back but took out his anger on Lana, actually choking her unconscious on one occasion. As a result of this tension, she became anxious and jittery, and the quality of her performance began to suffer. So quickly that Lana couldn't have interceded had she elected to, the studio contacted Scotland Yard, which was able to deport Stompanato. Lana felt disproportionately guilty about the whole affair and, regretting what had been done to her lover, began sending him passionate, purging letters. "My beloved love," she would write, "I adore all the truly beautiful things you say to me . . . every line warms me and makes me ache and miss you more each tiny moment. Know how dearly I love you, angel. . . ." The letters cried for more than forgiveness. She pleaded for Stompanato's love, for his embrace—Lana's way of capitulating to Stompanato's vanity, his need to be powerfully "male," factors that had been severely compromised by the deportation.

When *Another Time, Another Place* finished a few months later, Lana headed back to Los Angeles via the Netherlands. Deplaning in Denmark, she was shocked to find Stompanato waiting for her. The press was also there in force, and she could not avoid holding a brief press conference. To this day, Lana does not know how she got through the interview. Stompanato, she said, had taken her arm the instant she left the plane and did not let go until they were both back on board. She described him as eyeing her "like a cat watching a canary" all through the press conference, smiling but not missing a single move she made. Once they were airborne and alone, Stompanato made no mention of being kicked out of England; he didn't have to. Lana's self-punishing letters had all but left her groveling.

Lana felt that with 1958 off to such a trying start, she had earned a vacation. While in Mexico, she learned that she had been nominated as Best Actress of the Year for her work in *Peyton Place*. Since Lana wanted very much to look rested and tan when she made her appearance at the Academy Awards show, she decided to visit her favorite vacation spot, Acapulco. Naturally, Johnny Stompanato was along.

The seven-week Mexican idyll was anything but relaxing, for it was then that Lana and Stompanato fought the hardest. In all that has been written over the years about their stormy relationship, no one has ever chronicled the reason for these rowdy arguments, which Lana explained to me. The catalyst was something simple, which was par in their surprisingly two-dimensional relationship. Lana had given Stompanato affection, and she had given him money. She had given him everything except what he wanted so much: public acknowledgment. He needed that recognition because his dream was to become a motion picture producer; his only means of gaining instant legitimacy was to be seen by Lana's side at industry events. Accordingly, Stompanato was adamant that *he* escort her to the Academy Awards. Now, as foolish as Lana may be in her private life, she is no fool when it comes to her public image. She knew that no matter how magnetic his manner, how polished his exterior, this man's past could bring her nothing but bad press. As she always did when her career and private life collided, Lana opted to preserve the former. Thus, when they returned to Los Angeles, Lana came to the very difficult decision that she must get Johnny Stompanato out of her life for good.

There was a witches' brew of trouble the final night Lana informed Johnny of her wishes. Apart from the damage to his colossal ego, Stompanato had run up gambling debts that he'd counted upon Lana to pay. She probably wouldn't have been unreasonable about that, but she never got around to making him an offer. It was eight in the evening, and the couple was in Lana's bedroom at her newly rented home on North Bedford Drive. They had been arguing for most of the day, friction that had fortified Lana's desire to end the relationship. Quietly, and with genuine compassion and regret, she told Stompanto that this would be their last night together. Earlier, Lana had told Cheryl that there would probably be very harsh words that night, and the teenager said she understood and would try to be strong. But neither she nor Lana was prepared for the fury that swept through Stompanato. As soon as Lana had announced her decision, Stompanto was up and about the room like an enraged bobcat, dark and angry, screaming and punching at the walls. The violence of his outburst was such that it caused Cheryl to sneak nervously from her room and stand quietly outside her mother's door.

After his initial, disbelieving outburst, Stompanato faced Lana and snarled, "I'll *never* let you go. If I tell you to jump, you'll jump, and if I tell you to hop, you'll hop!"

Lana did not want to hear any more, and announcing that the matter was concluded, she turned to leave the room. Pulling open the bedroom door, Lana found Cheryl standing there. Mother and daughter stared at one another for a long moment before Lana implored, "Please don't listen to this." Cheryl nodded vaguely, and Lana shut the door, turning on Stompanto. "That's *great*," she yelled. "The child *had* to hear all that!"

Stompanato was unmoved and used Cheryl to hammer away at Lana. He threatened to hurt both Cheryl and Mildred if Lana didn't rescind her decision; when that tack failed Stompanato vowed to attack Lana herself.

"I'll cut you up," he threatened. "I'll get you if it takes a day, a week, or a year! I'll cut your face up. I'll mutilate you so you'll be so repulsive you'll have to hide forever! And if I can't do it myself, I'll find somebody who *will*."

Cheryl had not yet left; instead, she was standing in the shadows of the corridor. Panting with fear, she ran downstairs to collect her wits. Near tears, she wandered into the kitchen. Looking for something to chase Stompanato from the house, she snapped up the first weapon she could find: a nine-inch butcher knife. She sped upstairs just as her mother was screaming, "I'm absolutely finished, I want you to get out!"

Stompanato mumbled something in response, and as he opened the door, Cheryl screamed, "You don't have to take that!" Cocking her arm, she ran at Stompanato. Lana thought

Cheryl had hit him in the stomach with her fist. The first indication she had of something more dire was when Stompanato, gurgling horribly, his eyes wide with shock, staggered toward Cheryl. He hovered for a long moment, then he twisted and landed on his back.

Cheryl ran from the room while, gasping for air, Stompanato clawed at his throat. Lana ran to him, unaware of what had really happened until she rolled up his sweater and saw blood oozing from his belly. Lana hurried to the bathroom to get a large towel and, after draping it around the wound, called her mother. Mildred was at that time living in an apartment of her own on Charlieville Drive in Beverly Hills, just several blocks from Lana. Lana called her mother in a state of hysteria and instructed Mildred to call Dr. Mac. Mildred, when she finally got through to him, gave the doctor the wrong address. For this reason, he took longer to reach Lana and Stompanato. Stompanato was dead when the doctor arrived. Many people have questioned why it took so long for help to arrive. Stompanato's family later contended that he might have been saved if given proper medical aid in time. Stephen Crane, whom Cheryl herself had phoned, arrived soon after.

Before even examining Stompanato, Dr. Mac told Lana to call for an ambulance. Then, kneeling beside the body, he shot Stompanato full of Adrenalin and tried mouth-to-mouth resuscitation. But his efforts were futile, the young man dying while Lana hovered over him. Dr. Mac rose and, realizing that Lana's troubles were just beginning, suggested that she place one more call, to attorney Jerry Geisler. She did as he suggested.

"This is Lana Turner," she said upon reaching the famed lawyer. "Something terrible has happened—could you please come to my house?" When Geisler heard what had transpired, he hurried over. He was to prove a pivotal figure in the ensuing trial, as he had in acquitting Errol Flynn for rape and defending Bob Mitchum after his marijuana bust.

The police arrived shortly after the ambulance, and Lana pleaded with them to report that it had been she and not Cheryl who had wielded the knife. Beverly Hills Police Chief Anderson persuaded Lana that it would be better for everyone's sake if they just stuck to the truth. Lana had no choice but to agree with the advice, and along with Stephen Crane, she accompanied Cheryl to the police station. The girl was held there until a hearing could be arranged.

The trial was a spectacular one. It is ironic that Johnny Stompanato, the man who had wanted the eyes of the world upon him, was able to realize that dream only in death. The letters Lana had written to him after he left England found their way into the hands of the press and began appearing on front pages the nation over on April 9, 1958—less than five days after the killing. They were rumored to have been snatched from Stompanato's home by Cohen hirelings, who fed them to an eager press to punish Lana for the murder. Coincidentally, I think they were also annoyed at having been tagged for the funeral expenses.

Cheryl was acquitted with a verdict of justifiable homicide, and so the "legal" trial ended. For mother and daughter, however, the personal trial would never end. At first, Lana and Cheryl had to endure the predictable condemnation from religious quarters and from the press, not to mention every psychiatrist and bartender in view. There was also talk of Lana being declared an unfit mother and Cheryl being taken from her. To his credit, Stephen Crane did not press this, but Cheryl *was* made a ward of the court and left in Mildred's care. Cheryl remained so until her eighteenth birthday, even though she was in and out of psychiatric or delinquent centers throughout the four years of her probation.

Though the headlines eventually faded, the question that lingers to this day is whether a fourteen-year-old girl was capable of stabbing the 175-pound ex-Marine and mob bodyguard—or whether Lana herself stabbed Johnny and convinced her daughter to stand trial for it. In spite of the corroborative testimony and evidence, it's a mystery that titillates Hollywood to this day.

There is no doubt but that Lana persuaded the *jury* of her innocence. Intentionally or not, she gave the greatest performance of her life when she was on the stand, sobbing and swooning and all but fainting as she gave her testimony. When she had finished, the jurors were out for barely over a quarter of an hour. However, there are several discrepancies between the recorded testimony and what Lana revealed to me over the years about the murder. Memory fades, it's true, but I feel that the complete story of that night is something Lana will carry to the grave.

Without in any way regarding myself as an amateur Perry Mason, I find one of the most curious puzzles about the trial to be Lana's statement that she and Stompanato had gone shopping on the afternoon of the murder and returned home at approximately five-thirty. She testified that she found two friends waiting for her and that they asked Lana to join them for dinner that evening—without Mr. Stompanato. Lana agreed, testifying that Stompanato became angry because she had accepted an invitation that specifically excluded him. At *no* time during the trial was it ascertained just who the two friends were, and I find it astonishing that they were never put on the witness stand, let alone identified. Even more puzzling is that during the many times Lana and I discussed this subject, never once did she mention these two persons.

Lana also insisted on the stand that as they had just returned from Acapulco, the luggage was still sitting downstairs waiting to be unpacked. Another discrepancy is the stated manner in which the stabbing took place. Lana testified that she went to the bedroom door and opened it, whereupon Cheryl ran in and appeared to punch Stompanato. Yet, Lana told me numerous times that it was Stompanato who opened the door and that he literally walked into the knife.

My opinion about the murder is, withal, the same as that of the court. Lana does all of her "killing" mentally. She is comparatively charitable and forgiving toward women, but she does away with any man who lets her down. Whether this is a psychodrama of her own father's death, I'm not qualified to say. In the same breath, I must admit it seems incongruous that Cheryl simply up and decided to join in the argument that fateful night. Cheryl had to have heard enough of Lana's loud spats over the years to be immune by then. What some suspect is that Cheryl actually had a crush on the handsome gigolo. A lonely and confused girl, she would have been ripe for a Johnny Stompanato. For whatever reason, Stompanato had labored diligently to establish a warm rapport with Cheryl. He took her horseback riding and water-skiing, and in return, he often received very affectionate letters from Cheryl. They were always signed, "Love ya, Cherie." In fact, her letters to him were friendly and loving, more so than those she wrote to her mother. This has led more than one

observer of these events to speculate that it was rivalry
between Lana and Cheryl for Stompanato's affections that
spurred the killing.

In any case, whatever is cruel and impetuous in Lana's
nature, murder is not among those qualities. I suspect that
the different versions of the evening were subconsciously
cued by Lana's protectiveness of her public persona. Wanting
to have dinner alone with friends is an intimate gesture;
rebuffing Stompanato for the Oscars doesn't have quite as
neighborly a ring. Having gone shopping with her lover is
nice and domestic; true or not, it softens having fled with him
to Acapulco, which is hedonistic and illicit by comparison.
Even at a time of emotional upheaval, Lana instinctively
knew what was best for people to perceive of Lana Turner.
The great tragedy, then as ever, is that when Lana put her
best foot forward, no one paid any attention. It was only
when she stumbled that people sat up and took notice.

Lana married Fred May, husband number five, on
November 27, 1960.

May was a real-estate tycoon, whose efforts were concen-
trated in the highly profitable Malibu area. Lana says that at
the time they met she was rather weary of the state of
matrimony. However, May seemed too good to be true.
Physically, he bore a startling resemblance to Tyrone Power.
It was one of the first things *I* noticed when I happened to
meet him, and the resemblance surely did not go unrecognized
by Lana. Secondly, May passed the Dun & Bradstreet check
that for the first time Lana had her business manager, Jess
Morgan, run on a prospective spouse. The report was glowing, and he gave his blessings to go ahead with the marriage—
for the first time, it should be noted. Thirdly, May had the
fortitude to rough up a reporter who had written an unfavor-
able article about the actress and her relationship with Cheryl.
That fit in nicely with Lana's need for chivalry, and it brought
back very fond memories of Greg Bautzer to boot.

The impulsive Lana had already been living "out of
wedlock" with May for quite some time before they married.
However, it was a well-kept secret, and no one worked more
studiously than Lana to keep it. Whenever they went out
together, Lana tried to move incognito. She told me one story
about how when May ordered a new automobile, the two of

them decided to fly to Detroit and personally drive the car back to Los Angeles. Lana preserved her anonymity by wearing a black wig, and the two of them had a fine time on the road. The sole dark spot of their odyssey inspired Lana to establish an important ritual, which she was never to break.

One evening, tired from a long day's drive, they pulled into a lodge and registered, asking that a bottle of liquor be sent to their room. They were horrified to learn that it was against the state law to sell alcohol after five o'clock and that it would be virtually impossible for them to get a drink until the following day. Lana said that although their inclination was to drive on to the next state, they were simply too tired. However, while unpacking, they discovered a small bottle with just one shot glass of liquor. Each refused to allow the other to finish off the bottle ("How do I love thee? Let me count the ways..."). They just sat it on the dresser, in plain sight of both. To make temptation worse, they could hear one of the other guests on his balcony, clinking the ice cubes in his glass as he enjoyed a cocktail. The next morning, after exercising their willpower, the couple scrambled into their new car and sped into the next state. Today, as a result, Lana never goes on a trip of any kind without a well-packed, portable bar. In airplanes, it always rode with us since neither Lana nor I cared to be at the mercy of the stewardesses who seemed to take forever serving drinks. Not that Lana is a raving alcoholic, as columnists have claimed over the years. Sometimes she did drink too much, causing public appearances, interviews, or other engagements to be canceled. At best, she did drink a *lot* and was never able to give up liquor for long. But she was rarely dead drunk, and certainly she imbibes less than many of the famous drinkers who populate the industry. She drank to fortify her basically shy nature against the rigors of her life and profession. She drank on planes because she detests flying. Never mind that it's against regulations to carry alcohol on board; Lana usually had a glass in her hand prior to takeoff.

It was during her marriage to Fred May that Lana sold the Beverly Hills estate and bought the largest beach-front lot available in Malibu. Just to *reach* these superexpensive homes, one had to pass a security guard quartered in a small white booth at the colony's entrance. Lana decorated the new house from top to bottom, ripping out walls, installing a swimming pool, and erecting a wall of surfboards around the pool, the boards being hinged so they could be folded back to reveal the vast expanse of sand and ocean beyond. She and May also bought a working ranch in Chino, California, and another in the hills of Malibu. Lana's mother moved into the house at the Malibu ranch and lived there for several years, helping to tend to the livestock. Lana herself spent weekends there, getting up at five o'clock in the morning, feeding the animals, and in general seeing to their needs. Lana was particularly fond of her thoroughbred racehorses, and she managed to acquire one particularly fine stallion, whose brother was the legendary champion, Kelso. Lana named her horse Grey Host, and he became the favorite of her five thoroughbreds.

At the time, Lana's private secretary was a woman named Lori Sherwood. I've always liked Lori, a cheerful, bubbling lady with a terrific sense of humor. Lana credits Lori with being a great help to her not only professionally but also during the waning months of her marriage to May. As it turned out, although Lana loved her husband very much, she found him too dictatorial for her high-spirited nature. She now rather lovingly refers to him as "the frustrated cruise director." May was the sort of man who would attempt to dictate every waking activity of Lana's day. Up at five, fishing or whatever by six, lunch at noon, appointments beginning at three, dinner at six, and so on. He was a compulsive scheduler and Lana, ever the late one, simply could not keep up with his demands—though she did try. Her tardiness and his impatience were the cause of many long and loud fights between them. Lori would intervene, but because May didn't like her very much, the situation would become even more tense, and Lana would find herself trying to make peace between her husband and her secretary. The advantage of Lori's efforts was that they helped put on the back burner whatever May and Lana happened to be arguing about in the first place.

At this time, Lana was starring in *Who's Got the Action?* with Dean Martin. Indicative of how bad things had become, she and Lori would be headed home in the studio limousine when Lana would begin to shake in anticipation of the fireworks awaiting her at home. Further aggravating the situation was that May found himself in a terrible financial bind. He didn't want to admit these troubles to Lana, who had the pressures of making a movie on *her* shoulders. But it's impossible to keep anything from Lana for very long; apart from being extremely intelligent, she's frightfully intuitive. She discovered that her husband needed eighteen thousand dollars to keep his business solvent, and Lana immediately ordered Jess Morgan to advance him the money. May reluctantly accepted, though to show Lana how much he appreciated what she had done, he took a chunk of the loan and bought her a baby-blue Lincoln Continental. When the car arrived, tied with a huge red bow, Lana blew up. She was shocked by her husband's irresponsibility and yelled, "I don't *want* the goddam thing!" The couple tumbled into their biggest fight yet, Lana storming out—fittingly, in the new car—while May stayed at home fuming.

Lana drove aimlessly until she found herself at one of the many small bars that dot the Pacific Coast Highway. This one was called the Cottage, later to become one of Lana's and my favorites whenever we were in the area. Lana sat at the far end of the bar and had a few martinis, as well as a meaningful dialogue with the attractive bartender. Upon leaving, she went directly to a telephone booth and dialed the Cottage.

"This is the woman from the end of the bar, the woman who just left," she began, and she made arrangements to meet the bartender later that evening at his beach-front apartment. Although casual sex is not in Lana's nature, as I've said, this was different. The liaison was her way of rebelling against her autocratic husband. Lana's only two mistakes regarding the rendezvous happened to be major ones: she left the Lincoln outside the bartender's apartment, and she casually threw her fur coat over the downstairs sofa before heading upstairs with her lover. May, by this time, had decided to go out and look for his wife. It took a bit of cruising before he spotted the car but far less time to peep through the windows of the apartment and recognize the fur coat. He wasted no time laying fist to door and shouting Lana's name.

The bartender managed to hold off May while Lana grabbed her fur coat. She dashed out the back door and ran down the stairs to the beach. Since her car was in front of the apartment—along with the enraged Fred May—Lana chose to walk home along the beach. She was wearing only the fur coat and her sunglasses, and she did her best to ignore the

puzzled stares of those who were out on the shore for an
evening stroll. Even in Southern California, Lana looked a
sight! Capping off what Lana today considers a rather humorous story, her mother happened to be passing the bartender's
apartment at the time and saw both May and the blue
Lincoln. Mildred uncharacteristically took her son-in-law's side
when the legal fighting began, and the couple was formally
divorced on October 15, 1962. The bottom line was "irrecon-
cilable differences."

Lana took a breather from marriage, dating on occasion,
making largely unmemorable movies, and being out of the
spotlight for the first time in decades. The one exception was
the time she accepted Bob Hope's offer to tour the Far East,
entertaining American service personnel. She had just worked
with Bob on *Bachelor in Paradise* and thought very highly of
him. Lana also couldn't help admiring his selfless efforts on
behalf of his country, and she agreed to the tour. She found
the odyssey brutally exhausting but more rewarding than any
enterprise she had undertaken since the war years.

Upon her return, Lana found herself oddly undirected
and hungry for companionship. Dropping by a Beverly Hills
party, she was drawn to a tall man with dark brown hair and
an electric personality. The fellow's name was Bob Eaton, and
the aspiring actor/director/entrepreneur introduced himself
to Lana. It was in his nature to be quite candid about himself,
and though he had no way of knowing, his honesty and wit
were qualities on which Lana thrived. She parried and thrust
right back in matters pertaining to Hollywood, life, and love,
and when they weren't sparring, she was quite entertained by
anecdotes about his many romances. Lana was particularly
fascinated by his affair with a foreign actress and the story
that Eaton had to climb a rope ladder to the actress's bedroom whenever they were to make love. The actress not only
didn't want the servants to know with whom she was sleeping
but also thought that the rope was more romantic than simply
allowing her inamorato to stroll in the front door.

Lana and Bob Eaton were married on June 22, 1965, and
he moved into her Malibu house "officially." As per custom
he had been living there long before their union was sanctioned
by law, and Lana fondly recalls how once, in this spring of
their relationship, she and Eaton had spent five days in her
bedroom, just making love and being together. It was the

height of romance, the kind of physical and emotional luxury that money *can* buy!

After I had been working with Lana for a year, we were visiting a friend of hers, a Beverly Hills socialite. This woman had given over her palatial home on Angelo Drive for Lana's wedding to Eaton, and five years after the fact she had an incisive observation to make. "You know," she told Lana, "if you had just left Bob in the one good suit he owned when you met him, you'd probably still be married to him." She'd hit the proverbial nail smack on its head. When Lana does anything, whether it's getting married or taking a trip, acting or partying, she does it with all her heart. Bob Eaton needed an expensive operation to repair the vision in his one bad eye; Lana paid, and his eyesight was restored. She outfitted him with clothes from the finest men's shops in Beverly Hills and put up the money for his long-neglected dental work. In short, she made him outwardly worthy to be married to her.

Concurrently, Lana reluctantly allowed him to turn her lovely Malibu home into a party house. There was, according to her, a never-ending stream of persons unknown, who would visit the house on a daily basis. They ate the food and drank her booze, and while she tried to be a good hostess, she seldom even knew the names of her guests! She would invariably retire to the upstairs bedroom early each night, though she was unable to shut out the festive sounds rising from below. Through the large picture window Lana would catch glimpses of partygoers using her swimming pool, or if she ventured downstairs, she might find several people asleep in the living room. The ashtrays were always overflowing, empty liquor bottles were everywhere, and Lana found herself each morning apologizing to her maid Carmen, who would have to clean it all up. Lana very quickly grew weary of these excesses in a relationship that, unfortunately, had been founded in plenty.

Daunted by these problems and looking for a way to clear her head, Lana accepted another offer from the USO, this time to visit American bases in Vietnam. While she was on tour, Lana lived in barracks with the female nurses. There were no luxuries for her, but she enjoyed her stay, singularly impressed with the spirit of the fighting men under the most oppressive circumstances imaginable. Lana did not return home unscathed, however; she broke her ankle while jumping a ditch, and she still laughs about how the doctors fought over which of them would be permitted to tape it up. Her voice was always bittersweet when she recounted spending Christmas in Vietnam. She said that the soldiers decorated an ordinary tree with lights and ornaments, singing Christmas carols even while they kept an eye out for enemy soldiers on patrol. To this day, Lana proudly displays the many green berets that were given to her while she was overseas, mementos that hang over the bar in her condominium. Her least agreeable memory of the Bob Hope tour is of one of the other celebrities in the troupe, a young singer by the name of Anita Bryant. Long before Miss Bryant became a controversial spokesperson against the gay community, she was dubbed by Lana, "the most difficult person I have ever met." Lana boasted of the fact that, contrary to what certain members of the company might have expected, she herself behaved like a dream while Miss Bryant was demanding, temperamental, and made everyone's life miserable.

If the situation with Eaton had been bad before the trek to Vietnam, it worsened upon Lana's return. Eaton had been seen in all the popular night spots, drinking heavily, and he had hosted endless parties at the Malibu house. His carousing began to creep into the gossip columns, and the Hollywood community began to speculate about the durability of yet another of Lana's marriages. Lana herself was undecided until shortly after her return, when as Lana related it, Mildred urged Carmen to show her what she had found. Silently, the maid brought forth an armload of sheets that had been used while Lana was away. They showed, unmistakably, that Eaton had been having sex in their bed. As Lana said to me in recounting the sordid revelation, "He didn't even have the decency to go to a motel room!"

Lana picked up the phone and called Eaton at the Sunset Boulevard offices of her production company, Eltee Productions. Eaton protested that he was in the middle of an important business meeting, but Lana didn't care. She told him she wanted to see him *now*. When her husband arrived, Lana simply pointed to the stained sheets. Eaton went white and tried to accuse Mildred and Carmen of conspiring against him, but even he knew that that tack was lame. Lana told him to pack his things and get out. Those of his belongings that he couldn't carry, Lana sent to him later. The next order of business was to have the bed taken from her home and disposed of, something she did at the end of any serious relationship. Lana and Bob Eaton were divorced on April 1, 1969.

Barely one month later, on May 9, 1969, Lana stepped back into the wedding ring, surprising friends and family alike by marrying her seventh husband, Ronald Dante. The couple had met at a Beverly Hills discotheque called the Candy Store, where Dante convinced Lana that, as a hypnotist, he could help her give up smoking. He didn't even do *that* much for her when all was said and done.

Dante was definitely the lowest end of the totem pole insofar as Lana's romances are concerned. He was not a handsome man at all and had pop eyes, like those of a frog. I thought he was strange that day I first met him at the door of their home, and to this day I cannot understand why Lana married him. I can't say I'm a better man for having been on hand from the midpoint of Lana's seventh marriage through to its incredible, turbulent end. However, seeing how Dante tried to use his wife and witnessing the courage that she managed to collect to deal with his perfidy made me respect my new employer all the more. It was the very intimacy of these needs, wants, and soul-baring times that helped to propel the two of us into one of the most challenging relationships ever enjoyed—or suffered—by two human beings.

Chapter Two

It was Southern California beautiful on that morning of August 15, 1969, the air hazed but warm. Despite the raging butterflies in my stomach, I was optimistic as I swung my car off Lankershim Boulevard onto the lot of the world's most famous motion picture studio. After identifying myself to one of the two uniformed guards, I was directed to Miss Turner's dressing room. I managed to negotiate the narrow alleys bordered alternately by looming sound stages, where the movies are shot, and by squat, gray bungalows, the offices of producers and stars. When I reached the one belonging to Lana, I nosed up against the wall and slid from the car, smiling as I noticed the nearby spot marked Burt Lancaster. What caused me to grin even wider was that a car rolled in and out stepped Burt himself, an unfiltered cigarette dangling from his scowl. He saw me and said in that world-famous voice, "Good *maw*ning," and headed on to his office. His frosty brown hair was a jumble; his slightly paunchy torso was draped in a tasseled Indian-style vest. He cut an unlikely figure, yet I couldn't help staring. One thing about the major stars: no matter *how* they look, there's an innate aura that commands attention. It's just one of the qualities that distinguishes them from mere actors.

A horn sounded behind me. I turned and saw an enormous Lincoln Continental limousine, which must just have pulled around from the side. Its occupants were waving in my direction. I recognized my employer through the tinted windows, then I noticed Jack beside her. The driver slipped out and opened the door.

"Get in!" Lana said, beaming, "we're going to the set."

I squeezed into the jump seat across from Lana as she introduced me to Cherie, her hairdresser, and her wardrobe lady, Grace. The four of them were on their way to the sound stage, and we continued on to where they were in the process of shooting an episode of "The Survivors."

The sound stage was the equivalent of one city block away. By the time the five of us had scrunched into the limousine, gotten comfortable for the trip, then climbed from the limousine again, we could just as easily have walked. Of course, the act of walking is not really "Southern California," but Angelenoes *do* do it on occasion. However, Lana Turner walks nowhere unless it's absolutely necessary. At first I supposed that this was necessary to conserve her strength for the rigors of the long day on the set, a day that began with Lana's arrival at the studio before seven o'clock to go through the rigors of makeup and ended with her departure some twelve hours later. In truth, Lana doesn't walk to conserve her strength but because she finds it unseemly that a queen walk anywhere when she can be chauffeured.

I must say that under daylight conditions, Lana did not look as lovely as she had at her home. Mark one up to my naiveté. To compensate for the fact that film is not as fast as the human eye, movie makeup is applied quite thickly, literally like clown makeup at times. Lana was wearing this heavy, pink pancake makeup and looking like a carefully sculpted manikin. However, when I got used to it and began looking at her as the camera sees her, I realized that she was anything but unlovely.

Outside the hangarlike sound stage sat our destination, a large blue mobile home. The sign on the door read Lana Turner, and we all piled from the car and into the junior dressing room.

The first touches I noticed in this dressing room were the soft stereo music already playing and, beside a sumptuous couch on which Lana would relax between scenes, a table with a makeup mirror. This wasn't *just* a makeup mirror, mind you, it was a tall, three-sided mirror that enabled Lana to inspect every inch of herself before she faced the cameras. I don't mention Lana's fastidiousness in a snide or derogatory manner: apart from being a natural-born perfectionist, Lana Turner is keenly aware of what her fans and peers alike expect from her. They want the epitome of beauty and glamour, and Lana would go mad if she thought she let them down. Besides, she's extremely self-conscious about her features, describing her face as "an empty plate." This isn't so much false modesty as an accurate observation because Lana lost her eyebrows in 1938 while filming *The Adventures of Marco Polo* with Gary Cooper. To pull her Western eyes into an Oriental slant, the makeup department had glued a fine fishnet to her forehead, with false brows penciled on. After each day's filming, the mesh was ripped off—tugging with it a chunk of hair. By the end of shooting, Lana's eyebrows were quite literally gone, and they never grew back.

We made it onto the sound stage at ten o'clock, and I honestly don't remember which scenes they ended up shooting that day. I was walking around in a fascinated and disbelieving stupor, at the same time preoccupied with not *showing* my awe. But the morning's work must have been going well, because everyone seemed busy and happy. My job, for the moment, seemed to be limited to the number of ways it was possible to hold a gold cigarette case and offer Lana a light with her Cartier lighter whenever she returned to her very tall director's chair between takes.

It was well after noon before someone called for a lunch break. Jack told Lana that he and Cherie were going to the commissary and would be back in plenty of time to freshen Lana's makeup and hair. The commissary sounded pretty exciting to me, a chance to catch a glimpse of some of the other stars working at Universal that day, so I tagged along. When I learned my way around the industry a bit better, I discovered that few stars *ever* eat at studio commissaries. When they do it's usually the lower-echelon stars who don't have a bungalow, or celebrities who have to give an interview and don't want to cram themselves, a publicist, the interviewer, and often a photographer and their own secretary into a trailer. As for Lana, while working she usually ate nothing more than Triscuits or some such snack for lunch. In the privacy of her bungalow, she would stretch out and review her dialogue for the afternoon filming.

This routine didn't vary, regardless of the film or television project. The only social contacts she allowed herself during the day were with those few people with whom she was intimately working, such as Jack, Cherie, me, or on occasion one of her co-stars. It was as if Lana wanted to carry the ambience of the show and the character she was playing with her at all times. The only exceptions were those rare times when people literally thrust themselves upon her. The most vivid such instance occurred when we had finished shooting early one afternoon, time earmarked for Lana's bleach and manicure. Jack, Cherie, Lana, and I were in the bungalow, along with Lana's manicurist Sherry Peck. As always the limousine was parked at the front door at the star's beck and call, and Lana sent me out to get something she had left on the floor of the backseat. While I was bent over the cushion, with my tail sticking out the door, I heard a vaguely familiar woman's voice calling—not loudly, mind you, just sort of sailing on the wind—"Lanah . . . Lanah. . . ."

I glanced through the back window and saw a woman whose long red hairpiece framed a face smeared with black soot. Though she was quite disheveled, having just filmed a scene involving a fire on a riverboat for a television movie, I recognized the woman's wide eyes and broad smile immediately.

My God! I thought as I stood and turned to greet her. She walked up to me and offered her hand.

"Hello. I'm Joan Crawford."

As if I didn't know. I introduced myself and choked out some novel little phrase like, "I'm so thrilled to meet you!"

Joan smiled as if to say, "Of *course* you are, honey," but she simply asked if Lana were in. I said yes and gestured lamely toward the bungalow. The actress turned and strode toward the door, with me at her heels. We ascended the three steps, and when I tried to escort her inside, Joan stopped, poked her head through the door, and continued calling, "Lanah . . . Lanah!"

Before I could edge around Joan and announce her, I heard Lana call with exasperation, "Who *is* it?"

"It's *Joan*," the visitor all but boasted.

Lana gushed, "Well, for God's sake come *in!*" Only then did Joan cross the threshold. It wouldn't do for a superstar to just stop by; she required the formality of an invitation.

Climbing from her makeup chair, Lana apologized for not being able to clasp Joan's hand, since she was right in the middle of her manicure. Instead, the two legends kissed the air alongside each other's cheek.

Lana made the introductions all around, after which the

women generally bullshitted one another about how they must try to get together more often. I hoped they would for my own selfish stargazing, though I marveled that the two were even on speaking terms. Joan, like Rita Hayworth and Bette Davis, was one of those actresses with whom Lana was hotly competitive in the 1940s. It was not always a one-to-one battle, since there's no question that Bette could have acted any of them under the table; rather, it was a matter of who was the biggest box-office star and who could wring the most concessions from their respective studios. However, as their heyday passed and old resentments crumbled, most of the *grandes dames* of the cinema became quite sociable. There were a few exceptions, people I was to meet over the years, including one awful encounter with Barbara Stanwyck. For now, however, I was content to enjoy rather than psychoanalyze the incredible film history that was gathered in the small room.

Suddenly Joan turned to the open front door and called out, "Yes, yes, all right . . . I'll be there in a moment!"

She and Lana resumed their repartee during which Miss Crawford, at her suggestion, gave me her private home address and very private home telephone number. I dutifully transcribed both into Lana's equally private telephone book. Then, for the second time, Joan turned and called out, more indignantly this time, "Yes, *yes*, I'm coming right *now!*"

The surprisingly thin, frail woman then turned back to Lana and the others and excused herself with profuse politeness, explaining in an agony of detail how she was needed on the set, had had in fact a hell of a time breaking away. Lana thanked Joan for coming by, even though the latter was already walking out the door, then returned to her makeup chair.

As I'd not yet finished my chore at the limousine, I followed Joan out the door. Much to my complete befuddlement, there was no one else out there. I looked to the right and to the left and, sure enough, Joan Crawford was hurrying down the street all by her lonesome. Unashamedly puzzled, I returned to the living room, where I stood rather quietly for a while. After some moments I said, "Lana, you know how Miss Crawford kept yelling out the door, telling someone that she was coming?"

"Yes, dear," said Lana innocently.

"Well, I just don't understand it—but there was nobody *there*."

Even before my declaration had died, the quartet erupted into laughter. Without knowing what I'd done, I obviously felt like an ass. Lana saw my features crease with chagrin and crowed, "Oh, Taylor, that's just Joan's *way*. She always has to make a dramatic entrance and a dramatic departure. Everyone expects it and puts up with it."

Lana later elaborated that Joan had an even more engaging way of leaving a party that she happened to find boring or uncomfortable. Rather than blame a headache or anything so mundane, she would simply pick up the nearest telephone— whether it had rung or not—and registering enormous shock would say, "What?! Oh my *God*! No! When did it happen? Yes, yes, of course, I'll be right there." She would slam down the receiver, grab her coat, and go off. She never bothered to advise the hostess or any of the guests what had transpired, preferring to send a note the following day. These letters were cherished in Hollywood, for they always explained some horrid happenstance but ended with the inevitable phrase, "Thank God everything turned out all right."

Intrigued by Lana's explanation and smitten with curiosity, I subsequently drove to the address that Joan had given as her own. The street was called Norton, located in a very ordinary middle-class section of West Hollywood. I was not surprised to find a very plain, run-down apartment at the address she had provided, and I'm quite certain that Joan Crawford never set foot in it.

As much as Lana may never have become a great actress in a class with Joan or Bette, it was not for want of effort. She lavished superhuman effort on "The Survivors," just as throughout her career she has always given every ounce of energy and preoccupation to her films. Actor Keir Dullea, who played her son Clay Anderson, Jr., in *Madame X*, once told me, "Lana was a woman honed in to what she was doing with absolute concentration. She was also very giving to me as an actor, didn't play what one might consider 'the star bit' at all. I'm not saying that she didn't ever do that or isn't capable of it, but I never saw it." The only times Lana would become difficult on a set were when some insensitive actor or director tried to walk on her or compromise her integrity. I saw that happen several times on "The Survivors" and on subsequent projects, though never to the extent of Lana's most famous rebellion, which occurred behind the scenes on *Madame X*. It began, I was told, when Lana called producer Ross Hunter to her dressing room, explaining that she could not have her hair one color for the morning's scenes, then have it changed without rushing for the afternoon, when scenes were slated to be shot in which her character, after years of drink and prostitution is no longer a radiant blond. Hunter heard her out, then lost his temper, screaming that Lana was holding up production. Lana broke into tears, and Hunter stormed from the trailer, refusing to capitulate. Each ended up meeting the other halfway after whipping up some mutually unflattering headlines. After four enormously successful blockbusters, including *Imitation of Life* and *Portrait in Black*, Lana and Hunter parted professional company. Hunter went on to make *Airport* in 1970, and, though she never said anything after we saw the film, I suspect Lana regretted not having been a part of that production. However, she never let her falling-out with Hunter affect either her performance or her behavior toward her fellow players. She even made up with him.

Producers are rarely on the set, which makes friction with them easier to handle than with members of the cast or crew. Considering the fact that she has made fifty-four films, Lana has *had* surprisingly few fallings-out with actors, and these have not tended to be over trivial matters: for example, Anthony Quinn, who in 1960 accidentally broke one of her front teeth while kissing her violently in a scene in *Portrait in Black;* Glynis Johns, her co-star in *Another Time, Another Place*, whom Lana described as "the bitch of the world"; the late opera star Ezio Pinza, with whom she worked on *Mr. Imperium* in 1951 and categorized as a nonactor and an egomaniac. Even so, Lana would rarely hold up production by fostering tension on a set. She has too much self-respect to be the cause of that kind of environment. As for minor problems, these were always dealt with then and there and put from her mind.

As much in control as she was in professional matters, Lana had remarkably little authority in her private life. This is doubly surprising considering the experience she had dealing with husbands. The biggest problem Lana had was that she tried to be a good wife. That would be admirable if the men she had married hadn't tended to be such heels. Being a mentalist, Dr. Dante would sometimes be booked into clubs far from Los Angeles, in places like Phoenix, Arizona. On such occasions Lana would surrender much-needed rest to travel with him. It was really the only extended time they *could* be together, as Dante never rose with her at five o'clock, and as the date for the show's debut neared, Lana often found herself working until nine or ten at night with wardrobe fittings or doing some last-minute dubbing.

When Lana went on these trips with Dante, she would go to the club and sit in the audience for a time, then return to the hotel room and watch television. It seemed to me self-defeating to travel all that way and then duck out shortly after the lights went down, but Lana attended the show to demonstrate to her husband that she cared—then departed because her presence proved distracting. It *might* have been possible for her to stay unnoticed, except for the fact that as many times as she asked Dante *not* to, he would always introduce her to the audience. Lana would always stand and put on her most radiant smile, waving to the audience and looking rapturously at her husband. As even a hayseed would have to recognize, his innately small spotlight would have to expand to include her, and even after she'd left, the afterglow made him shine that much brighter. Though Lana felt most uncomfortable being exploited, she allowed it to continue for love of Dante.

All of this club hopping was exhausting, but in Lana's mind being married meant being with your spouse whenever possible. However, those around her sensed disaster. If Lana harbored similar feelings, she closed her eyes and ears to them, trying to remain the incurable romantic. I remember vividly those uncomfortable times when Dante would call Lana in her dressing room. She'd coo and giggle into the phone while Jack, Cherie, and I waited discreetly in the next room. The conversation would be punctuated with frequent terms of endearment, breathless utterances that were embarrassing to hear, since we all felt Dante to be an opportunist and a fraud. Our discomfort was such that once Cherie just stared at the floor and uncharacteristically muttered,

"What a jerk." I wondered, at the time, whether she was referring to Lana or Dante or both.

My own suspicions about Dante were reinforced not only by the way he took advantage of Lana's celebrity status but by the dubious quality of his professional achievements. Dante had published a book on hypnotism, which any responsible librarian would have filed under the heading of science fiction; he'd also cut a record, one side of which was supposed to hypnotize the listener into losing weight, while the other side made one stop smoking. I never saw the album in stores, though there were hundreds of them piled high in a closet at the house.

About the time I joined Lana, Dante's entrepreneurial skills were in full flower. His record and book, even his nightclub act, were small potatoes compared to a budding brainstorm that he called Stack-Sack Houses. These were homes built from sacks of cement stacked one atop the other, and they seemed ideal to me for something like the Maginot line instead of a home. But Dante was convinced these economical, sturdy dwellings were the wave of tomorrow. Accordingly, he believed that if he had a piece of property on which to build a model, no investor could resist backing his enterprise.

Dante knew how much Lana wanted him to stop performing, at least until "The Survivors" could be successfully launched. Lana hadn't had a hit film in quite some time, and the television series was proportionately important to her. Besides, for a major film star to appear in a small-screen television series was in Lana's mind a step down—and it was indeed quite a novelty at the time. The theory in Hollywood is that a true star makes people come to her in the theater rather than going to them in their homes. The primary reason she had accepted "The Survivors" was that it was several notches above anything that had ever before been created for the medium. The series had been created by best-selling novelist Harold Robbins, and it was being touted as the first "visual novel," with a new chapter aired each week. It also had the distinction of being the most expensive program in television history, which it remained for ten years until Universal's science fiction epic "Battlestar Galactica" hit the airwaves. Still, "The Survivors" *was* television. If the part wasn't played with precision, if Lana didn't project the magic she radiated on the big screen, her reputation would suffer. In short, the challenge was enormous, and Lana could have used far more emotional support and love from her husband.

Instead of helping Lana, Dante used his nightclub dates to push her against a wall. She wanted to be with him, but he wouldn't give up his performing, claiming that he had to work to raise money for his model Stack-Sack. As always, Lana paid for her playmates; she was about to pay again, more than she could have imagined.

Worn down by the trips with Dante, Lana offered to put up the thirty-four thousand dollars he said he required on the condition that he stop performing and stay home where he was needed. Dante agreed, and Lana contacted Jess Morgan, instructing him to draw a check for the full amount. Jess is nothing if not the most cautious, albeit brilliant, business manager in the world. He had already had several meetings with Dante to discuss the Stack-Sack undertaking, and he was not convinced that it was a sound investment. I personally believe that Jess, apart from his business acumen, clearly saw Dante for what he was and was trying to protect Lana within the boundaries of their professional relationship. But Lana, who over the years has referred to Jess as "Mr. Conservative," elected not to listen to his advice. The check was to be sent by messenger the following day.

The carrier arrived at Lana's bungalow on a Friday afternoon, Lana already having told Dante to come by for lunch. The memo accompanying the check was never seen by Dante, but it stated, "According to your wishes and against my own personal advice, I am enclosing the attached check." Interestingly, this was the only time Lana elected to use the bungalow's spacious dining room. I'm not sure why, though I suspect it gave the event a secure, familial touch—something Lana needed to reassure herself that she did indeed have a loving husband. She had also invited her co-star George Hamilton, the only member of the cast with whom she was genuinely friendly. George had worked with Lana eight years before in *By Love Possessed*, playing a character with the unlikely name of Warren Winner. There had been some short-lived resentment when the two had signed for "The Survivors," George having come on board for $5,000 more than the $12,000 Lana was earning per episode. He was deemed to be a more bankable attraction for what advertisers consider one of the most desirable blocks of viewers, young women. Lana's bruised ego was preserved partially by the fact that, as in any project she undertook, she was allowed to keep all of her wardrobe once filming had been completed.

George kept us in stitches throughout the light meal by telling us about his romantic escapades, tales that would put Don Juan to shame. One of the boldest tales was about his almost being caught in bed with a very married lady. Her husband had just come home and, totally nude, George said he had to exit her boudoir through the window and inch his way under cars parked along the street until he reached his own. George was so convincing a raconteur that never once did I wonder whether the vignette were true, only whether he slid from car to car lying on his stomach or on his back.

When the lunch break ended and George left, there was no one in the bungalow but Lana, Dante, and me. I was seated at my small desk tucked in a corner of the living room, and I remember very clearly how Lana made a joke of giving her husband the check. She held it in front of him and waved it in a playful manner, as if teasing a child with candy. Dante was slightly piqued by the time he managed to get his hands on it, but he had the decency to give Lana a hug and a kiss before he quickly cut a path from the bungalow. Lana watched him go, then stared for a long moment at the closed door. I said something devilishly original like, "A penny for your thoughts."

Lana slowly turned her eyes toward me. She replied, "Money isn't what I need right now," then returned silently to her vanity. I feel she did not sense by then what we had all suspected, that "something was up."

Domestic fears and suspicions aside, our attention was fairly well monopolized by "The Survivors." Despite Lana's best efforts, the show was not evolving to her satisfaction. The role she played was tailor-made, that of a fabulously wealthy woman by the name of Tracy Carlyle Hastings, the daughter of a banking magnate with the unlikely moniker of Baylor Carlyle. Baylor was played by the distinguished Ralph Bellamy. George Hamilton co-starred as Tracy's uppity brother Duncan, while Jan-Michael Vincent was on hand as her son Jeff. Rossano Brazzi and Diana Muldaur were also featured players, and Lana's character was unhappily married to one Philip Hastings, played by Kevin McCarthy. Philip's one redeeming trait was that he had married Tracy when she found herself pregnant, and not by him. In exchange, of course, Baylor had to provide this ne'er-do-well with a cushy job at the bank. Not that Philip was ever at his desk—he spent the bulk of his time and money womanizing.

For having concocted all of this froth, Harold Robbins, who wrote some fine novels early in his career, had been paid a cool one million dollars. Despite constant rewrites, the basic scripts were weak and confusing, even to me—and I had a headstart on the audience, having been able to read the scripts. Not that this was a recent problem. Two years of planning had been lavished on the hour-long weekly show, a period that saw innumerable writers and producers try to make sense of the plots. That ABC and Universal Pictures went with the hodgepodge that emerged is indicative of Hollywood's shortsightedness; the producers succumbed to pressure from corporate offices that were anxious to get *something* on the air and generating revenue. They were confident that the actors and directors could salvage the god-awful scripts, despite warnings from the producers that, as even I very quickly learned, *nothing* can rescue a bad script. As for the executives, maybe they were hoping the viewing public wouldn't notice.

As if the atmosphere going into the project weren't strained enough—or maybe because of the sense of doom— the relationship between Lana and at least one of her co-stars, Kevin McCarthy, became unusually tense. People who had seen completed episodes predicted that he was going to be far more popular than Lana, and she resented that. I felt that it was the attraction a louse always seems to have, whether it's J.R. Ewing or the Wicked Witch of the West, but Lana disagreed. She claimed that Kevin was upstaging her in very subtle ways. I was not yet schooled enough to notice whether or not this were true, although one day the friction between them did come to a head. Lana was delivering her dialogue while Kevin stood behind her, taking practice swings with an invisible golf club. Actions such as these may well be in the nature of a character, though they tend to distract an audience. When it became evident to Lana that the director was going to permit Kevin to continue, she just stopped dead in the middle of her scene. She snarled, "Cut!" then spun to face Kevin. "If you *ever* try that again, I will annihilate you. Now, we're going to do this scene again, and you, *Mr.* McCarthy, will not so much as move a muscle." All Lana had to do was to say it once; the coldness in her voice left no doubt but that she was prepared to enforce her edict.

George Hamilton, on the other hand, managed to infuriate Lana in another way entirely, one that had nothing to do with the show per se but distracted her all the same. Though he had the flair and good looks of a leading man, he had difficulty remembering his lines or hitting his marks properly. That always threw Lana off, and she does not like to divert from the way a scene has been rehearsed. This is not unique to George; I've seen serious, seasoned pros like Richard Basehart and Robert Culp do the same. But not as consistently as George. Lana, able to hit a scene on target and to the director's satisfaction by the second take, would become edgy when a scene had to be shot more than two or three times through the fault of another actor. Lana has earned the nickname of "Two-take Turner" in the industry. Although she could never stay angry at George, Lana often admonished him that if he could just be *himself* in front of the camera, not stiffen up or go blank, he could easily be another Cary Grant. At that point, however, George wasn't able to muster that level of confidence or interest. As a result, though he was relaxed and good-natured offcamera, his performance was never quite believable. It's been gratifying to see that he has finally hit his professional stride with films like *Love at First Bite* and *Zorro, The Gay Blade*.

Telling facets of Lana's personality revealed by her dealings with fellow actors were not only her professional methods but her prejudice as well. Lana respected Ralph Bellamy very much, though they never saw one another off the set. I suspect that's because he was a character actor, a breed of performer specializing in flavorful supporting parts rather than leading man roles. Hume Cronyn, Lana's co-star in *The Postman Always Rings Twice*, told me that character players were considered second-class citizens, and an old bias like that dies hard. "If I'd given Lana the slightest hint," one of her leading men once confided over drinks, "she'd have wanted me to make love to her. I think that's the old fading movie queen syndrome. It's not me, it's just that I was the leading man." Lana earnestly enjoyed Bellamy, who was one of her few contemporaries on the show; but Lana, like Joan Crawford and others of that era, is a victim of protocol.

During the last week of October, Lana received an invitation to be guest of honor at a large charity event in San Francisco, a dinner at the Museum of Natural History in Golden Gate Park to raise money for the Presbyterian Children's Hospital. Lana was flattered, of course, and felt that this was something she would like to do. She finds it nearly impossible not to attend any benefit that will help children. Whether this is because of her own sad childhood is something I'm not sure even she can answer. Lana discussed the invitation with the people at Universal Studios, and they agreed that it would be a wonderful gesture. As long as it could be handled in such a way as to avoid creating the impression that she was going to San Francisco solely for the publicity, she wanted to try to help promote "The Survivors." It had just come on the air, and though it was still too early to determine its fate, every little push would help. The fact that the program had taken a critical trashing neither surprised nor daunted Lana; many shows, from "The Beverly Hillbillies" to "Batman" had taken drubbings in the press yet gone on to be large hits, while highly lauded efforts such as "The Defenders" and "East Side/West Side" went down the drain.

There were many preparations to be made for Lana's appearance in San Francisco. Since she seldom wore the same clothing twice, a suitable gown had to be created for the occasion. Her designer at the time was Nolan Miller, who had been hired to create her wardrobe for "The Survivors." He was actually the second man to hold that post; another top-notch designer by the name of Luis Esteves walked out after several disagreements with Lana. These were not displays of temperament on the part of my employer: better than anyone else, she happens to know in which clothes she looks the best. She also has an uncanny eye for color, and she would have been without peer had she become a designer or interior decorator. Esteves did not necessarily disagree with her recommendations, but he understood better than Lana that craftspeople of television shows don't operate with the same comparatively generous budget or liberal schedule of a feature-length film.

For the benefit, Lana and Nolan decided on a red crepe jump suit over which she would wear a fabulous, red, floor-length lace vest. The lace proved to be very expensive, handmade in Spain, and there was only one such bolt in captivity. Lana instructed Nolan to buy the entire bolt so that no other woman would ever be able to appear in that same lace. The cost of that particular indulgence was charged to the budget of "The Survivors."

Lana was glad to get away from Los Angeles on a minivacation with Dante. We left the day after she had given him the check, and as promised, he hadn't booked himself some professional engagement.

That Lana was relaxing in San Francisco gave the weekend a Brontësque flavor for me. Heathcliff had returned to the home that held such unhappy memories, memories of poverty and of death. However, unlike the protagonist of *Wuthering Heights*, Lana had come to raise rather than to destroy. No matter what I came to think or feel about Lana over the years, this early impression of her as an "angel of mercy" always warmed me.

Our party consisted of Lana, Dante, a representative from Universal, and me. Arrangements for our stay had been made by Phillip Sinclair, the San Francisco public relations man and Lana Turner buff, who had put the gala together. According to our schedule, after departing from Burbank Airport on Saturday afternoon, we would have just enough time to go to the Mark Hopkins Hotel and change. There, Lana wouldn't need more than an hour to prepare for the affair. Jack and Cherie had come to the house to prepare her for the evening's festivities, and as a result, she looked absolutely striking from the neck up—her shimmering blond hair done up in a soft chignon above her very chic, very dark glasses. Insisting that even for the forty-five minute flight she must be no less glamorous from the neck down, she donned a red sweater and matching slacks, both of which fit her like a second skin. Over that she wore a red coat whose ankle-length hem was trimmed entirely in black fox. It all seemed to me a little much for the Burbank terminal, though it made a hell of an impression on the crew of Pacific Southwest Airways.

Due to Lana's lengthy preparations, we missed our scheduled flight and had to be booked on a later one. Even *that* flight we cut close, though the advantage of being Lana Turner is that you don't have to wait in lines. Not that our fellow passengers seemed to mind when Lana was boarded ahead of them. Seeing her walk to that famous, sashaying stroke, smiling and nodding ceremoniously in their direction, was apparently ample reward for being otherwise slighted.

It was late in the afternoon when we finally landed in San Francisco. Though we were pressed for time, Lana suggested that we be the last to deplane. It made sense: we wouldn't be crushed in the crowded aisles, and we could stay together more easily. However, before the aircraft was quite empty, a frantic Phil Sinclair came on board, fearing that we'd missed this flight as well. Charging through the door, he reminded me of Buster Crabbe racing through Sky City in search of Jean Rogers. When he saw Lana, he nearly fainted with relief.

"Thank God!" he gasped, not bothering to introduce himself. "And how thoughtful of you to come dressed for the evening. It saves us having to go to the hotel first."

Lana just laughed, explaining to Phil that this was a mere traveling outfit. His jaw fell to his knees, and we beat a hasty retreat to the exit.

As we made our way through the San Francisco terminal, Lana had to keep constantly punching the Universal rep in the back to straighten him up. He'd been drinking at the house while we waited for Lana, and he'd been weaving around the vast living room even before we left. He had continued to calm the nerves that *all* publicists seem to have while we rode to the airport in the studio limousine, and he kept up the pace once we were airborne. By now he was very drunk and showed it.

There was a limousine waiting for us outside the terminal, along with two motorcycle officers to help speed us into the city. I felt self-conscious about all the pomp, but everyone else seemed to enjoy it. When we arrived at the plush Mark Hopkins, there was a crowd of fans waiting in the lobby, and Lana lingered to sign a few autographs. I noticed that she rarely signed anything more than her name plus a salutation like, "love" or "always," or on rare occasions the individual's name. She will write *nothing* else for the public in her own hand, wary of speculators who might want them to sell her autograph for a large profit. Memories of the Stompanato days died hard. . . . Anyone who tried to peddle an autographed photo would receive no more than ten or fifteen dollars from collectors; anybody who received one through the mail—which happened only if they had enclosed a stamped, self-addressed envelope—would get even less, since for the sake of convenience, these were signed in my own hand rather than Lana's.

Growing anxious over the lateness of the hour, Phil Sinclair gently maneuvered Lana toward the elevator and ushered her to her suite. It took over an hour for her to put on her gown and for Dante to don his tuxedo. It took considerably less time for me to pull on a plain brown suit. Alarmed when she saw my attire, Lana instructed me to buy a tuxedo for subsequent affairs, though she didn't help to underwrite the expense.

Incredibly enough, we made it to the function, though we were some three-quarters of an hour late and without the benefit of our p.r. man, who had gotten too drunk to stir from the hotel. Our tardiness was my initiation to a facet of Lana's character that I would be forced to accept first with annoyance, then with resignation, and finally with fearful displays of temper: she is rarely on time to *anything* that isn't film-related. Movies are her lifeblood, and she'd sooner slit her wrists than endanger a film with lateness. Not so a play, dinner engagement, or affair of any kind. Having said that, I must add that when Lana does arrive, she is always so lovely and so disarming that any hostility that may have festered instantly vanishes. That fact did not help in my ultimately futile efforts to wean her from this practice.

Lana was forgiven when she made her entrance that night. The applause was enthusiastic, accented with whistles, cheers, and assorted "We-love-you-Lana's." The sit-down dinner was quite pleasant; Lana circulated through the spacious but packed hall in the museum while the crowd danced to the music of a live orchestra. Dante hugged Lana's side all evening, though it was all *I* could do to stay within shouting distance of the couple, such was the press of adoring humanity. I remember at one point mentioning to Dante that he keep an eye on Lana's jewelry, though I'd have done better to allow it to be stolen in light of events that were soon to pass.

That night was a special one for me, not only because it was the first of many trips I'd take with Lana but also because my mother was able to attend. She lived in Burlingame, twenty miles to the south, and I freely admit getting quite a charge when she saw me with this woman whom she had admired for so long. I was even able to introduce the ladies after dinner, and Lana made a special effort to spend a few minutes chatting with her. My mother later told me how dazzled she was with Lana's sincerity.

The evening took its first sour turn a half hour later, when it came time for Lana to go onstage and say a few words. By this time she was a bit dizzy from the long day, a condition abetted by the vodka-and-tonics she'd been sipping. Her speech was slightly but noticeably slurred, though people didn't begin to suspect that maybe she'd had a wee too much to drink until Lana decided to *sing* to the audience. It would be charitable to go on record describing Lana as not quite the vocalist that she is an actress. Her singing voice has been dubbed in various films, and justifiably so. However, what was worse than the act itself was that midway through "I Left My Heart in San Francisco," Lana forgot the lyrics. The banquet-goers, myself among them, began to squirm with embarrassment for her. Dante, who was onstage beside her, stepped back a pace, as if to dissociate himself from impending disaster.

There she was, this incomparably radiant woman—stuttering, then humming, then by the grace of some guardian angel remembering that salvation was out there somewhere, that *I* was a singer. Lana called to me with a face-saving, "Taylor, what are the words we rehearsed?" and I stood and belted out the rest of the song with her. Lana was able to finish to surprisingly appreciative applause, though no one clamored for more.

Phil sighed audibly when Dante escorted his wife offstage, and we exchanged a few words of mutual congratulation for an evening well managed, all things considered. Though the evening wasn't quite over for those who had paid to attend, one of the rules of Hollywood-style partying is that a superstar never stays until the end, even if she or he is the guest of honor. The routine for an event such as this is for the star to make an entrance, pose for the press, ease her or his way through the room, then disappear. Through sheer force of personality, they manage to leave the impression that they have given something of themselves to each and every person in the room. It's a real art, and Lana is its da Vinci. She was able, whenever she chose, to get in or out of any social situation at a moment's notice, and without the contrived histrionics of a Joan Crawford. She would simply up and leave, as if no one expected someone so important to have stayed in the first place. What usually followed is that Lana, taut and agitated from having been on display, would unwind by painting the town red. So it was that night in San Francisco. The job done, the money in the coffers, Lana wanted to visit some of the city's more colorful locales.

After stopping at a club to see flamenco dancers, entertainment that rated high on Lana's must-see list wherever we went, we pushed on to Finnochio's, a cabaret famous for its female impersonators. We waited in the limousine while Phil went inside to advise the owner just who was waiting outside; there was a long line of people waiting to get in, but needless to say, there was no wait for our party. Lana caused a flurry of excitement as we bypassed the queue and went right inside.

More drinks were ordered, and the show began. It was a lot of fun, and I remember how the drag queens would make their entrances and turn at once to stare at Lana, as if measuring themselves against her own indisputable beauty. One of the performers went so far as to introduce Lana to the audience; Lana surprised him by being no less forward, climbing right up on stage and joining in a number. Lana enjoyed herself thoroughly, due to the intimate, impromptu nature of the performance, and all of us had by this time imbibed enough so that her singing was very good indeed.

Since California establishments are not permitted to serve liquor past two in the morning, that left us no alternative but to go back to the Mark Hopkins come the fateful hour. Still in a partying mood, however, Lana suggested that we get some submarine sandwiches and take them back with us. Though we were all a little tired and feeling our drinks, when the Star wants to play, everyone else should want to play as well. However, dressed as she was and wearing close to one hundred thousand dollars in jewelry, Phil suggested that the limousine first take Lana, Dante, and me to the hotel and that he go for the sandwiches. Lana agreed to the plan. When we arrived at the entrance to the Mark Hopkins, Dante rather impulsively said, "Taylor, you take Lana upstairs. I'll go with Phil." I thought that was rather sociable of him, and so did Lana. She nodded, blew Dante a kiss, and we headed for the lobby.

Lana was admitted to her suite by a security guard, who was the only person with access to the keys that opened a pair of sturdy locks on her door. Sidestepping the p.r. man who lay out on the living room floor, Lana and I entered the bedroom. I helped her remove the diamonds draped around her neck and wrists and unzipped the back of her gown. As I was fixing the two of us another drink, the telephone rang, and I scooped it up. Phil Sinclair was on the line, calling from the lobby. He wanted to know if it was all right to release the limousine. When I asked why he didn't just ok it with Dante, Phil replied that on the way to get the sandwiches, Dante had ordered him to stop the car a few blocks from the hotel, where he left without a word of explanation and hailed a taxi.

One reason I survived so long with Lana is that, whatever my skills as a secretary, I'm usually steady in even the worst of crises. I told Phil that he should wait for me in lobby, I'd be right down. Lana naturally wanted to know where I was going and why. As I didn't want to alarm her, I said, very calmly, that Phil wanted to show me something and that I would be back shortly.

Downstairs, an increasingly agitated Phil repeated the story he had told me over the phone. It was a total mystery to us as to why Dante just got into a cab and split. Dressed in his tuxedo, wearing some very expensive jewelry, and carrying several hundred dollars in cash, he had to know that he wasn't exactly inconspicuous. Oddly, though, his safety was not as important to me as Lana's state of mind. She was still a powerful, largely mysterious figure to me, and I wanted desperately not to upset her. Also, I didn't want to let her down by mishandling a clutch situation so early in our professional relationship. That may sound a bit self-serving, but it wasn't as if Dante had been kidnapped. He'd run off! The only obligation I had was to do what was best for Lana. I considered trying to track Dante down but dismissed that as impractical. Besides, if he had wanted to be followed, he'd have told Phil where he was going. Maybe Lana would have some inkling as to where he'd gone; regardless, she had to be told.

I let the limousine go and informed Phil that I'd call him in the morning. If *he* had any news, he was to call us at once. He agreed, and I turned toward the unhappy business before me. I couldn't believe that I was going upstairs to tell one of the world's best-known women that her husband was missing. That sick old joke popped into my mind: "Other than that, Mrs. Lincoln, how was the play?" It seemed particularly distasteful just then. So did San Francisco, for that matter. The suite that just a few hours earlier had looked like a wonderful place for Lana and her husband to be at ease now loomed like hell itself.

Lana had changed into a robe, and the look on her face as I entered the bedroom told me that she suspected something amiss. As I've indicated, she may not be psychic, but she reads people instantly and with remarkable accuracy. She is also quick to accept an unpleasant truth, something of a trademark with her and one that was about to be tested to its limit.

As tactfully as possible, I explained what had happened. Lana's response was understandable. She sank down on the bed and began to weep, repeating over and over, "Oh, my God, *why*?" However, she regained her composure after a time, and the two of us sat alone on the bed trying to reason the situation out. Lana hit upon the idea that her husband might have friends in San Francisco whom he'd decided, on the spur of the moment, to visit. She never really believed that, though, and spent the next few hours trying to make sense of it all. It was a very long night for both of us and a wrenching experience for me to see Lana in this kind of pain.

Sometime near dawn, overcome with exhaustion, we both fell asleep side by side atop the covers.

I don't remember what time it was, but the sun was barely up when the telephone rang. Phil was on the line, wanting to know if Dante had returned. The answer was negative, and I told him we'd stay in touch. Lana and I sat there, then, aware that we had to come up with a plan of action. As unfeeling as it may seem, Lana said that it was important to try and keep Dante's disappearance out of the newspapers. A few months before, someone had taken a shot at him in a subterranean garage. The attack made the front page just because he was Lana Turner's husband, and neither Lana nor "The Survivors" needed a rerun of the seedy

speculation his latest escapade would inspire. There have
been times—this was not one of them—when pictures have
been helped by the sensational lives of their stars. The most
memorable are Errol Flynn's rape trial and the spectacular
impact that had on his back-to-back releases *Desperate Journey*
and *Gentleman Jim;* the offcamera dalliance of Elizabeth
Taylor and Richard Burton on *Cleopatra;* and a few of Lana's
own doings. But when the headlines die and the gawkers
crawl back into their holes, the long-term impact is almost
always negative—witness the fall of stars from Fatty Arbuckle,
who was acquitted of manslaughter in 1922 but barely worked
again, to John Garfield, who never recovered from investigation
by the House Un-American Activities Committee in 1951, to
Charlie Chaplin and his 1943 paternity suit. In the long run,
people expect their stars to shine, not to dim with slander.

By this time Lana and I could hear the intrepid p.r. man
up and nursing his hangover, which was considerable. Lana
called him in for a briefing, and I'm sure the dazed fellow
wondered if he weren't still asleep. She instructed him to get
right back to Los Angeles and not tell a soul outside the
studio what had happened. As he gathered up his things, it
occurred to Lana to phone the house on the off chance that
for some reason Dante had returned home. There was no
answer, and we proceeded to try a few of the clubs where
he'd performed. Most were closed, and those that weren't
couldn't help us.

We sat and stared at one another for a long time until,
faced with no option, Lana suggested that we wait it out in
San Francisco for the day. If Dante didn't show up, the two
of us would fly back to Los Angeles that night. Having
reached those decisions, Lana surprised me by undergoing a
swift change, becoming positively defiant. It was as if she had
had enough of worrying about her husband; Lana was
determined to get out and see some of the city by day.

I went to my room and showered, then I crawled into
some fresh clothes. Lana slipped on an orange wool dress
with a matching turban that she had fashioned herself. There
has never been a woman before or since who looks as good in
a turban as Lana. Completing the ensemble were a Chinese
squirrel coat that had been used on "The Survivors" and the
obligatory pair of dark glasses.

As contradictory as this may sound, by the time we had

crossed the lobby and reached the waiting limousine, we were in rather high spirits. Lana's metamorphosis from depression to elation follows a quick pattern of grief, acceptance, resentment, and ultimately, inevitably, conquest. Lana had *made* herself happy, and, since it was she and not Dante for whom I was really concerned, I became rather giddy as well.

It was an unusually clear day, utterly lacking San Francisco's famous fog banks, and the sharp, morning-yellow sunlight was invigorating. We slid into the car; Lana ordered up some soft music, and the mood was definitely right for some decadent exploration.

Though Lana's bearing was "all movie star" and people stared at her, the turban and dark glasses allowed us to wander from shop to shop unrecognized. Only when I slipped and mentioned her name once or twice did people make the connection and ask for her autograph.

Lana is a compulsive shopper, though she usually gives away most of what she purchases. She spent a lot of money that day on what she calls "fun things," items to entertain her in the car or divert her at the hotel: novelties, books, postcards, assorted San Francisco kitsch, and tic-tac-toe-style games. After an hour or so, laden with bags and boxes, we headed back to the car. As we approached, we passed directly before two young hippies leaning against a brick wall. This being San Francisco in 1969, there actually *were* hippies everywhere; these two just happened not to be stoned silly and thus were able to determine that the woman walking by them was a person of some means.

When we swung past the delinquent pair, one of them snapped, "Hey, rich lady, got any change?"

Feeling more like Clark Kent than Superman just then, I said to Lana through the corner of my mouth, "Just keep walking."

As I was to be constantly reminded, no one tells Lana Turner what to do. Whether rebelling against my selfless command or indignant at the way the two young men had boldly intruded upon her privacy, Lana was two steps past them when she turned and confronted them.

"*What* did you say?" she commanded. The two young men just stared. She snarled, "Are you *deaf* as well as impertinent? What did you just ask me?"

The youths had to feel like they were back in the

principal's office. With a tremor in his voice, one of them shot back, "I wanted to know if you got any change."

"The phrase is *have* any change, and I want to know what you plan to do with it. Are you going to buy pot?"

Feeling that the young man had been dutifully chastised, I timorously suggested that now might be a good time to return to the car. Lana just waved me aside and stepped closer to the hippies. After scrutinizing them for a long minute, her expression softened, and she struck up a conversation. Her tone was less domineering than before, but no less commanding. She learned that the two had just arrived in San Francisco and had come from Fresno in the back of a truck belonging to some friends. They explained that they were panhandling in order to get enough money to buy food. When Lana inquired about their friends, the boys said they were inside a coffee house down the square, but they didn't have enough money to spare.

The interview lasted a good twenty minutes, during which Lana asked their names, ages, and if their parents knew what they were doing. The interesting thing to me was that after the initial exchange, she got respectful replies from these two rather unsavory-looking characters. All this time the young men had no idea with whom they were talking, though I suspect that, as they were only nineteen, it wouldn't have made any difference.

After listening intently to their story, Lana opened her purse. I remember clearly her telling them, "OK. Now I'm going to help you, but you have to promise me something. I don't know you, and you don't know me, and we'll probably never see each other again, right? But I want you to promise that you'll take this money and buy yourselves a *nourishing* meal. Then get an inexpensive room somewhere and find yourselves jobs."

When her terms had been agreed upon—twice per anxious hippie—Lana reached into her purse and handed each of them a fifty-dollar bill. Never have I seen two faces light up so spontaneously. They actually began to dance around her, and Lana laughed with them; then she suggested that they join their friends. Before they left, she reminded the pair not to forget their promise.

The two ran ahead, whooping with delight, and again we set forth toward the waiting limousine. I was in the process of telling Lana what a generous gesture she had made when, before us, the door to the coffee house flew open and what seemed like a dozen young hippies came storming in our direction.

"Oh, my God!" I cried. "They're *all* going to want a handout!" For one insane moment I considered dropping the packages, grabbing Lana by the wrist, and making a dash for the car. But the flock was upon us too quickly. Fortunately, and much to my surprise, they had run out not to accost their friends' benefactor, but to *thank* her. None of them asked her for money; they just kept thanking her as they took the packages from our arms and helped us to the car. We were like Dorothy and Toto in Munchkinland.

By this time, the commotion they were stirring had caused other people to stop and see what was going on. It was at this point that a young tourist, a girl of about eighteen, looked very closely at Lana and asked, in a Southern drawl, "Say, are you who I think you are?"

"I don't know," Lana returned. "Who do you think I am?"

"Are you *Lay*-na Turner?"

"Yes, I'm *Lah*-na Turner." She laughed. "What's your name?"

The girl did not reply. She simply slapped her cheeks and screamed, "My mother's going to shit when she finds out I met you. She's just going to *shit!*"

Lana grinned appreciatively as we climbed into the limousine and the crowd milled to her side of the car. She rolled her window halfway down to shake hands with people who came by and wished them all well. In the meantime, several of the hippies had moved into the street and stopped traffic so that our car could pull away. Lana closed the window and sighed as she sat back in the seat. "Isn't it wonderful how you can solve people's problems with just a little money?"

I didn't respond to her rhetorical question, and we fell silent. I'm sure the both of us were thinking the same thing: money couldn't solve Lana's problem. Whether *anything* could remained to be seen.

Fisherman's Wharf was our next stop. During the course of lunch, I casually called Lana's attention to a jacket the maître d' was wearing. Though I'm not particularly fashion

conscious—would not, in fact, consider myself a connois-
seur of anything except fine singing—I can recognize the
quintessentials of food, drink, and fashion. And this jacket,
made of herringbone tweed, was cut more elegantly than any
I had ever seen. Lana agreed it was fine indeed, and when
we rose to leave, I expressed my admiration to the headwaiter.
He confided he'd found the garment in an old trunk, that it
had belonged to his grandfather. Lana was intrigued, and she
impulsively asked the young man how much he wanted for
the jacket.

Taken aback, the maître d' stuttered, "I—I don't really
want to sell it."

"Come *on*!" Lana persisted as if she were haggling over a
melon in the market. "How much do you *want* for it?"

"Really, m-madam, it isn't for sale. It's an heirloom!"

"I'll give you one hundred bucks, right now."

The headwaiter insisted that he needed the jacket for his
job and that this was the only one he owned.

"With a hundred bucks you can buy a new one and have
money to spare," Lana reasoned, which was true back then.

Hearing loud voices and noticing his employee's discomfort,
the manager came over and asked to know what was going
on. This attracted the attention of the people at the bar, and
now that Lana had an audience, she turned the contest of
wills into something of a show.

"One hundred and twenty-five dollars," Lana offered.

"Madam, I—"

"One-fifty."

"Please, you don't—"

"One-seventy-five," taunted Lana.

"But—"

"*Two hundred dollars*," she promised.

By this time the manager had caught on and was grinning
while, with enthusiasm to match the spirited bidding, the
people at the bar encouraged the confused maître d' to take
the money. Finally, the flustered young man turned to his
employer. Noticing the manager's smile, the maître d' said
sheepishly, "I would be a fool not to take it, no?"

The manager nodded. "Take your dinner early. I'll cover
for you while you buy another jacket."

Without hesitation, Lana dived into her purse and counted
out two hundred dollars while the people at the bar cheered.

The maître d' doffed the jacket and handed it to Lana, whereupon she told me to take off my brown sport jacket and put the new one on. I did so, and it was a perfect fit.

Laughing and flashing the crowd at the bar a V for victory, Lana shook me from my slight stupor, and we returned to the car. When we reached the hotel, neither of us was surprised to learn that Dante had neither returned nor called. Lana was not going to wait around. As promised, she phoned Phil Sinclair, and he came to the suite to check us out. We would wait at the house and, if we didn't hear from Dante by Monday night, I would return to San Francisco to check out the city morgues. Macabre as that sounds, it's the direction in which our minds had begun to drift.

There was an unusual footnote to an already unusual day; as we boarded the plane, two men in their early twenties recognized Lana. We happened to sit right behind them, and once we were airborne they knelt in their seats and talked to us. Lana was very friendly, as she tends always to be with her public, and after a short time one of the men initiated a sing-along. It struck me as rather odd that a woman who no longer knew whether her husband was alive should be singing "Row, Row, Row Your Boat" at thirty thousand feet in the air. But Lana, as I've said, lets *nothing* depress her for very long.

The studio limousine met us at Los Angeles, and it took us half an hour to reach the house. The place was quiet and empty, and one of us kiddingly referred to it as the "White Mausoleum." Considering the part of her life that Lana was about to bury there, it was a more-than-fitting sobriquet— and so we called it ever after. The first thing we noticed upon our arrival was that Dante's fancy Italian motorcycle was missing from the driveway. I told Lana to wait in the car, that I would check out the house in case there were an intruder afoot. Just where *I* got my sudden bravery, I'll never know. Making my way toward the back of the house, I switched on every light I could find. There was nothing at all amiss until I reached the bedroom, where I saw that Dante's closet had been stripped to the bone. Further, there was every indication that it had been done in a terrific rush, because books, toiletries, and other items had been left behind.

I hurried out to the car and, as gently as possible, broke the news to Lana that Dante had apparently come and gone.

In retrospect, I'm sure she had expected something of this sort. Nonetheless, when I escorted her into the house, her reaction to the vacant closets was one of shock. She was clearly in a daze, trying to figure out why this had happened. Only later did she admit to me that what bothered her almost as much as Dante's departure was that her home had been violated—it had been enjoyed and then pillaged by someone who cared neither for the owner nor about her feelings.

For reasons of privacy, Lana's staff was not live-in. Consequently, the house was absolutely still as I walked her through every room. My first impression had been correct, that only the bedroom had been hit. However, the most unsettling discovery of all awaited us in Lana's private bathroom. Taped to the mirror, above the vast marble sink, was a note from Dante. He had had the gross insensitivity to use her personal stationery, a pale, delicate blue with her name embossed at the top. I myself was slightly annoyed because he had used my typewriter, which I kept in the office at the other end of the house.

I can still feel the anger that bubbled inside me as I stood with Lana and read the letter that dangled before us. In essence, the note said that Dante felt he simply had to get out and "do his own thing." There were no apologies for his actions or for any mental anguish he might have caused by skipping out this way. The letter was not only entirely self-centered but it was signed, with heartless audacity, "Muggs" —Lana's pet name for her husband.

As bizarre as unfolding events continued to be, I was totally unprepared for what happened next. Lana, who had been standing to my right as we read the note, let out a small half sigh and promptly collapsed onto the sky-blue carpeting. I was less alarmed than perplexed. Nothing like this had ever happened to me, and I didn't know whether to leave her, to try and bring her around, or to call Dr. Mac. I considered throwing water in her face, but I dismissed that as undignified and knew it wouldn't work for me the way it did in the movies.

Suddenly, and I don't exactly know *why*, I remembered the thirty-four-thousand-dollar check Lana had given Dante. That son of a bitch.

I knew what to do then, knew that Lana needed a shock to get her on her feet. I dropped to my knees and, folding her hands within mine, softly called her name. She moaned and seemed to be coming around. The instant she had a toehold in sensibility I said quietly, "Pardon me, Lana, but didn't you loan Dante some money the other day?"

Never before or after have I seen those hazel eyes fly open so fast. Still board-stiff on her back, she barked, "Get Jess Morgan on the phone." I offered to help her to her feet, but Lana wrested her arm away and stiffly repeated her order.

It was by this time very late on Sunday night. Jess was home, and after I had breathlessly offered up a digest of what had happened, that loyal wizard made banking history. God only knows how, but he managed to put a stop payment on the check before it could clear the following morning. Dante thought that he'd been clever by breaking Lana's check into smaller cashier's checks made out to a variety of fictitious names; however, in light of Jess's ninth-inning play, Dante's loaded bases were worthless. Only one check, made out to Harry Firestone in the amount of three thousand dollars, was ever successfully cashed. In order to insure the bank's cooperation, Lana had to put sixty-eight thousand dollars of her own money on the line, which she did without blinking an eye.

Chapter Three

Dante had come into her life when she was at an emotional nadir, and though she would have been perfectly content to let him come home and spend the night, he proved too magnetic to put out. He must have charmed the pants off her, for Lana acknowledged that she at first felt very safe and loved with Dante.

People outside Hollywood tend to look at a Lana Turner or Elizabeth Taylor and self-righteously proclaim that having seven husbands is not only sinful, it's excessive. But it isn't, really, if you consider the milieu in which these women have lived most of their adult lives. One of Lana's directors, Alexander Singer, who guided her through *Love Has Many Faces* in 1965—the film with the famous "million-dollar wardrobe"—once got onto the subject of stardom. Alex, a chum of Stanley Kubrick, is one of Hollywood's most perceptive and articulate directors, and I think he hit the nail on the head in his discourse. I was so impressed that, a compulsive "saver," I made copious notes for posterity.

"I have a certain amount of pity for Lana," he began. "In this decade, the women's movement has permitted women to grow as people so that a young actress, a Susan Sarandon or a Candice Bergen, develops skills outside herself. Inevitably, this enlarges the frame of reference of her interior life. Lana was a very ordinary young woman in terms of interior resources. On top of that, she and her contemporaries were glorified out of all proportion, spending twenty or thirty years in this extraordinary, luminous posture that is an artificial creation of the first order. They're elevated to a position of inhuman adulation, see their face reproduced everywhere, are made incredible goddesses of beauty. That's not fair. All the studio wanted was to squeeze twenty good years out of Lana in front of the camera; there was no concern given to her psychological health. As a consequence, actresses of that era were encouraged to be and do things that were really quite destructive."

Singer is dead right. MGM needed Lana, so she was allowed to demand, wheedle, get her way professionally and materially. Her friends and associates were in awe of her, and after Lana began supporting her mother early on, even Mildred started to tread carefully when telling her daughter what she really was thinking. Only Jess Morgan and a handful of others openly have disagreed with Lana—as in l'affair Stack-Sack—though she usually just ignores their advice. For emotional support, then, Lana never had any choice but to turn to husbands. And as each, in turn, let her down, she moved to another. And another. Then still another. Until finally, she was desperate enough to allow herself to be wooed and taken by Dante—taken as *fast* as possible for as *much* as possible. It was possibly the most savage blow of her adult life because she had so obviously been used, yet she hadn't seen it coming. When I dared confide that Cherie, Jack, myself, and others had been derelict by averting our eyes from the big, bold writing on the wall, Lana admitted what those who knew her longer than I had recognized, that she'd not have listened anyway. "After all," she said, laughing hollowly, "love is not only blind but deaf." Perhaps. Yet, I'm convinced that if Lana had had someone close to her with whom she could have talked things over, she'd never have made the many marital mistakes she did.

It's a gross simplification to say that I just happened to be in the right place at the right time to become that sounding board and, thence, the most important man in Lana's life. True, we had shared the trauma of Dante's leaving, an event that could not help but bring us closer together than just employer and employee. However, what *kept* us together for so many years was our mutual fascination with one person: Lana Turner. I was the only individual throughout the ensuing decade in whom Lana confided completely. And, in accord with my prediction, *because* she had someone to play devil's advocate, she made fewer bad decisions of a personal or professional nature than at any time in her career. It's not that I'm any kind of genius; if I were, Lana would have done better than she did, professionally. She still made all the decisions. I was simply able to point out all the alternatives. As a result, she came to rely on me, and we saw more of one another than the average husband and wife. We ate together, worked together, traveled together, shared the same hotel suites, slept together, drank ourselves silly together, fought together, and had wonderful fun together. We were a great team, and the only reason we never married is that, for once, Lana felt no need to reassure herself through an official pact of a man's devotion. I'm still quite flattered by that, although I personally would have preferred matrimony in order to calm the whip-hand tendon that she occasionally tensed in our professional relationship.

Lana was due on the set of "The Survivors" the next morning. With millions of dollars on the line, not to mention her reputation, Lana did not want to start juggling schedules and risking delays just to ease her personal burden. Thus, she was up at five and ready when the studio limousine came by an hour later. I had stayed over at the Mausoleum, crashing in her guest room around one, and because she very kindly allowed me to sleep, I did not arrive at her bungalow until nine. By then, she was fully made up and openly sobbing to Jack and Cherie about the fact that every newspaper on which she could lay her hands had wasted no time announcing that the husband of the ill-starred Lana Turner had walked out on her in San Francisco. She didn't even care how the leak had occurred, but she later resented the fact that by the time the extent of Dante's thievery was made public, the press considered the breakup old news. At the moment, providing readers with a full picture of his artifice was not, however, foremost in her mind. Lana said she felt like a fool and was mortified every time she thought of what everyone on the set must think. It was awful having to watch this woman gather herself together, put on an elegant face, and walk onto a sound stage to perform before the cameras. She was able to make it through the day thanks to her own considerable professional reserves and the fact that, despite her understandable fears, everyone on the set extended her the utmost courtesy. There was no doting, but rather an absence of the hectic crowding that one finds behind the camera. The crew and co-stars alike were giving Lana space and quiet, which she desperately needed.

Actually, I was not surprised. Years later, when I was visiting a friend at CBS's Studio City, where Mary Tyler Moore's ill-fated variety series, "Mary," was being taped, I saw a dancer fall right in the middle of an extravagant production number. While the dancer slowly rose and hobbled offstage to massage her ankle and the set was rearranged so the company could begin from the top, Mary came backstage for a slug of Tab. I asked her why everyone had walked away, leaving the dancer to her own resources. She replied, "Everything is magnified in show business, the highs and the lows. Making a mistake is embarrassing enough because of the number of people who see it, so the last thing another performer wants to do is heighten the embarrassment by calling attention to it. Better to leave the person alone." It's a courtesy that show people just naturally extend; it's also a silent acknowledgment that, in this capricious industry, it's only a matter of time before everyone from Mary Tyler Moore to Taylor Pero each needs that moment of privacy.

At day's end, I found myself bothered by the thought that Lana would go home, dismiss the hired help, and be left alone in that rattling big vault on the top of the hill. I offered to stay with her again, and smiling appreciatively, Lana accepted. It would be several months before I found out why she didn't respond to my alternative suggestion, that she go to Cheryl's house.

Up at the Mausoleum I settled into the guest room, which happened to adjoin my office and came complete with a bath, refrigerator, Dante's heat lamp, and anything else I might need. Carmen Cruz, who had been Lana's maid for over twenty years, stopped by on her way out to thank me and tell me how very happy she was knowing that someone would be there to look after Lana. She added, in her innocent way, that she hoped I'd stay "many, many nights."

I ended up staying at the Mausoleum for a few days, engaged in no more than my normal, solely professional routine with Lana. There was nothing at this point of a sexual nature between us, and not because I found Lana undesirable. Just the opposite was true: I often fantasized about making love to her. Sex, to me, is not only the most pleasing but the most multifaceted of all activities. I have slept with women and men alike and have discovered that there is no end to the kinds of pleasure a person can give and receive. In Lana's case, however, I simply and honestly didn't want to ruin a fine working relationship. In that sense, I made a grave error when I volunteered in due course to sublet my one-bedroom apartment and move into the guest room. My offer was genuinely motivated by concern for Lana, inspired one morning when we were reviewing her agenda at the studio and she said, "It's comforting to have a *dependable* man around." But I was not ignorant of the dangers involved. Neither of us was so naive as to overlook the obvious: never mind whether or not there was a mutual physical attraction; we'd be so convenient for one another that sex was inevitable. Still, it would make my job easier by cutting an hour from my travel time; besides, when Lana *accepted* my offer, I felt ten feet tall. And so, taking a page from the book of my glorious employer, I damned the torpedoes and steamed full ahead.

Because Lana is such an intuitive woman, I think, in retrospect, that she wanted me around for a calamity she sensed was yet to come, rather than to commiserate over her husband. Not only had "The Survivors" premiered to miserable reviews, it was not doing well in the ratings race. One of ABC's rival stations had gone so far as to blunt the crucial debut episode by scheduling *Madame X* against it. Chief among the problems cited by critics and viewers who wrote to the network was that the story line was disjointed, convoluted, and preposterous. No wonder, since writers and directors continued to be hired and fired almost daily. Worried by the magnitude of this public rejection, Lana renewed her complaints about the scripts to the studio heads. She did not presume to tell them how to do their jobs, but she did recognize that she, at least, would be unable to help the show unless they gave her more to do than show off smart new Nolan Miller outfits. The producers assured Lana that these matters *were* being taken care of but that it was too late to do anything about the thirteen episodes already in the can. Their sole concern at the moment was promoting the show, not improving it—as though the two were mutually exclusive.

Meanwhile, rumors spread quickly over the set that the series was bound for an early grave. But they were only rumors. Lana had signed for twenty-six episodes, and it seemed reasonable that with all the money riding on "The Survivors," ABC would at least give it a full season to find an audience.

During these trying days, domestically, at least, all was comparatively well. The Mausoleum was large enough so that Lana and I could have our privacy, yet small enough so that we were never more than a very loud holler away. Each morning, as Lana was about to head for the studio to have her hair and makeup done, she would come into my room and wake me very gently, often with a kiss. I'd watch her sweep from the room, wearing her "working mink," and begin to pull myself together. The studio was minutes away, just down the hill, so I could take my time getting ready and enjoy not having to worry about traffic on the freeways.

Because Lana and I did not arrive in tandem, I was able to get a jump on yet one more calamity. One morning, a few weeks into the new season, I arrived at Universal and happened to bump into Cherie. She was walking from the sound stage toward Lana's bungalow, and when she didn't return my wave but scurried over, I knew that something was wrong.

"Today's the final day," she said breathlessly. "I just heard it from Brad, the assistant director. It's over, finished, they're not going to complete the remaining episodes."

My first thought, naturally, was for Lana's state of mind. I asked Cherie how she had taken the news, and my mouth fell open when the hairdresser replied, "She hasn't been told. I don't think anyone's got the guts."

Recovering from my shock, I protested that surely someone from the Black Tower—Universal's executive offices right on the lot—surely *someone* must have phoned. Or Lana's agent at the William Morris office—*he* must have called. Cherie just shook her head. Disgusted, I hastened toward the bungalow. Jack was putting some finishing touches on Lana's makeup; I could tell from his dour expression that *he* knew. I couldn't imagine what grim tale he must have concocted to cover for his obvious depression. In fairness to both Jack and Cherie, it wasn't their place to inform Lana that her show had been canceled. Nor had I any desire to be the bearer of bad news. Still, she had to be told, and, "tag," I was it.

I approached the makeup chair from behind, and Lana smiled at me in the mirror.

"Good morning, Taylor, dear. Sleep well?"

Jack backed away, pretending to gather a few items from his kit. Cherishing her smile before it faded, I said, "Forgive the lack of tact, but I think you'd better call whoever's in charge of this show."

"Why?" She frowned. "Is something the matter?"

"I believe so. According to the assistant director, we're all through."

Lana's eyes narrowed, and when I'd filled her in on the little I knew, she just sat back in the chair while Jack finished his work. When we arrived at the sound stage shortly thereafter, she searched the busy set like a hawk. Spotting Brad, she took him discreetly aside.

"I want you to tell me whether or not today's our last day."

Brad stared at her with a blend of confusion and embarrassment. "You mean, nobody in the Black Tower told you?" Lana indicated that they had not, and Brad courageously did the executives' dirty work. Lana thanked him sincerely and retired to her mobile home. Considering how deeply she had just been humiliated, her bearing was nothing less than regal. It was my first lesson in falling from favor in Hollywood. When you're a star, you get first cabin treatment. When you're on a sinking ship, they won't even heave you a life preserver.

Lana did the day's work like a trouper, though there were more than a few tears all around when shooting was wrapped. Lana had grown especially fond of what she called "my crew," a habit with her. Working on any project, performers get so caught up in what they're doing that it becomes their life. The people behind the camera literally replace one's family and friends, and this is especially true with Lana, who has an almost supernatural respect for the talent of movie crews, from the cinematographer to the lighting hands. Now there was nothing. "The Survivors" was to be disassembled down to the team that built the sets, each member being an employee of Universal Studios and, like soldiers, shipping over to new projects. Universal, by the way, finally called Lana's agent at four o'clock with word that the show had been dropped.

After spending so many months on the program, Lana's

spirits fell understandably low. There was no longer a set to go to, no lines to memorize, and for the first few nights she'd mostly lie in semidarkness in her bedroom. I'd hear her crying and go to her, but Lana would collect herself and insist that she was fine. It took about a week for her to come to grips with the cancellation.

"So," she announced one afternoon as I was handling some correspondence, "we've had two swift kicks in the ass. So *what*? I've had them before and survived, and I'm sure you have, too. I'll survive these."

It was glib, I'll admit, but all I could think to say was, "Well, that's *one* survivor ABC ain't gonna cancel!" Lana cracked up, more from relief than from my fast wit, and we went to the bar. I proceeded to fix us some drinks, and we had one of our drink-talk marathons. She recounted all the high hopes everyone had had for the show. There had been an enormous bash at the ritzy Bistro in Beverly Hills to announce the series and location shooting on the French Riviera—which was unheard of for a television budget. The September debut had been publicized like no other in the history of the medium, and surveys showed that the viewing public was ready for this kind of glorious soap opera in the tradition of "Peyton Place," the smash television series based on her own hit movie. "Now," she said wryly, "there are enough press clippings to reach the moon, and good and bad script pages to come back again . . . but no show." What Lana *did* have, she enthused, was a future to build and a loyal secretary to help haul over the bricks and timber. That was enough, she claimed, to help her shut the book forever on "The Survivors."

One turn of Lana's personality that I discovered during the next few days was that when she's not working, she's most definitely a night person. Lana prefers to stay up all night and then sleep until two in the afternoon. As a rule she used to spend her nocturnal hours at restaurants or parties, though in the wake of her television debacle, she wanted to avoid the press and cherished nothing more than the privacy of her home.

In the bar area of the Mausoleum there was a small bumper pool table. Lana is an expert player, and I delighted in watching her. She has the most beautiful hands I've ever seen, and it was always a pleasure just drinking in the graceful manner in which she handled a pool cue. For her part, Lana, by God, loved to win. She taught me how to play the game and took me to the cleaners nine out of every ten times we had cue in hand.

Lana and I would play every day after the mail had been opened and we'd taken care of whatever little business was on the docket. Eventually, the hired help would leave for the day—Carmen always smiling at me—and we'd continue our games well into the night. Toward the end of a bumper pool session, it was not unusual for us to be alternately screaming with laughter or swearing fluently over miscalculated shots. Lana was inclined toward the more traditional "oh, shits" and "fuck-its," though I was able to come up with bluer, more evocative phrases such as "scum-sucking *dog*," which Lana loved. It was closely akin to primal therapy, using this silly little game to shout out our hostilities and frustrations.

As we played we drank, which was the reason the table had been placed by the bar in the first place. I drank a variety of beverages at the time, over the years coming to favor scotch. Lana, however, almost exclusively drank vodka and tonic. And it had to be prepared just so: two, not more than three, ice cubes in a highball glass, filled half with vodka, half with tonic, squeeze of lemon. One reason I have to laugh at reports of Lana's "habitual drunkenness" is that it takes Lana forever to finish a drink. Unless she's at it for hours, she rarely nurses her way through more than two or three drinks. The only time she tends toward a hastier pace is, unfortunately, when she's at a public engagement, where she knows that people will be sizing her up from head to toe—or, as she puts it, "Getting close isn't enough. They want to count your pores." It takes a lot of vodka to encourage Lana to sally forth as the larger-than-life movie star, and on such occasions the alcohol sometimes gets the better of her. I think, frankly, it's unfair that male stars like Richard Burton and Peter O'Toole, who have been known to be heavy drinkers, are tolerated and even cheered by the press, whereas females who sometimes walk a tipsy course are the objects of pity and contempt.

Days came and went at the Mausoleum, with very little change in the daily pattern. The household staff would arrive at midmorning and go quietly about their cooking and cleaning chores, and the telephone answering service knew not to put through any calls until I rang that it was all right to do so. Then on to the mail, business, drinking and bumper pool, sleep. . . .

I have never fully understood how, for a woman who smoked and drank and starved herself as much as Lana; who, save for a modest daily routine of stretching, shunned exercise utterly, refusing to play tennis, swim, or even dance for fear of developing unladylike muscles; who would not even play golf for fear of damaging her manicure—how anyone so antifitness and nutritionally irresponsible could possibly be so health conscious. She'd pop a Contac at even the remotest hint of a cold, and she had both a drawer and a travel case stocked with all manner of medication. There was no ailment for which she was unprepared, from muscular tension to a fever, and even potential sicknesses had met their match in Lana: if she had to be around anyone with a cold, she insisted that that person wear a face mask. If the individual reacted with irritation or embarrassment, that was simply too bad. Not that these idiosyncrasies bothered *me;* illness and the threat of neutralization of same were the only distractions in our otherwise pleasant but innately dull activities.

At this time, Lana and I were still primarily employer and employee, though we had obviously become "pals" as well. There was devotion and affection with a modicum of sexual innuendo ("Look at those buns!" Lana would say while holding a hamburger, though it seemed her eyes were locked squarely on my derriere), though nothing as yet more intimate. As for me, with a failed marriage of two-years' duration fast becoming ancient history, I was more than pleased to have Lana as even the platonic lady of my life.

Naturally, I was by no means a captive of Mulholland Drive. At night, I was free to take my little blue convertible and go whenever I wanted. This being Southern California in 1969, that meant either going to a bar, a movie, or watching the tar bubble at La Brea. I tended to stay at the Mausoleum, since I genuinely enjoyed Lana's company, and quite honestly, due to the modest nature of my wages, I was always low on money, and she was very generous in providing me with food and drink.

Lana tended to pass most of her afternoons on the phone and early evenings watching television. This included watching her own films whenever they were on. She regarded these as "photo albums," summoning up memories good and bad. The good memories were about the likes of Clark Gable and John Garfield, both of whom generated with Lana a rare, engrossing screen chemistry. Her bad memories were usually about films rather than about people, many of whom she'd banished from her mind. She would often entertain me during the commercial breaks with recollections about the making of these lemons—for example, *The Prodigal* in 1955, which she credits as one of her least-favorite films. Made at the height of the Cecil B. DeMille-inspired sex-and-Bible cycle, Lana told me how she gave the censors heart failure when they saw the amount of flesh she was revealing. Her principal costume was originally designed with a minimum of fabric but scads of beads with just a hint of nudity; Lana ordered the wardrobe lady to cut some of them away, a snip here and a strand there until there was nothing but the two pieces of cloth connected by eight widely spaced strings of beads. Lana says that it was the only way she could get back at MGM for forcing her into this five-million-dollar fiasco.

When Lana wasn't reminiscing, she was busy studying the television commercials, actually sitting there with a notepad and jotting down the name of each new product. It didn't matter whether it was a new popcorn popper, a doll that wets when it laughs too hard, or a miracle seed grower. She had to have it all, and it was one of my jobs to go out and buy her these things. She'd look them over, try them out, then give them to me or to Carmen. Lana never tired of acquiring things, often very juvenile items, another habit no doubt inspired by her deprived youth.

The one aspect of Lana's televiewing that was most interesting to me was the way she'd perk up for the talk shows. She rarely went on them herself, though on occasion I'd learn something about Lana from one of the guests. Typical was one afternoon Fernando Lamas and his wife Esther Williams were guests on "The Mike Douglas Show." Mike asked how they had come to meet, whereupon Esther said that her dressing room at MGM used to adjoin that of a very important star whom Fernando was dating at the time. It was a tempestuous romance, since Fernando had a typical Latin temper and the star was known for having spunk of her own. Esther said that she used to overhear their fights and

also their romantic encounters and that she made up her
mind to meet and marry this fascinating man. As Lana and I
watched the interview, she sat in her chair and with a
knowing smile turned to me and said, "Yes, dear, it was me."
A few years later Lamas was put forth as a possible co-star on
one of Lana's films. Although he had been happily married to
Esther for many years, Lana didn't even need words to
convey her feelings about him. Just the coolness of her eyes
and the slow side-to-side movement of her head brought to a
dead halt any further discussion of him. Never mind what
magic they may have brought to the screen. To Lana, Lamas
was dead. The nonchalant way in which Lana had dismissed
the suggestion rather belied, in fact, what had been one of
her most torrid flings. Esther Williams had only scratched the
surface! Lana and the Argentinian actor had met on the set of
The Merry Widow in 1952. MGM was thrilled when their
most popular and most promising stars had hit it off and
encouraged them with publicity and the development of
other co-starring vehicles. But the relationship came crashing
down when Lana asked Lex Barker to dance at the Johnny
Ray party. Lamas, indignant, accused her of being indecent
and, rather spitefully, of being a disaster in bed. Ironically,
Lamas went on to marry Barker's ex-wife, Arlene Dahl. By
ending his relationship with Lana, Lamas also unfortunately
crippled his film career: MGM elected to hire Gilbert Roland
for *The Bad and the Beautiful* and elected to replace Lamas
with Ricardo Montalban in *Latin Lovers*.

Most of the time, however, our viewing hours were not
so informative, and often they became downright annoying.
Lana has a positively unnerving habit of leaning forward and
scrutinizing everyone who comes on the tube. If we were
watching "Dinah," Lana would go into a litany the instant
Dinah Shore appeared.

"Look at those terrible shoes! Why is she *wearing* those?"

"I don't know."

"And look at that *dress*! It makes her look huge. Why is
she *wearing* that?"

"I don't *know*!"

"Jesus, will you *look* at Goldie Hawn's hair! Why would
she appear on TV looking like that?"

"I just *don't know*!!"

By the fifth or sixth time, I would give Lana a look,

whereupon she'd sink down in her chair and say, "I think I'll just shut up." But she'd start again within moments and continue until you wanted to kick in the television screen. Nor, by the way, was Lana's critical eye restricted to what she saw on television. It roved constantly, no matter where we were. She would wonder who designed a stewardess's ugly uniform, how a waiter could walk in such tight pants, why all the women in Chicago seemed to have such fat asses. It took me a while, but I finally realized that Lana's preoccupation stems from more than just her interest in clothes and appearance. The sad fact is that she rarely has anything more important to worry about.

There was another "T" that made life interesting. In addition to Television, there was Telephone. And never was the telephone more interesting or unpredictable than when Lana made her nearly daily calls to her mother and her daughter.

I met "Gran" first, which is what we called Lana's mother. Every time I think of her, even today, I'm reminded of amethysts. Lana had given her boxfuls of magnificent jewelry over the years, but the violet gems were Gran's favorites.

Mildred is a very quiet and perceptive woman. Although she'll side against Lana when she feels her daughter is wrong, Gran is above all protective of her. This was as true when I met her as it was at the beginning of Lana's career. Yet, she is an evenhanded woman. I think Lana would have done better over the years had she chosen to solicit Gran's opinions more frequently. In terms of Gran and me, we became very close friends from the start, not only because of our common interest in Lana but because the old woman was the only reliable source of stability in the entire Turner family.

I have to admit that as much as I saw of Cheryl, I was never very close to her. She was usually friendly enough toward me, yet she generates an aloofness that she carries like a shield. The only time I *ever* experienced anything approaching warmth from her was several years after we first met when she came to Denver to see Lana in *Bell, Book and Candle*. She subsequently wrote me a note that said, "You are a marvel. I never realized what a twenty-four-hour job you have, and I wanted to let you know how much I appreciate the wonderful care you are taking of mother." Even then, the tone was more one of admiration for my stamina than an expression of friendship.

In her defense, Cheryl had spent most of her life in an emotional wringer. As a child, she had been overindulged, so much so that Cheryl's youth was really little different from that of a princess. She had the most expensive wardrobe of any child in Beverly Hills, and she knew the feeling of ermine and satin against her skin when she was barely able to walk. Anything she wanted was provided by Lana, Stephen Crane, her grandmother, her Scottish nanny, or the servants. It was easy to arrange for the hero of the day, Hopalong Cassidy, to put in an appearance at Cheryl's birthday party, scoop her onto his horse, and ride around with her—after which Lana presented her daughter with her very own pony. Or, at the invitation of Fred MacMurray, to spend a summer with his children and the children of other movie personalities on his vast ranch in Wyoming—where, according to Lana, everything each child did was tabulated and, at the end of the youngsters' stay, a bill presented to each parent. (MacMurray later informed me, "That's a lot of crap. I don't know what she's talking about!")

One can hardly blame Lana for having tried to give her daughter the fairy-tale childhood she herself would have relished. This is obviously every parent's ambition, though the monied citizens of Hollywood can realize it more conveniently than most. It follows, not coincidentally, that child rearing in Hollywood also so very often turns out all wrong. The reasons are many, though two are predominant: the unusually high number of divorces and the fact that celebrity parents spend so much time performing, often away from home, in order to pay for their luxuries. As a result, there is wealth but very little attention given to these children. There are also the ever-present comparisons between parents and offspring, analyses that even the most well-adjusted offspring find difficult to accept.

The list of Hollywood children whose lives have gone wrong is sadly limitless; Cheryl, at least, has made a life of her own. The same cannot be said for many, many others, such as Paul Newman's son Scott, dead in his twenties; Gregory Peck's son Jonathan, who shot himself to death at the age of thirty with a .44 caliber revolver; Mary Tyler

Moore's twenty-four-year-old son Richard, also dead of a
gunshot wound, as is Charles Boyer's twenty-one-year-old
son Michael; James Arness's daughter Jenny, who gulped
down a lethal dose of sleeping pills when she was twenty-
four; not to mention the drunken demise of Charles Chaplin,
Jr., and Edward G. Robinson, Jr., plus so many others. If
there is a common denominator in the lives of youngsters
who *did* rise above the pitfalls of being celebrities' children,
such as writer/producer Fraser Heston and attorney Bela
Lugosi, Jr., it is that whatever indulgence there was seems to
have been of a cultural rather than a baldly material nature.

In Cheryl's case, rather than being spoiled, she very
early on came to resent the cornucopia, and she fought
having to live in the shadow of a mother who was not only an
international celebrity but one of the world's most beautiful
women. Lana's fame was grating for as far back as Cheryl can
remember. One of the earliest memories she has is, at the
age of two, of being torn from her mother by a mob of fans
outside the Sherry Netherland Hotel in New York. Cheryl
told me that she never understood who or what a "Lana
Turner" was. "It was my *mother* they were always mobbing,"
she would reminisce, "and that's a frightening thing." Lana's
beauty was another matter entirely. Although Cheryl is very
attractive in her own right, she simply does not possess the
legendary face or figure of her mother. Though she was
always the best-dressed child in Beverly Hills, Cheryl often
heard friends and strangers alike comment aloud what a pity
it was that she hadn't her mother's physical perfection. Nor
does Cheryl attract people with the force of her personality
the way Lana does. Select outsiders could hope for no deeper
peek into her soul than to read her poetry: "Loneliness,"
"The Tinseled City."

Because of this—and then the horrible tragedy of her
involvement with the Stompanato murder—Cheryl was a
frequent runaway from the age of thirteen and, later, she
fought constantly with her mother.

However, Cheryl was always close to Gran. Gran's and
Cheryl's mutual affection became even stronger when the
Turner matriarch moved in with Cheryl and a friend, Joyce
LeRoy (known as Josh). Neither Cheryl nor Lana saw any
reason for Gran to pay rising rents at her small apartment,
a decision that drove them to convert the downstairs of

the Calabassas house into private, self-supportive rooms.
I think Cheryl exhibited a great deal of love and concern
allowing Gran to move in; as much as Lana loved her
mother, she doesn't like being silently watched or judged and
didn't want her living under the same roof. This was, as it
turned out, a painful setup for Lana. On weekends, Lana and
I would drive out to the house so that she could spend time
with her mother. Cheryl was not always at home when we
arrived—a coincidence, we usually allowed. But there were
exceptions. One Monday afternoon I came to collect Lana,
who'd spent the weekend with Gran. On the way home she
broke into tears, revealing that she'd heard footsteps and the
stereo from above all weekend, yet not once did Cheryl come
downstairs to say hello. Nor did Lana go up, it's true; a
mother's conceit, I submit. My heart went out to Lana, and I
argued not for the first time that she was too forgiving of
Cheryl. But Lana had learned to remain silent or conciliatory
just to keep the peace. And because Cheryl *was* her daughter, after all, she wanted her to be happy—even at her own
expense.

In short, there was a surfeit of heartache, and I spent
more than a few long nights easing Lana's pain and self-
reproach in matters pertaining to her daughter. As a result of
this and of Cheryl's and my fundamentally different natures,
while there were many holidays and birthdays that I cele-
brated with the family, I was never entirely comfortable in
the woman's presence. But, and I was thankful for this,
neither she nor Gran was ever dull.

Maylo, my daughter, was included whenever possible in
all of our "Turner" family holidays. One Christmas, when
Maylo was about eight we drove out to Cheryl's to drop Lana
off for the weekend. Cheryl always decorated her home like it
could be photographed for *Better Homes and Gardens* and
Maylo was suitably impressed with the giant Christmas tree
that went to the top of the two-story living room. More
impressive were the vast array of beautifully wrapped gifts
that lay under it. Cheryl had thoughtfully placed a present
under the tree with Maylo's name on it. After we had been
visiting around the fireplace in the warmly appointed living
room for about an hour, Cheryl took Maylo over to the tree
and helped Maylo find her present. Maylo then brought it
back to the couch and, in front of Gran, Lana, me, Cheryl

and Josh, she made a great ceremony of opening it. I truthfully don't remember what the gift was.... However, the punch line of the story is that Maylo shortly afterward found she could not hold back her tears. None of us could figure out what on earth was the matter as she tried bravely not to cry. Finally, through her choking half-sobs, Lana was able to find out why Maylo was so upset. It seems that since she was the only child there, she had naturally assumed that ALL of the presents were for her. Well, we all had to laugh at that one, but then Lana took great pains to explain to Maylo what the situation was... that she was still Gran's little girl and that Cheryl was still HER little girl and so on. Maylo was able to comprehend what Lana was telling her and everything was soon smoothed out... although Maylo kept eyeing the remaining presents until it was time for us to leave.

I recently asked Maylo what she remembers about Lana and her immediate response was, "her mouse collection." Lana has an extensive collection of mice. Some of them are stuffed and comic, others are extremely rare, one in particular which is made of solid gold with ruby eyes mounted on a fabulous chunk of unpolished turquoise. Each piece of the collection is equally important to her and when Maylo would come to visit she and Lana would often go through the vast collection. Lana has names for each member of the collection and she and Maylo would often fantasize about how, at night after everyone was asleep, each of the little creatures would come to life and play the night away, only to return to their places with the first light of dawn. Such is the stuff of imagination that stirs the creative juices of the actress and the impressionable child. I do feel that Lana's subliminal influence on Maylo was valuable in helping her toward her determination of her life's goal of acting which, happily, Maylo appears to be reaching.

Although "The Survivors" was gone, in the small minds of some people it was not yet forgotten. The telephone rang one afternoon, and I took the call in my office. Lana's agent was on the line, calling to try and make a deal on behalf of Universal Studios. He asked me to find out if Lana would settle for fifty cents on the dollar of the monies the studio still owed her. I thought it strange that a high-powered agent should ask Lana's secretary to convey such an important question—but once again, I was discovering that no one wanted to deal with the star herself.

I told him I'd call back, then I walked to Lana's bedroom, where Nolan Miller and his top seamstress were fitting her for a new gown. As I leaned against the doorway, Lana turned slowly and asked, "Who was that, dear?"

"It was your agent."

"Oh? And what did he want?" Lana turned back to her full-length mirror.

"He called to ask if you would settle for half the money owed on your Universal contract." The implication, I added, seemed to be that if she didn't, she'd never work there again.

Lana's face remained unchanged. She turned toward me, she shook her head and answered in two words:

"Every . . . dime."

Then she calmly gave her full attention over to the fitting, with the air of one for whom this matter has been settled.

I strode directly to my office to call the agent. Suffused with the flush of power, and doing a bad impression of Lana's own resolute manner, I said, "In answer to your questions, sir, Miss Turner has replied, 'Every dime.'"

The meek-sounding voice on the other end of the line sighed. "Ah . . . yes, well, I guess I'm not surprised."

Later that night, when Lana and I talked about the call, she explained to me the sound, very sound, reasoning behind her decision. She had signed their contract in good faith. She had done what they'd asked of her, even going beyond her duties and pointing out exactly what was wrong with their stinking scripts. It was not her fault that the public did not want to watch. In fact, people who *were* polled or wrote to the network said that the only reason they had bothered to tune in was to see Lana. There was no question about giving Universal *anything*. Besides, as Lana revealed, she had already given the studio quite enough. In 1959, Universal had been in a bad way financially and had just enough money for one more film. They selected *Imitation of Life*, asking Lana to star as a Broadway actress who puts her career before the well-being of her teenage daughter. In deference to Universal's troubles, Lana agreed to take a minimal salary up front but to receive half of the profits plus interest. That was a chancy proposition: if the film had flopped, she'd have ended up doing the film virtually for free. As it was, *Imitation of Life* grossed more than fifty million dollars worldwide, one-quarter of which was pure profit. There is no doubt but that Lana saved the studio, and it was appropriate that when Universal first began its popular tours, one of the stops was a visit to the Lana Turner dressing room. Though Lana had never set foot in it, the attraction was a thoughtful gesture—certainly more appropriate than what the studio had tried to do to her on "The Survivors."

After the money had been duly paid, it was Lana's turn to twist the screws a bit. She and I drove her Eldorado down to the studio, where she went through her entire wardrobe and took what she wanted of the gowns, shoes, and accessories—just as her contract had stipulated. Lana wanted these items, it was true, though she really didn't need them all. It was just her way of thanking the studio for the way she'd been treated. Her agent was furious when he learned of Lana's escapade, as was the stunned head of wardrobe at Universal. Lana and I were quietly amused by it all.

Chapter Four

During this period of professional inactivity, Lana looked for more than just television and bumper pool to occupy her. One of her more ambitious undertakings grew from having asked her decorator for a new king-size bed. She wanted the bed she and Dante had shared *gone*, as per ritual; in fact, Dante had earned the dubious honor of being banished more thoroughly than any of Lana's previous exes. She refused to speak his name, and while one was free to allude to something about him, if anyone uttered his name Lana would interrupt and quip, "Oh, you mean the Evil One!"

Lana's decorator is Vince Pastere, one of Lana's few true friends. Vince drove up from his home in Palm Springs, some three hours away, to find Lana a bed. While he was at the house, Lana impulsively decided to get rid of some of her old bedroom furniture as well; by the time he'd measured the bedroom and returned to the living room, Lana had decided to replace the furniture there as well. While there were certain pieces with which she would never part, such as her white leather game table, she ordered the rest of it carted away. In came a new nine-foot-long white leather sofa, new tables, armchairs, a white sheepskin area rug, and paintings. I inherited a custom-made coffee table, and Vince was given the stunning white baby grand piano. That may seem generous, and it was; however, Vince and I were being paid rather minimal salaries and worked our tails off for those "gifts." Through it all, Lana had insisted that everything be brought to her gratis for inspection. If she liked something, she didn't bother asking the price. If not, the chairs, lamps, end tables, or whatever had to be carted off to their trucks and hauled back to the showroom. Actually, people are surprised when they meet Lana at her home. She happens to have excellent taste, assiduously shunning the blazoned crystal-chandelier formality of her public image, preferring an environment that is comfortable, inviting, and most of all *alive*.

Most of the activities Lana whipped up were diversions, nothing more. She was marking time for the public and the industry alike to forget about the egg on her face and give her another chance on some new project. Unfortunately, because Lana had elected to remain semi-isolated for a while, we were obliged to turn down a good many potentially fascinating social engagements. During the ten years that I was with her, Lana received an average of five invitations a week to attend any number of parties, industry galas, and the like. This included an annual request to attend the Greek Film Festival in Athens. Though the sponsors would have paid her travel and hotel expenses and thrown in a luxury cruise of the Greek islands, she chose not to go. Lana could never get over her dislike of being "scrutinized" away from the protection of a camera. Not that this was the only reason she shunned certain affairs. Sometimes she just didn't care for the people involved.

One rejection that is burned in my mind because it was something *I* wanted to do was when Lana received a call from Elizabeth Taylor to spend "Thanksgiving" with her and Richard Burton in Palm Springs. Though it was only June, Liz explained, "We're celebrating early because I have a taste for turkey." Lana accepted because she disliked being hounded— and then, as was her habit, declined at the last moment due to "illness."

Lana had known Liz since their days at MGM, though there was never any real competition between Lana, the love goddess, and Elizabeth, the child star, who was eleven years her junior. She liked Liz a great deal, but Richard Burton she simply couldn't stand. Her feelings toward him had been formed on a motion picture set in 1955, when they had co-starred in *The Rains of Ranchipur*. According to Lana, he possessed an ego so all-consuming as to be offensive. Years later, when I asked their co-star Fred MacMurray about Burton, he said, "Gee, I found Richard very pleasant. Lana, too. But then"—he shrugged—"I was just the town drunk in that picture."

When the Taylor/Burton romance was busy splitting and mending every other day and filling the gossip columns, Lana would invariably remark, "Ugh! How can Elizabeth sleep with that? He's a pig! He's got that pockmarked face!" and so on. Personally, I always felt that his voice and talent more than made up for these "faults," if flaws they were.

As a result of Lana's intransigence and insecurities, although she was just forty-nine and boasted on more than one occasion that "my juices are still flowing," very few people were allowed inside her life at this time. That really was a shame, for as much as she could have used the fellowship, she is also a wonderful guest. She remembers names and faces with amazing speed and accuracy, and she is never faced with the problem of meeting someone a second time and not being able to recall not only their name but where they met and what the occasion had been, no matter how many years have passed. Her warm and enthusiastic manner of greeting people makes them feel like old friends and puts them immediately at ease. But she preferred the security of her home, wanting to lick her wounds before risking new ones. Not surprisingly, life tended to become quite lonely for us both. I, at least, had a job to do, though as 1969 crept to a close, more often than not that meant just keeping the press at bay when they phoned or stopped by in search of the "inside" story of Dante or "The Survivors." Lana remained adamant about not discussing either, and as politely but as firmly as possible, I informed each news hound that Miss Turner was too busy thinking about the future to worry about the past. Not that that stopped any of them from making Lana the subject of cruel, "inside" reports.

Considering how Lana was being roasted by the press, our Christmas was surprisingly merry, indeed. Neither of us was inclined to brood over our lot; Lana actually got angry when she found herself failing to get into the festive spirit of the approaching holiday. Two events in particular distinguished that holiday season, the first of which was a call one afternoon from Nolan Miller to inform Lana that a Beverly Hills furrier with whom he did business was liquidating his stock. Lana happens to love fur and made an appointment for us to visit the salon after hours when Lana would not be bothered by the presence of other patrons. Upon our arrival, the furrier, Mr. Hennessey, showed Lana and Nolan a selection of things.

The prize of his collection was a Somali leopard coat that went to the knee and had a detachable black seal, floor-length skirt. Somali leopard was not yet on the endangered species list, but it was still extremely rare and quite costly. Lana tried it on, consulted with Nolan, then indicated that the outfit be put aside. Next she tried on a Persian paw stroller with a fitch collar and asked that it, too, be set aside. She snuggled into several other furs and ordered a few more placed on the settee.

In time, Mr. Hennessey walked over and asked me if Miss Turner might be keeping anything from the pile of furs that was mounting up. I turned from a coat I'd been examining and said that I honestly didn't know but would find out. I walked over to Lana, and asked if she intended to keep anything in the stack. She just looked at me with a half smile and said, "Yes. I want them all."

I saw the furrier go slightly weak in the knees. Forty-three minutes after we had arrived, Lana walked from his shop having purchased five furs. The price tag was in the neighborhood of $30,000 in 1969 currency.

When we got back to the Mausoleum, I followed Lana into her bedroom to hang up some of her purchases. Others had been left behind so that her initials could be sewn into the linings. I was helping to arrange them when Lana turned to me and said, "Taylor, I'd like your help with something. I don't want you to fight me on this, I simply want you to call Mr. Hennessey and tell him to put aside the fur coat that you were looking at this afternoon. Tell him you'll be in tomorrow for alterations."

If looks were benedictions, Lana would have been the most blessed creature on earth. I went through the obligatory motions of protest, but Lana stood firm, thank God. As soon as we'd finished in her bedroom, I called Mr. Hennessey and acquired my first and only fur coat, a double-breasted marmoset that went below the knee and had a green paisley lining, very masculine-looking. By the way, though it didn't trouble Lana, *I'm* not an advocate of turning live creatures into coats. However, Beverly Hills is a barrier against good taste and conscience. I was spending so much time there that I was seduced by its decadence, and things that previously hadn't seemed such hot ideas were suddenly all right.

The second memorable event of the season was *my*

Christmas present to Lana, a chance for her to see my former
boss, Johnny Mathis, in concert. It proved to be one of the
most awkward moments in my life, if not in the history of
Western civilization. Johnny was appearing at the Theater in
the Round in the San Fernando Valley, and the place was
jam-packed. I was really happy to be at the concert, not only
because we were actually on time for the first act but because
it gave me an opportunity to see his performance from the
point of view of an audience. Johnny happens to be a
mesmerizing entertainer, despite the fact that he engages in
very little banter with his audience. And it would be good
just to *see* him, since we'd had a wonderful three-and-a-half-
year association. Johnny is a down-home, very earthy person
who has nothing of the egotistical star trip going. He is a man
of eclectic personal interests, from golf to gardening, and he
quietly contributes money to many good causes.

When the lights went down and Johnny strolled onstage,
I found myself growing misty-eyed with nostalgia. At least, I
thought it was nostalgia as he went through the program of
which I'd been a part for so long. What I was really feeling
was affection, not for the music nor for the memories but for
two of my favorite people, my former boss and my present
one. I realized how lucky I was to be able to feel that way
about my employers and to sincerely enjoy the work I did for
them. Only once in a while, listening to Johnny and noticing
his backup group of almost entirely new faces, did I have a
jealous urge to leap up there and belt my heart out. . . .

Lana thoroughly enjoyed the first half of the program,
particularly Johnny's more romantic numbers. However, at
intermission she expressed the desire to skip the second half
and get a drink. That was fine with me, since it was her
evening, and I'd seen enough of the show to be sated. Before
we could leave our seats, however, an usher came by to say
that Johnny had heard we were in the audience, and would
we do him the honor of dropping by his dressing room?
Though Lana was very gracious in accepting, I knew she felt
trapped. Were it not for my feelings, I'm sure she would have
declined.

We followed the man backstage, and I was surprised to
find a half-dozen guests and friends already there, sitting
around the room in folding chairs. Johnny himself was at the
far end of the dressing room wearing everything but his shoes

and slacks and, at five-foot-eight, looking rather like a pixie. Eyes lit up and smiles broadened when Lana stepped in, and one of the guests actually applauded. I introduced Johnny to Lana, and the two of them exchanged somewhat uncomfortable hellos. Though Lana is shy, she has nothing on Johnny; he may sing like an angel, but he's so shy he never knows quite what to say to people. That's why he seldom speaks during his performances, and it was the reason he and Lana just stared at one another until Johnny had the presence of mind to ask if either of us would like a drink. We both requested a vodka and tonic, and Johnny's valet prepared them while Lana sat down. Everyone was seated now except Johnny and me, the two of us standing in the grip of a *second* deafening silence. Suddenly, poor Johnny broke the hush. Donning a cheek-splitting grin he came toward me, arms outstretched.

"Taylor, you shit! How have you been?"

I prayed for quicksand to swallow me up. Johnny's crazed outburst was not the end of his welcome. He proceeded to hug me. My head happened to be turned slightly to one side, and I could see Lana sitting there, her eyes like saucers, her mouth agape. This kind of display was definitely taboo.

I knew that Johnny was merely ill-equipped to strike a moderate salutatory note, and with as much good humor and Pero aplomb as I could muster, I managed to disengage myself from his hug. Someone mercifully got the conversation rolling again, though the intermission seemed interminably long. When it was finally over, Lana and I were escorted back to our seats. Since the concert was about to resume, there was no way for us to sneak out, nor did Lana seem inclined to do anything except sit there and steam.

After the show we politely refused an invitation to join Johnny and the others at a party. As we sped home along the Ventura Freeway, Lana accused me of conspiring to make her jealous with our loving display, and I rather naively remarked that that wasn't true, and even if it *were*, what was there to be jealous *about*?

"You were my escort," she reminded me, "and there's an element of fidelity in that."

I replied that she was not incorrect, though I admitted that I hadn't realized our relationship for the evening had been so formalized. That comment set Lana off for a few

minutes, lecturing about how a man owes a woman certain
courtesies like respect and devotion. I felt as if she were not
only defining a relationship that went deeper than I'd presumed ours to be, but that I was also taking a dozen extra
lashes for Dante's actions. Since there's no fighting an idea
once it's in Lana's head, I sat there quietly while she fumed.

When she had finished, and an unspoken truce was in
effect, I suddenly burst out laughing.

"What's so funny?" Lana demanded.

I turned to her, still chuckling, and said, "How many
men do *you* know who have taken Lana Turner on a date and
ended up being hugged by Johnny Mathis?"

Lana couldn't help seeing the humor in that, and her
anger dissipated. However, as I look back on that evening
now, it was clear that Lana's possessiveness had begun to flex
its muscles. She paid me (she'd given Dante money); she'd
clothed me (as she had Bob Eaton); she'd allowed me to move
in with her (as Fred May had done prior to their marriage). A
pattern was beginning to emerge, though I didn't recognize it
then. It was a question of power, a tug-of-war that was to
cause the bulk of our troubles in later years. Unlike her
husbands, I didn't love her so little that I could just leave in
order to preserve my self-respect.

Lana resented much more my independence than what she
would consider libertine perversion. I had never concealed
from Lana the fact that I'm bisexual, nor is this so unique in
Hollywood that it would cause eyebrows to raise. Some
people go to great lengths to conceal their sexual bent,
though this is more in deference to the folks in Idaho and
Mississippi than for the local community.

Lana, in turn, revels in control, in power over people
and situations. When this eludes her, or threatens to as it did
the night of the Mathis concert, the game playing begins. This
can range from mind games to heated arguments and violent
outbursts. Whether it takes a minute or a decade, Lana
allows no one to beat her, not Universal Pictures or Johnny
Stompanato. She managed to get me right back into line
because I was still in awe of her. Future bouts were never
again so simple.

After the debacle of the Mathis concert, I stayed well out
of our plans for the next holiday. Not surprisingly, New Year's
invitations arrived by the sackful, and the one Lana chose to

accept rather shocked me: it was from Harold Robbins and his wife Grace. I had thought that Lana would want to have nothing to do with anyone who was even remotely associated with "The Survivors." I was wrong, but then Harold and Lana had had a bizarre relationship from the start.

Harold had first made an impact on show business in 1964, when his novel *Where Love Has Gone* was made into a motion picture. The story was an unabashed retelling of the Stompanato killing, with Susan Hayward in the Lana role and Joey Heatherton playing the part of Cheryl. Bette Davis was also on hand as Gran. I had known about the book and the film, though Lana and I had never discussed it; common sense seemed to indicate that it would be a very sore subject. I was wrong. After Lana accepted the invitation, I asked her about Robbins. I could understand where she would appear in a prestigious show that he had helped create; that was a professional decision. But this—? Lana admitted that she'd been deeply hurt by the publication of *Where Love Has Gone* and upset that someone would be so callous to, as she described it, "market another human being's misery." However, in time she came to realize that if Robbins hadn't done it someone else would have, and at least he'd created a property with the gloss of class rather than trash. Her feelings were further mollified when Harold managed to convince her that he had researched the book at juvenile hall in San Francisco, where he had found many, many cases wherein a child had slain his or her parent's lover. Maybe so, I remember thinking, but it's doubtful he'd have written, nor anyone have published, his opus were it not for the Stompanato slaying.

Accordingly, and in spite of Lana's own forgiveness, I managed to harbor enough bitterness against him for the two of us, mumbling nasty words under my breath as I dressed. But my animosity toward this man I'd never met was short-lived. He proved blunt but intelligent and charming, in an unpolished way. On top of that, Grace Robbins is one of the most lavish party givers in Beverly Hills—which means in the world—and the gaudy magnitude of the affair would envelop me as we walked in the door, turning me from Sir Lancelot to Uriah Heep. I would see why the Robbinses' affairs were always number one on everybody's list, a fact that had helped Lana make her decision regarding which bash to attend. If she were going to show her face in public, it would be at the biggest New Year's Eve party in town, one that at the same time showed the world how quickly *she* could forget "The Survivors," since she'd be partying with its creator.

Speaking of being seen, Lana was not unaware that *I* would be seen as well as she. As we were getting ready to leave for the big event, Lana asked me over to the bar for one last drink. While we were casually sipping away, Lana looked me straight in the eyes. "Taylor," she said somberly, "I have to warn you. The press will *make* something out of this."

Since there *wasn't* anything at the time, I replied, "I don't care if you don't care." That wasn't entirely true, I chastised myself the instant after I'd said it. I did care. After all, I *was* a singer in my spare time and not averse to publicity. I would never have *sought* to use Lana the way other men had, but I can't feign idealism since, aware of the benefits to be gained, the true idealist would have on principle refused to accompany Lana. I, on the other hand, went. Actually, Lana made it extremely easy for me. Whereas she had refused to make a public appearance with Johnny Stompanato, she was going to do so with me; gladly, it seemed, for as she sailed into the bedroom for her habitual last-minute freshening up, she sang, "You are I are going to be an *item*." I felt like I was lifting her spirits, doing her some good. I didn't realize that that was only partially so, that I was both helping and harming her. In the film business, where appearance often means more than talent both in establishing and prolonging one's career, being seen with an obviously much younger chaperon can work wonders for the press of a film queen whose time may be passing. On the other hand, people who live in Hollywood find this *Sunset Boulevard* syndrome frightening because it's an open admission of middle age. They keep you at arm's length, as though fearful the disease will spread. No one acted like this to Lana's face, but I overheard comments behind her back and had a few self-conscious jokes hurled in my direction. They'd have been easy enough to ignore if they weren't emblematic of how people actually perceived Lana and to some extent governed the kinds of parts she was—and wasn't—offered. I had to take solace in the fact that while I *am* twenty years Lana's junior, never once did I manufacture or contrive any aspect of our relationship with other than genuine fondness or admiration.

The Robbins party was held at the Beverly Hills Hotel because there were simply too many people for even the couple's large home on Beverly Drive to accommodate. Lana had elected to wear the same red lace gown that she had worn during our disastrous evening in San Francisco, as if she were daring fate to fling more trouble in her direction. As for me, I was dressed in my not-brand-new tuxedo. I'd bought it at the Hollywood Glamour Shop, not a place where the stars shop but rather where they donate their used clothing. I paid twenty-five dollars for the outfit and discovered, upon getting it home, that it had been made for Vic Damone. A good omen for an aspiring singer, and an excellent argument for the worthlessness of omens.

The party was lovely, not to mention star-studded. We arrived quite late; Lana always timed her entrances to occur at a point when photographers are hungry for a new face to shoot. Sure enough, as we walked into the hotel lobby, there was an instantaneous and constant whirring of shutters. Lana posed and gave them good pictures, though I knew I appeared slightly uncomfortable, particularly after one reporter asked for my name. I said that it wasn't important, but Lana disagreed. Not only did she tell them who I was, she spelled my name so they would get it right.

For me, the most educational and satisfying part of the evening was watching the jealous stares of the other women when they saw Lana. It was just as catty and sly as in every Robbins novel you've ever read about the superrich. In addition to Lana's natural beauty and regal carriage, she was wearing a fabulous necklace made of emeralds surrounded by diamonds, with earrings to match. She also had on her $48,000 bracelet.

We were seated at a large table, where Lana had a fine time talking with Marty Allen, one of her favorite comics and favorite people as well. He was dressed rather incongruously in diapers as the Baby New Year 1970, but he didn't seem to mind. Rona Barrett was also at our table, and for a time after our arrival couldn't take her eyes off either Lana or the jewels. However, it wasn't long before Rona left us, retreating once she had been informed that the jewelry was real.

True to Lana's word, the publicity that stemmed from this one evening was overwhelming. The following issue of every motion picture magazine featured photographs of the two of us, and they insinuated a far deeper attachment than there was at that point. Said *Photoplay,* "Lana Turner quickly overcame the blues of her busted marriage. Her date these days is Taylor Pero." Echoed *Hollywood Dateline,* "In the old ball game, it's three strikes and you're out. But Lana Turner runs her life with different rules. So far, lovely Lana has been married and divorced seven times, and she's not quitting the game yet. Our photogs captured the happy mood when they snapped a picture of Lana with Taylor Pero, who's said to be a candidate for the number eight position on Lana's long list of husbands." So we had become an item.

Chapter Five

Though Lana had wiped the slate clean for the new decade and prepared herself for fresh challenges, none were forthcoming. That meant there was little for me to do except to keep Lana entertained. However, she was convinced that work would be forthcoming, and so we both hung in there.

I found it unusual, and a bit frustrating, that Lana refused to divert herself with a little entertaining at home now and then. I almost begged her to have over some of the fascinating people she knew. It didn't have to be a Frank Sinatra or Bette Davis; I'd have settled for a few laughs with Tommy Smothers or screaming "Drop the gun!" at passersby with Efrem Zimbalist, Jr. But no, Lana did not want to have guests. What put her off hosting parties, she confided, was that with Bob Eaton she had entertained *too* much, bacchanals that still caused her to shudder. Rather than confront the problem, she simply did away with the cause.

In an effort to relieve our boredom, Lana accepted an invitation from Vince Pastere to spend a few days as his houseguests in Palm Springs. We had a delightful, quiet time, but after a week Lana became restless, and we returned to the Mausoleum. We reached Beverly Hills late in the evening, and as I entered the house I noticed that the white drapes that covered the sliding-glass doors to the pool were billowing in the night breeze. I held out my arm to block Lana's entrance, then silently gestured toward the open sliders. We stood there for a long moment trying to comprehend what could have happened. Carmen would never have done such an irresponsible thing, and we knew that neither of us had left the doors open. I suggested that, instead of

going in, we call the police and have them search the house
with us. Lana reluctantly agreed, and I telephoned them
from the living room phone several paces from the front door.

While we stood there, awaiting the arrival of a squad car,
Lana asked if I thought it would be all right for her to use the
bathroom. I said of course *not*, but she perked up and said
defiantly, "This is *my* house, and I'll be damned if anyone's
going to scare me from my own john!"

I knew it was pointless to argue and sought instead to at
least minimize the danger. "Let me check it out first," I
suggested, hoping she'd decide it wasn't all that important
now that she thought about it. But Lana agreed, and was
brave enough to accompany me.

To reach the bathroom it was necessary to pass through
the entry to Lana's bedroom where, even in the dark, I could
see that the doors to one dresser were open and all the
drawers pulled out. I flicked on the light and saw that jewelry
had been thrown all over the floor and on the bed. Lana cried
out and ran at once to a small drawer that had been pried
from its lock. She moaned, exclaiming that that was where
she kept all of her best jewelry. Though we were both in
shock, there was little else to do but begin cleaning up and
hope that the police could make some sense of this. It was
like a rerun of the day we had found Dante's belongings
gone, both of us obviously upset but at the same time
outraged that a person's home could be so easily ravaged.

When the police arrived, they found us still on our
hands and knees picking pieces of jewelry and loose stones
from the carpet. They proceeded to scour the house from top
to bottom for clues, determining immediately that this had
been a professional job. The Mausoleum had been entered
from my office, where the louvered glass windows were
simply lifted out so the thief could enter. The intruder had
been careful to open every door leading to the outside, which
the police explained is the first thing a professional does. This
insures his escape in case the homeowner returns while the
robbery is in progress. Judging from the amount of valuables
that had been left behind, the police felt that this is what had
happened to us. I told Lana to be grateful that the burglar
hadn't decided to jump us rather than flee, though she was
hardly consoled. Cataloguing the losses, which included the
diamond bracelet she had worn to the Robbins party as well

as one of the largest black star-sapphire rings in the world, I think she'd have *preferred* a crack at the burglar.

Because of the magnitude of the theft, the FBI was summoned. The agents were polite and friendly, even if they *did* suspect for a time that Vince and I had had something to do with the theft. They hypothesized that we'd lured Lana away so we could have the place robbed, though I convinced them that my many years as a cat burglar had taught me never to wait until the evening my victim returned and to phone my accomplices if there was a change in plan. The agent in charge did not find me humorous in the least, nor did my wit cheer Lana when he told her that there was little hope of recovering the jewelry. A pro would already have the stones out of their mountings and the larger gems cut. The only stone that could not be cut was the star sapphire, which would probably end up on the finger of a mobster's girlfriend, never again to be worn in public. The G-man was correct; the case was never solved, although I believe Lana was right in speculating who had set it up. The intruder had had to pass through the dining room, where there was an armoire filled with silver, and through the living room, decorated with valuable oil paintings. The thief had gone directly to the one small, locked drawer in the bedroom, where the most valuable jewelry was kept.

Unfortunately, adding injury to misery, the jewelry was not covered by Lana's Lloyds of London policy because she had neglected to inform her insurance representative that the jewelry had been moved to her home from the bank vault in Malibu where it had been housed.

Once again, spurred by defiance rather than practicality—the horse had already been let from the barn—Lana instructed me to hire two twenty-four-hour guards to patrol the grounds. Personally, I was less perturbed about the prospect of another interloper than I was sitting in her living room, engrossed in a television show, and seeing flashlights periodically poking through the darkness into the window.

As the weeks of cohabitation became months, it was increasingly apparent that the temporary living arrangement was doing neither of us any good. Lana had come to rely on me too much, and although I enjoyed her company and the accommodations, I sometimes felt trapped and wanted to return to my own apartment. By sad coincidence, the brutal murder of Sharon Tate just a hilltop away did not make Lana feel particularly secure where she was. When I brought up the subject of Lana herself moving, she did not disagree, going so far as to say that she felt this was an evil house because of all that had happened to her while she was living here. Lana's primary objection was with my suggestion that she move into one of the many beautiful apartment buildings in Beverly Hills. Except for during her childhood, she had always lived in a large house and had come to cherish the sense of ownership and retreat that that implied. I countered that an apartment would provide not only round-the-clock security, but she wouldn't rattle around quite so much in a smaller place. Thus, over her protests, I was allowed to go searching for a suitable abode, with the provision that it have a ceiling at least nine feet high to accommodate the armoire that housed her silver collection.

More than one realtor gave me a strange look when I asked the height of a ceiling before we even discussed price or cost. That ceiling stipulation quickly exhausted all of the possibilities in Beverly Hills, so I began moving out toward the ocean. At last, virtually on the shores of the Pacific, where Sunset Boulevard ends its winding trail west, I came upon a complex of luxury apartments called the Edgewater Towers. As fate would have it, a beautiful penthouse was available for immediate occupancy, one that overlooked the ocean *and* had ceilings exactly nine feet tall. Vince Pastere was summoned from Palm Springs, and the three of us went at once to view my proud discovery.

The apartment boasted a long passageway from the front door, leading past the kitchen and into a living room that was half the size of the one in the Mausoleum. Off the living room was a spacious terrace, across from which there was a white marble-faced fireplace. There was also a den with a closet that Vince said could easily be made into a mirrored bar. The master bedroom was spacious and had a bath-dressing room, plus a fairly adequate closet; an adjoining guest room could serve as my office.

Although Lana loathed the thought of opening her front door onto an impersonal, common corridor that led to the elevators, there was no suitable alternative. This was to become her home for the next two years.

It took weeks to get ready for the move. Lana refused to trust the moving company to wrap her valuable dishes, silver, and such, so Carmen and her temporary staff were kept busy with cartons, tissue paper, and crumpled newspaper for days on end. The new residence was good therapy for her, I felt. Moving day itself was quite upsetting, more from the fear of things new or unknown than from fond memories. Lana averted her eyes from the whole affair, going to my one-bedroom apartment before the movers arrived and remaining until late in the afternoon of the following day, by which time the job was nearly completed. Unhappily, we reached Edgewater at an inopportune moment, just as the movers were hoisting a large leather sofa up the side of the building. I could tell from Lana's pained look that she felt sick seeing her possessions hauled around like so much meaningless baggage. I also knew that things were bound to get worse before they got better. As soon as we were inside the penthouse, Lana examined the boxes piled high to the ceiling, eyed the furniture that was only approximately in place, and began to cry.

"Let's leave everything the way it is and find another place," she wailed. "We'll *never* get all of my things put away here."

Vince and I worked very hard to convince Lana that what was really upsetting her was the disorientation but that everything would be fine, which it was in a matter of days. All it took was a lot of sympathy and hand holding. Throughout, I could not help but wonder if I'd have taken this job had I known that comforting Lana would be my primary responsibility. I'd expected *some* "weeping with them that weep," as the saying goes, but I'd also hoped to gain some more valuable experience in show business. So far, it had been exclusively the former. Not that I was disappointed in Lana herself; she was a lesson in tenacity and noblesse oblige. I just wished my responsibilities were less domestic than they had been to date. However, I convinced myself that I was being overly harsh, that the past few months had been unusually difficult. It was not every woman who lost a husband, a home, a television series, and some of her most prized jewelry in less than half a year. If that had happened to me, I'd have required a minimum of one shrink per problem. Lana was, in fact, a helluva gutsy lady. In any case, I was sure that the worst was over, that normalcy was about to rear its lovely head. I should have realized that if you want normalcy, you move to Muncie, Indiana.

Shortly after we had both moved into our separate abodes, Lana puckishly conspired to thwart my efforts at independence by booking us both into the Sands Hotel in Las Vegas, where Elvis Presley was about to make his first personal appearance in a long time at the International Hotel.

We reached the hotel a few minutes before the performance. I had called ahead; and though there was a long line of people waiting to get into the opening night show, we had a ringside table at our disposal. However, Lana decided she wanted to spend some time playing the slot machines.

In her younger days, Lana had had quite a fondness for gambling. It was common for her to spend days on end in Las Vegas, not paying attention to her winnings or losses, tipping one-hundred-dollar bills right and left. She learned moderation only after running up a deficit in excess of one hundred thousand dollars. Nowadays, Lana is content to settle for the pleasure of playing the nickel slot machines. As she explained, it wasn't the money that made her happy but the *sound* of winning, the triumphant jangle of coins as they tumbled into the metal bowl.

As people in the casino began to recognize Lana, a small crowd gathered in our vicinity. They were too sophisticated to come right up and watch her play; they just started using the machines nearest her and mindlessly feeding in nickels. Lana pretended not to notice that their eyes were upon her, though at one point she turned to me and whispered, "You know what they're all saying? 'Look at poor Lana Turner! She's so broke that she has to play the nickel slot machines.'" I don't think anyone really believed that, but I was glad to see her self-effacing humor back in gear.

I'd never really been an Elvis Presley fan, but I confess he won me over that night. He played, of course, to a packed house, and even before he made his entrance, you could feel the electricity in the air. Elvis was overweight then, but that didn't detract from the power of his performance. Never before or since have I been so dazzled by the energy that man exhibited that night.

In terms of memorable events, however, the visit to the

Sands was most noteworthy in that at long last Lana and I made love.

The first night we slept together was one of terribly mixed feelings for me. Emotionally, the very fact that I was sleeping with my boss was overwhelming. In just five months, Lana and I had gotten very close as friends. I'd had no desire or intent to become her lover as well; it just happened as a natural evolution of things, the final act of discovery. It also tore down the barrier of employer and employee in *my* mind, though not often in hers. That had been an important demarcation, since it kept our professional relationship from spilling entirely into our private lives. Except for the weeks I lived with her at the Mausoleum, we still had our personal affairs to return to. In a fit of mutual curiosity and desire, the two worlds were made inseparable. I remember thinking to myself on the plane home that I wouldn't let the Sands incident set a precedent. But it was too late. At the same time, I was on my own wild ego trip to think that this woman might actually be attracted to me. I was devoted to her, but to believe that the feeling was reciprocal staggered me.

What was important about that night in Las Vegas was that Pandora's Box had been opened, jumbling and intertwining sex and love, work and friendship, hope and hate. It was the end of a great platonic relationship, one I sorely miss even to this day.

Every year, on the grounds of the old Paramount Studios Ranch, where westerns were filmed when the genre was in vogue, Los Angeles mounts the Renaissance Fair. Everyone who attends is urged to dress in a costume suggesting Europe of the Middle Ages to go along with the spirit of the strolling musicians and fortune-tellers, booths where craftspeople sell handmade wares and foodstuffs, and stages where drama and mime are presented in the manner of the bygone era.

Cheryl loved the event, and every year she urged her mother to attend. Since Lana didn't really want to go, she always came up with some wonderful excuse. This year, however, I added my voice to that of Cheryl's. Convinced that her indifference was unfair to her daughter, Lana agreed to give the fair a try. There was only one problem. In order to find a parking space, Cheryl told her mother to be there no later than nine-thirty in the morning. When Lana is not working, she goes *nowhere* before two; however, since she promised Cheryl she would be there, she told *me* to hire a helicopter. The move was pure, flamboyant Lana. She had gotten into the spirit of the event and had rummaged through her closets and donned a tasseled, squawklike outfit along with a sandy-colored wig with bangs and shoulder-length hair. Then she put on a few dozen gold chains for good measure. She had had Carmen pack us a massive picnic lunch, and she was intent on having the best time possible.

One of the stipulations laid down by Paramount in giving us permission to land was that we stay well clear of the fairgrounds so as not to disturb the period flavor. Accordingly, as we arrived, we were all busy peering earthward for the men with red flags who we'd been told would show us where to land. It didn't take long to spot them, dressed like Robin Hood's Merry Men, and we began our descent. But a mere landing would never do for Miss Lana Turner. Feeling naughty, she told the pilot to arrest his descent and buzz the fair.

We swooped down like a vengeful mosquito, great clouds of dust rising into the air as the red clay was caught in our downdraft. People ran in every direction trying to escape it, looking like stampeding herds of giraffe. Those who were not running from the storm were hanging on to their small booths, trying to keep them from being blown apart. Since the first pass was so exciting, Lana ordered the pilot to do it again, and then a third time.

When we finally landed, the repercussions were mild because Lana was, after all, a superstar. She feigned innocence. We never did run into Cheryl, although we looked for her constantly. Cheryl later said that she and her group had been unable to find us as well. We subsequently learned that in fact, she'd decided to avoid us because she was embarrassed by Lana's dramatic entrance. Even though she'd had no notion of our plans, when the helicopter made its first pass, she had sighed and told one of her friends, "There goes my mother."

The Renaissance Fair, like Las Vegas, had been fun. Good thing, too, since fun was all we were having. There were no films in the offing, no scripts in the mail, no fundraisers or television guest spots or even solicitations for a magazine subscription. Denied honest work, Lana refused to slip back into a dejected state; like a shark, she had to keep moving or asphyxiate.

Not long after the fair, Lana and I were standing on her spacious balcony, looking out across the ocean. From there, Lana could also look down onto the terrace of actress June Lockhart, who at the time was going with an actor many years younger than she. Often, Lana and June would hang from their respective windows, just like in "The Goldbergs," hollering back and forth about whose romance was making bigger headlines. Though June's was then, I'm happy to report that Lana and I overtook her in due course.

On this particular day, Lana and I happened to be steeped in thought when her favorite radio station began playing Hawaiian instrumentals. Lana brightened.

"Let's go to Hawaii," she said. "Tonight."

How quickly we take luxury for granted. I replied that, yes, it was a nice idea but that I had a singing engagement later in the evening that I didn't want to break. Lana enjoined me to do so, but I explained that anyone who offered me a mike, an accompanist, and an audience got first dibs on my spare time. Lana persisted, but when it became clear that I would not yield, she pouted and said that it would be all right to leave the following morning. We retired to the bar, and much to my delight, Lana for the first time seriously asked me about my singing career.

Lana knew that I'd been singing almost every weekend night at the Pump Room, a club in the San Fernando Valley. Though she never went to hear me sing, I refused to let that demoralize me. However, I happened to have a copy of the recording I'd done a few months prior to meeting Lana, and I dashed to the car to retrieve the slightly warped copy. She listened to the record several times over and finally, after a long silence, lit a cigarette and said, "I can see it all now. I'm going to lose a secretary, but I'm going to make you a *star!*"

Though I tried not to show it, my pulse rate shot sky-high. History was coming full circle: Lana Turner, whom happy chance had made a star, was going to repay her debt to fate. How lucky that *I* was to be the beneficiary! We engaged in a long, far-reaching discussion about how she'd go about it, using her company, Eltee Productions, to manage and record me. Sadly, somewhere along the line, Lana chose to ignore what she'd said. I couldn't blame her; after all, she did have problems of her own. I just wish she hadn't brought it up in the first place. I know Lana meant well.

What was to have been a two-week stay in the islands blossomed into a disgustingly hedonistic month, one day sliding into the next as we luxuriated on the beach or in our $250-per-day two-bedroom suite with its one-hundred-eighty-degree view of Waikiki Beach and Diamond Head. It was not unusual for Lana and me to stay up all night talking, drinks in hand, not going to bed until well after dawn. Many mornings we sat on the terrace and watched the sun rise, followed by the first of the surfers wading into the breakers. We'd retire then, and I'd sleep until midmorning—at which time I'd go to the hotel pool and sleep some more in the sun. Lana, upon waking, would lash a bright red scarf to the railing of the balcony; I'd see it whipping in the breeze and call upstairs to see if she was hungry, after which we'd share a late breakfast together, then bum around for the day.

Our serious playing in Hawaii was done at night, when we'd do up the town royally at least every other evening. One evening in particular Lana was feeling down and decided that she needed to spark some of the old Turner fireworks. She put on a beautiful silk pantsuit, then playfully looped a necklace around me. I liked the way it contrasted with my tan and, before it became a California rage, decided to see how a bit more gold would look on me. Lana thought it was a great idea, and almost everything she could not get on herself ended up dangling from some portion of my anatomy. As a final touch, she donned a pair of earrings that were five carats of simple glass. However, as Lana very correctly observed, "On me, people will think they're real." Sounding like a pair of knights bedecked for the Crusades, we went clanking into the night to have some fun.

Lana and I saw three shows, after which we found ourselves on Kalakaua Avenue, the main street of Waikiki. I had spent five of my teenage years along this beat, working odd jobs as I attended high school. As we were strolling slowly along, much to our surprise and joy we bumped into Jack Freeman. Jack happened to be on the last night of his own vacation, and naturally, the three of us headed for the nearest watering hole. During the course of the evening, Lana persuaded Jack to change hotels and join us for a few more days at her expense. Jack was reluctant to accept her charity, but eventually he gave in. Few people are ever able to resist Lana when she wants something, and people who work for her are wise not to.

The three of us were like Porthos, Athos, and Aramis—the three musketeers—as we reveled on impulse here or there that night, and for several nights subsequently. However, Jack finally had to return to the mainland, where a film commitment awaited at Universal. Though Lana cringed at the mention of the studio, she reluctantly surrendered her friend to it. The two of us were alone again, and despite the emptiness without our comrade, we had no wish to return to Los Angeles. Still, things *had* fallen into a predictable routine, even here, and one night all the local hot spots seemed unusually dull. Lana wanted excitement, and having heard of a small gay bar on Waikiki called the Clouds, she decided that she wanted to see what just such a place was like.

The Clouds was actually a comparatively discreet bar, without the on-premises sex of many private or backroom establishments. When we arrived, we went to a table far from the men at the bar. Drinks were ordered, and we quietly engaged in conversation while Lana took in the sights. It was pretty dull, actually, a low-key pickup now and then but nothing out of the ordinary. Looking to stir up some commotion, I asked Lana why she didn't walk the length of the bar to see if anyone would recognize her. Quick to pick up on any dare, Lana left the table and subtly but sexily strolled from stool to stool, ignoring the looks she drew. Personally, I wondered how many of the men actually recognized her and how many thought she was simply a drag queen looking for a date. No sooner had she returned to our table than I got my answer. Three young men out of the thirty-odd at the bar came over and introduced themselves. They had identified Lana right away and were thrilled to meet her. My lady decided to hold court right there, and we all had a grand time buying one another drinks and luring more and more people over to our table. Finally, someone suggested that we go to another place, one mixed with straights and gays, to see how the patrons there would react. That was fine with Lana, who had grown a tad uncomfortable with some of the more affected patrons of the Clouds, so we trooped down Kalakaua Avenue to a famous strip joint.

Lana was instantly more at ease here, particularly when one of the girls came over after finishing her number. She was a friend of a young man in our party, and Lana seemed glad to have another female in the group. The two of them got along famously until, later in the evening, the girl began making overtures toward Lana and had to be informed in no uncertain terms that she was definitely not interested. That put a brief damper on things, but the girl excused herself, and the party regained its earlier momentum.

The delightfully sleazy little club closed at two, but as we were still in a convivial way, we all went to the hotel suite for a nightcap. That jamboree lasted until well past sunrise, and as we bid everyone good morning, we took the name and phone number of one particularly polite and witty young man named Tim Callahan. He invited us to spend some time with him at a large house he shared with friends on the windward side of the island. Lana felt that a less commercialized environment would be a welcome change of pace, and during the next few days we spent a lot of time on his private beach, where we could swim and relax without the ever-curious eyes of tourists.

We didn't return to Los Angeles until June 11, having spent a total of twenty-five days in Hawaii and running up a hotel tab in excess of six thousand dollars. However, Lana was refreshed and purged of a lot of lingering hostility, and she felt the expense was worth it. I couldn't agree more; those few weeks were the most carefree times we ever had.

Chapter Six

Hawaii taught me something about my sense of values. There's a worth that attaches itself to income, worth that is proportionate to the guilt you'd feel without it. Though I had a lot of fun during our vacation, I was "working" the entire time, collecting a paycheck for amusing Lana and seeing to her needs. I'd found that pursuit shallow in Los Angeles, where I knew there were other ways I could and should be earning a living wage. Yet, it made me feel not quite so decadent while enjoying a holiday I hadn't otherwise earned amidst the lazy delights of Hawaii.

Lana was not so lucky. Though she had needed Hawaii for her mental and physical well-being, and justified the expense on those grounds, she *wasn't* working. She managed to radiate an air of confidence in public, but when we were alone she admitted that she was worried. She wanted to go before a camera and be paid to act. It wasn't that she needed the money, since Lana is an extremely wealthy woman, at least on paper. Her jewelry and art, wardrobe and silver are worth millions. Even when she wasn't working, Lana still collected a weekly check in the amount of $2,000 for her work on that 1959 crap shoot *Imitation of Life*. Acting wasn't, for her, a matter of career any longer; it was pride pure and simple. Charlton Heston once told someone that he felt good getting scripts after nearly twenty years in the business, just to prove to himself that he was still employable. Lana, who had been around over thirty years, was no different, and every day that passed without a script or a feeler made her more and more anxious. People who know Lana sensed this trepidation, but only I saw it day and night.

Once again, while I don't blame Lana her insecurities, they became predictable and sometimes excessive. She would not go so far as to attempt suicide (yet), but she did sprain more limbs and digits than Jim Brown in his salad days, and she did manage to "misplace" an inordinately high number of cigarette lighters, pieces of clothing, and charge cards—acts of helplessness calculated to draw my attention. Fortunately, shortly after our return from Hawaii Lana was invited to attend the opening of a new hotel and casino at Lake Tahoe. The management of King's Castle had offered a select number of celebrities the opportunity to enjoy an all-expenses-paid vacation in exchange for being seen and photographed at the establishment. While Lana had never enjoyed endorsements of this sort, she must have felt as I did in Hawaii, that being paid to play was too good a deal to pass up just now. Thus, on June 30, Lana and I were on a jet heading north to Lake Tahoe.

We arrived a day in advance of the other celebrities so that Lana could get the lay of the land. She liked to know as much or more than her peers; as I learned over the years, one never knew when an upper hand might be useful in getting the best table at a restaurant or garnering an extra column of all-important press coverage. After we checked in, Lana was at once surprised and a trifle distressed to learn that one of the other invited guests was Barbara Stanwyck. I knew that Stanwyck's presence would add a dangerous touch to the event, since Barbara blamed Lana for the breakup of her marriage to actor Robert Taylor. The damage was alleged to have been done in 1942, during filming on the glossy gangster picture, *Johnny Eager*. Lana's version of what happened is the only one I ever heard, but I tend to believe it, if only because she and Taylor never became an "item." It seems, however, that Taylor fell in love with Lana during the shoot, misreading her friendship and habitual flirting as affection. Totally unbeknownst to Lana, Taylor asked Stanwyck for a divorce so that he could woo and win his co-star. Lana knew nothing about any of this, she said, until one night when she was having dinner with another gentleman at a Malibu restaurant. Taylor noticed her and, approaching the table, declared his love—adding that he'd just asked Barbara for a divorce. Shocked by his actions, Lana was forced to inform Taylor that while she liked him very much as a person and as a fellow actor, she had no romantic inclinations toward him. Crushed, Taylor withdrew from her table and from her life. The divorce from Stanwyck did not become a reality until ten years later when Taylor was filming *Quo Vadis* in Italy. There, he was linked with a lovely extra by the name of Lia de Leo—though Barbara never stopped blaming Lana as the one who really ruined her marriage. People who knew both Taylor and Miss Stanwyck say that no woman was responsible for the breakup, but rather Taylor's preoccupation with guns, flying, and sports, pursuits that he shared almost exclusively with male friends.

Because nearly three decades had passed and Taylor had died some time before the Lake Tahoe fiesta, I decided that it was time for the women to reconcile. When I broached the subject with Lana, she replied that she had no aversion to talking with Barbara, since the whole thing had been a misunderstanding in the first place. She *was* a little reluctant, fearful of losing face in the event of a frosty reception, but I prevailed upon her to be the bigger of the two and allow me to call Barbara's suite.

The operator put the call through, and I must admit I was unprepared for the harsh, masculine voice that barked into my ear on the second ring.

"What is it?"

"Miss Barbara Stanwyck, please."

"Who's this?"

"Is this Miss Stanwyck?"

"Yeah. What do you want?"

"Just a moment, please. Miss Lana Turner is calling."

Lana went into her bedroom and picked up the phone. I could hear only her end of the brief conversation as Lana made an ultimately futile attempt to be lighthearted and friendly. She explained to Barbara that she thought it would be nice to welcome her to King's Castle and said she hoped Barbara would enjoy the ensuing two weeks. There was a rather long pause on Lana's end of the line, after which she quietly returned the receiver to its cradle. She walked back into my room and said from behind a forced smile, "Would you care to help me chip the ice from my shoulders?" Barbara Stanwyck was never mentioned again.

The next few months were relatively quiet, with one day all but crawling into the next. Lana was sleeping later and later into the afternoon, which meant that today's work wouldn't get done until tomorrow. The fact that her business could wait a day is indicative of its importance. One day, obviously beset by guilt, she asked if I felt she were sleeping her life away. As diplomatically as possible I replied that I did—if only because her hours were out of sync with the rest of society, hours that could have been used more constructively. Lana murmured her assent, followed by her favorite expression, a bratty phrase that came to wear on me over the years. "I don't have to do *anything*," she asserted, "except breathe. And even *that's* my decision." Those proved to be prophetic words indeed, although for now it meant only that reform had the chance of a snowball in Haiti.

On a sunny afternoon in August, which seemed just like the sunny afternoons in January, February, and so on, we were watching television and halfheartedly debating whether or not to order a cake to celebrate my first anniversary with Lana when a phone call came that was to rejuvenate and expand her career and mine. The caller was Lana's agent at the William Morris Agency. He informed Lana that he'd had a firm offer from producers Lee Guber—who was at that time married to Barbara Walters—and Shelly Gross, owners and operators of a chain of theaters-in-the-round in the East, for Lana to star in a tour of the popular play *Forty Carats*. They were willing to pay her an astonishing $17,500 per week, the largest salary ever offered in the history of summer theater.

Lana found herself in a deep, deep quandary over the proposal. Just a few months prior she had refused an offer of even greater magnitude to take over for Lauren Bacall in the Broadway musical *Applause*. Her reasons for declining were semilegitimate. For one thing, Lana has enormous respect for Lauren Bacall and correctly reasoned that an actress stepping into a role Bacall had created would suffer by comparison. "She wears her balls for earrings" was the way Lana had couched her fears. For another thing, Lana had never even appeared in a high-school play, let alone on Broadway. The thought of jumping right into the major leagues was frankly terrifying to her.

But things had changed between the two offers. Anticipated movies had not materialized, and Lana's agent told her
in no uncertain terms that she had better weigh this deal
carefully before turning it down. An impressive amount of
money was being dangled, and if Lana didn't bite now she
might never again have the opportunity. Lana was disproportionately upset by her agent's edict, in that there were
really but two facts to consider: he was right, and Lana didn't
want to do the tour. It took her three days of consideration,
plus a lot of discussion with her business manager and me
before she very tearfully committed to the project.

I was able to allay many of Lana's fears by relating stories
of what life was like on the road when I toured with Johnny
Mathis. There would be good audiences and bad—the latter
at benefits, tickets to which were bought to support a group
or a cause rather than from a desire to see the play; there
would be long hours in transit and countless, faceless hotel
rooms. Lana seemed unperturbed by most of this, reserving
her gravest doubts for having to learn an entire play from
word one. For movies, she never had to learn anything more
than a scene at a time, forgetting about it once the shot was
in the can. Furthermore, she had always acted on a closed
movie set and was terrified of working before a live audience:
she realized you couldn't say "cut" if you blew a scene.
However, for each objection I was able to come up with a
workable solution. These all hinged upon learning the play,
and I promised her I'd come up with something foolproof. In
the meantime, I reminded her what fun it would be once she
had mastered the dialogue. To be able to *hear* an audience
cheering firsthand was something she should not deny herself, and besides, to leave an audience begging for more was
the supreme test of star quality, something she had by the
truckload.

Partly because of the pressure under which Lana found
herself careerwise and my own sense of mounting guilt/
joy/responsibility for her professional and personal well-being,
it was at this critical time that we stumbled into our first
serious argument, a real whopper. If I'd been smarter, I
would have seen that our relationship could never survive
her possessive nature. She refuses to kowtow to anyone, and
while one cannot help but be stirred when she turns her

wrath against Universal Pictures, it's considerably less exhilarating when one gets both barrels oneself.

I met a man named Ross Marlow in November of 1970 in
a bar in Los Angeles. He was, and still is, a highly successful
fashion model with that look of great health that is peculiar to
blond, blue-eyed, Southern California men. He also has a
brain in his head and is quite gallant, and we developed an
immediate and very close friendship. Ross lived an hour
away, in a wonderfully rustic setting overlooking the Pacific
Ocean. It was like a minivacation whenever I'd drive out to
his house for a weekend, something I did with frequency.
Ross gave me a photograph of himself, one that emphasized
his cobalt blue eyes. I liked the shot very much and took to
carrying it in my briefcase so I could look at it from time to
time.

It wasn't long before Lana realized that I was spending
weekends away from my apartment. It had been my habit to
phone her late on Saturday and Sunday afternoons to see
what was doing, but as I got more and more involved in
various activities with Ross, my calls to Lana became less
frequent. Eventually, I had to tell her about him. In the
beginning, Lana was agreeable enough. Though she wore an
insincere smile whenever we talked about him, she did not
seem to resent him. But as patience and discretion are not a
part of Lana's lexicon, it wasn't long before her true feelings
surfaced. No one, man or woman, takes a lover from Lana
Turner. She and I were by this time together often,
but as I reminded her more than once, we were not man and
wife—and I felt, further, that Ross was a rare enough find for
me to want to share a portion of myself. In an attempt to
convince Lana that he really was worth my time, I dragged
out his picture. With scarcely a glance, she flung the eight-
by-ten on the pool table and sneered. "Very nice. But can *he*
keep you like *I* can?"

Her question stunned me, and picking up a glass cigarette lighter, I angrily brought it down on the top of the bar,
shattering the lighter. "Nobody *keeps* me," I yelled. "If you
had to pay me by the hour for the amount of time I spend
with you, you'd fucking be *bankrupt!*" I confess we both
had been drinking heavily before and during this argument.

Lana was visibly startled by my outburst and, for want of

anything more decisive to do, darted toward her bedroom. I followed her, only to find the door locked. I pounded for her to let me in, but she refused with silence, which only made me angrier. Fortunately, I turned from the door rather than try to smash it in, which would have resulted in either her neck or my fist being broken. Instead, grumbling loud deprecations about how Lana was an old woman and a has-been, I staggered from the penthouse and wove my way home. Upon arriving there, I called to tell Lana through slurred speech that I quit, to which she responded by screaming, "You *can't* quit. You're *fired*."

"Suits me either way," I shot back and hung up. Dumping myself onto the mattress, I fell with monumental satisfaction into a deep sleep.

The following afternoon I drove back to the penthouse to clean out my desk and tidy up old business. I wasn't going to be a spiteful son of a bitch and leave Lana's affairs in confusion, as much as I felt like doing just that. I walked briskly through the den and saw the offending photograph still on the pool table. I walked over to retrieve it and, much to my surprise, saw that dear, sweet Lana had gone into the photo-retouching business. Printed boldly beneath each finger of Ross's hand, which was clasped beneath his chin, was the word E-V-I-L. Written much smaller, much less obviously, across the fingers of the other hand was l-o-v-e. *No matter,* I thought. *I can get another one.*

Emotionally drained, I couldn't even get upset about what Lana had done. I just thought the graffiti petty and vindictive, then I dismissed it as I went about my work. Lana didn't emerge from her boudoir until late afternoon. When we did happen to meet in the living room, nothing was said about Ross—though as a matter of courtesy we both apologized for having let our discussion get out of hand. Lana didn't ask me to come back to work for her, nor did I even care to offer. Yet, she *acted* as if I'd never left. Apparently, her apology was a blanket retraction of everything said in anger, including my firing. I knew that Lana was not conceding defeat; she was merely withdrawing her claws for now. She would accept having ninety percent of me, weathering Ross for as long as he was around, for as Jack Freeman had told me when I first went to meet her, Lana would rather stay with a person who is imperfect than have to break in someone new. However, whenever I would see another woman or occasionally a man, Lana did not hesitate to show me the price of my independence, making my life miserable with jibes and useless busywork. In her defense, Lana *needed* the security of one man's absolute devotion; in my defense, Lana does not give nearly so much as she takes and smothers; witness the collapse of her multiple marriages. It was my job and my pleasure to be nine-tenths her chevalier. To have given her ten percent more would have left me an empty husk with very little self-respect—"kept" was the word she'd used. That my being "kept" finally happened is a tribute to Lana's possessiveness and pertinacity.

In any case, the problem was forgotten for the time being, as our full attention was turned to *Forty Carats*. I must admit that the choice of vehicle for Lana's stage debut couldn't have been more appropriate. She played a forty-year-old New York divorcée, who is courted by a twenty-year-old Lothario. The part is equally comic and austere, and it fit Lana like a proverbial glove.

Preparing for the play left us with literally hundreds of different things on which to concentrate at once. Aside from the formidable obstacle of learning the dialogue, there were unexpected problems—such as Lana's voice being too soft for the stage. She would have to be body-miked, and all of her costumes had to be designed with microphones in mind. Another problem was Lana's makeup and hair, more accurately the fact that she wanted Jack and Cherie to travel with us. Though this would be an extremely costly luxury, her business manager gave in just to keep the nervous star contented. There is no understating how important it was to Lana that she have this cosmetic buffer, not only for the play but for the rehearsal period as well. God forbid one of her fellow actors should see Lana Turner with dark roots showing! As if the palace knaves didn't know that the queen went to the bathroom. . . . In an effort to talk Lana out of this indulgence, I told her a story related by a friend who was my counterpart with Betty Grable. The legendary sex goddess had been appearing in *Hello, Dolly!* at theaters-in-the-round across the nation. From Broadway to Juno, Alaska, matinee audiences usually consist of elderly, blue-haired women who have been bussed in with their garden clubs. Now, these little old ladies, even those sitting in the front row, bring their opera glasses to get a close-up view of the star. At one performance, Miss Grable was standing near the lip of the stage when she overheard one of those front-row ladies remark to a friend that the actress certainly did not look the way she had twenty years before. Much to the surprise of the actor who was singing "So Long, Dearie," Miss Grable turned to face the offending patron. Placing both hands on her hips, she boomed, "Madam, who the fuck does?"

Lana did not miss the point of the story but, as usual, didn't particularly give a damn. Jack and Cherie would be with us from day one. I'm convinced that, throughout her career, had Lana fretted over her acting as much as she worried about her appearance, she might have been a great actress instead of just a superstar. In fairness, I must add that Lana's diligence *did* reap the dividends she desperately sought. During every show, I would sit somewhere in the audience to listen to the reactions of theatergoers. At one show, in Chicago's Drury Lane Theater, I overheard a woman whisper to her lady friend, "Isn't she just *awful* in this play?" Her companion replied, "I don't care. . . . She's so pretty I'm just enjoying looking at her."

As soon as Lana had agreed to the tour, an announcement was made in the show business trade papers. No sooner was *that* done than Lana's agent received a panicked call from Guber and Gross. It seems that through a secretary's typographical error, which no one had caught, Lana was *supposed* to have been paid $7,500 per week rather than the $17,500 cited in precontract correspondence. Lana, who had accepted the offer in good faith because of the large sum, was unwilling to settle for less; since the announcement had already been made, Guber and Gross could not back out and maintain credibility for future productions. The bottom line was that $17,500 per week it would be.

At once, all of Hollywood began placing bets on just how long Lana's stage career would last. From the press to the studio executives, it was the cruelest kind of gossip imaginable, the oddsmakers saying she'd never go through with it. Most people believed that she'd never even make it as far as the first rehearsal in New York. Lana was not unaware of what was being said, though I tried to minimize the importance of what we heard secondhand. Lana endeavored to use each snippet of denigration as a rung in a ladder to help her climb from insecurity to determination. It was not an easy time for Lana, but as she herself pointed out, she had survived talk far more vicious than this.

One person who wasn't laughing was Lana's friend Dorothy Lamour, who had just trod the boards for the first time herself in *Mame*. She came to Lana's aid, not only encouraging her but recommending a director by the name of John Bowab. According to Dorothy, Bowab was "the best director in the business for a woman." His particular talent was acclimating ladies who had only worked in film, a medium that requires a different kind of performance than the stage. She added that Bowab was also young, vigorous, and quite a gentleman. Lana was sold, and she instructed her agent that it was up to Guber and Gross to obtain Bowab's services. They did, and from that point forward, the pace grew even more frenetic.

At my suggestion, Lana contacted a vocal coach and began taking lessons in projection. Even though she would be miked, I felt that the training would boost Lana's confidence. The instructor's name was George Griffin, and he had worked with many novices. In fact, among his pupils was one of my favorite actresses, Jennifer Jones. I had the good luck to meet her one afternoon as we arrived for Lana's lesson, although Miss Jones seemed slightly uncomfortable running into Lana. The two ladies said hello and, after the few verbal niceties, managed to extricate themselves from what was clearly an awkward situation. I later found out from Lana that Jennifer had been given the film *Madame Bovary* in 1949 after Lana had been put on suspension by MGM because she was pregnant. Lana felt that they could have postponed the film, and she was furious when they did not. Within weeks, she had one of her three miscarriages.

George Griffin was a patient and gentle man, but he didn't manage to impart much knowledge to Lana. Not only was she habitually late for her lessons, but when she *did* arrive, we usually sat around drinking and gossiping the hour away. When Lana really doesn't want to do something, she'll go as far as she must to shut you up and then not a millimeter further.

Dance classes were another activity designed to get Lana into shape for the rigors of the theater—that is, running up and down the aisles, standing onstage for nearly two hours, and so on. Needless to say, given her celebrity status Lana would not join just any dance class. At Nolan Miller's suggestion, she got together with producer Aaron Spelling's wife Candy, and the two spent an hour each week stretching, firming, and toning. I can't say how much of this was actually useful to her when the tour finally began, but it did a world of good for her attitude. Doing anything strenuous, anything that worked up a sweat served to encourage her that she was extending herself for the tour. One day we walked on the beach, which Lana later told the press was an everyday part of her training.

With Lana's body and psyche both to some extent looked after, I had other concerns, one of which was purely organizational. Having had a great deal of experience with theater managers during my years with Johnny Mathis, I knew how they worked and knew how to get from them whatever a star wanted. I knew that Lana trusted my judgment, but I explained to her that the title personal secretary simply held very little clout. I suggested with all due modesty that we change it to personal manager, though I didn't request a percentage of her income as a personal manager is entitled to do, offering to take on the added responsibilities with only her best interests in mind. Lana wholeheartedly agreed with me, and when I informed Jess Morgan about our plan, he said he frankly didn't care as long as it didn't cost Lana more money. I assured him that it would not, and I was hurt when he failed to thank me. As for Lana, she enjoyed the prestige my new title lent her—although whenever she was annoyed with me, my darling employer would make a point of referring to me once again as her secretary. I didn't let that bother me; either, since it carried all the substance of Lucy sticking out her tongue at Charlie Brown. There was a job to do, plain and simple, and I did it.

Overall, Lana was actually very good defining up front my position and authority to her colleagues. The first time I ever accompanied her on a business meeting at William Morris, she unexpectedly hustled me from the reception area into the conference room and announced to the producers and agents present, "Gentlemen, this is Mr. Taylor Pero. He is my other eyes and ears, and you can feel free to talk openly in his presence." Later I thanked her for that courtesy; she told me I'd earned her trust and she gave it freely. Well, that she did, too. After all, a secretary could never have strong-armed a theater manager into painting a filthy dressing room, whereas a personal manager could. Fortunately, I would also have some major duties on the road.

As May 20 and our departure for New York neared, Lana began to leave more and more time for what *she* considered to be most important: her wardrobe. Not less than three-quarters of her waking hours were spent on fittings for both on and off the stage. Lana had decided that she didn't have a wardrobe suitable for summer travel, and she asked Nolan to make clothes expressly for that purpose. Not only did every-thing have to be fitted impeccably and thoroughly accessorized but the garments had to be made from the best, yet most wrinkle-free, materials. None had to be machine washable, however, since everything Lana owns goes to the dry clean-ers. At least, I reflected, she had gotten quickly into the spirit of touring. For the show itself, Nolan designed an absolutely fabulous wardrobe that consisted of seventeen separate costume changes with a pair of bow gowns calculated to send the audience away with a flourish of old-style Hollywood glamour. The quality, let alone the amount of work he did was phenomenal, and it's a pity Lana refused absolutely to use him on any future projects when the wardrobe arrived in New York and she found that a belt was missing.

Another matter that was nearly as important to Lana as her wardrobe was her wigs. Since she perspires profusely under the hot stage lights and no ordinary hairdo can possibly hold up even to the first intermission, she has to wear wigs. The wigs for *Forty Carats* were carefully chosen by a commit-tee consisting of Lana, Cherie, and me—although none of us theatrical pros took into account how they would ultimately look under stage lighting. Early in the tour, most reviewers took pains to point out that Lana looked as though she were wearing a blond steel helmet, and we quickly learned to tone down the color.

Studying the dialogue for *Forty Carats* proved to be the least of our troubles. I devised what I thought was a clever means for her to learn her lines; we read the play into a cassette recorder, which Lana would keep at her side wheth-er she was creaming her face, taking a bath, or having her hair done. We'd act out the play whenever possible, Lana weaning herself from the script as the weeks progressed. She wasn't the quickest study in town, but once the play was in her head, it was there to stay.

During the last few weeks of our preparations, added incentive for Lana to excel came from the presence of John Bowab, who flew in to help Lana mold the part. Lana was immediately infatuated with the tall, handsome director.

Lana seemed reborn by all of this activity, but it proved to be a false front. She was aflutter with what she called "nervous energy," but it was really a severe case of anxiety. Just *how* severe it was hit home when my telephone rang at four one morning. It was Nolan on the line. He groggily told me that he had just had a call from Lana and that she sounded incoherent. I presumed that she was drunk but decided to call just the same. There was no answer. She might have fallen asleep, I reasoned, but then again—

Preferring to err on the side of caution, I put in an emergency call to Dr. Mac, who told me to get out there fast and to call him the moment I was in the penthouse. He said he would have an ambulance on alert, but he did not want to send it there unless absolutely necessary, since false alarms are frowned upon. Dr. Mac sounded urgent but not surprised, almost as if he'd been expecting this kind of thing. Rather than waste time demanding an explanation, I raced out to Edgewater.

I found Lana in bed, oblivious to the world but not quite unconscious. I tried to rouse her, but she could do little other than groan. I checked around the bed for empty bottles, and though I didn't find any, I was unwilling to pronounce her in the clear. She was too languid for anyone to have responsibly labeled her merely drunk. I called Dr. Mac from her bedside, and, as if she were being directed by Vincente Minnelli, Lana opened her eyes. They were bloodshot and clearly unfocused, though she was coherent enough to recognize me.

"Wha—What are you doin' here? Somethin' wrong?"

I asked Dr. Mac to hold on. "What did you do?" I demanded. "Is it just drink, or did you take something else?"

Lana shook her head. "I can' remember any—anything."

"Dammit, Lana, I've got Dr. Mac on the line, and he *has* to know."

Her features brightened slightly, and she propped herself on an elbow, asking to talk to the physician. I handed her the phone, then I went to the bar and poured myself a substantial belt of scotch. I rarely needed liquor to calm myself, but this was the first of many exceptions. When I returned to the bedroom, Lana was still on the phone. Her speech was so badly slurred that there was no sense allowing the conversation to continue, so I snatched the receiver from her, and Lana's head just kind of rolled back onto the pillow.

Dr. Mac said that Lana didn't sound as if she'd taken a lethal overdose of Seconal or anything else, and he asked if I'd mind staying the night with her. We agreed that it was better to be safe than sorry, so after I got off the phone, I made Lana comfortable and then threw myself onto the bed in my office. What Dr. Mac hadn't told me, and what I didn't learn until the following day, was that Lana was no stranger to having attempted suicide. In 1951, beaten by the collapse of her marriage with Bob Topping and the box-office debacle of the highly touted film *Mr. Imperium*, Lana had slit her wrists. She still bears the fine, clean scars of that laceration, which is one reason she always wears so many bracelets. Lana denies that she ever tried to take her life and says that she stepped into the shower, was stunned by the heat of the flow, jumped back, and fell through the glass door. I don't put much credence in that story quite frankly, because the nature of the wound smacks of what Lana had done the night I rushed over. Several tendons but no major blood vessels had been slashed, which makes for a pretty selective glass door. She seemed to be intent on hurting herself enough to be fawned over without seriously courting death. As ever, it was an effort to gain attention— albeit, in both instances a rather extreme effort. Like everything else about Lana, nothing in moderation.

I was quite literally bowled over the next morning to find Lana ripping mad at Nolan for having called me. I asked her what he was *supposed* to have done, and she replied, rather cavalierly I thought, "*Nothing*." I had a difficult time convincing Lana that what Nolan had done was because he *cared*. She didn't accept that, but in light of how irresponsibly she had acted in the first place, her opinion carried very little weight.

That evening wasn't the last time Lana pulled a stunt of this sort, but it was certainly her *mildest*. She told me that she'd only had a bit too much to drink, but I couldn't accept that excuse the second time around. A few weeks later, I received another early morning call, this time from Lana herself. This in itself was not unusual, as she would call me at all hours of the night for words of reassurance, of love, maybe even a joke or two. This call was different. I knew that she was drunk again, but her speech was not just slurred, it was *mushy,* as though her tongue were pasted to the bottom of her mouth. She kept repeating that she couldn't go through with *Forty Carats,* that she was letting everyone down and couldn't face that. I tried to tell her that that was nonsense, which it was, but she didn't hear me; there were long silences in her conversation as she dozed off with her mouth on the receiver. I'd yell loud enough to wake her, and she'd start babbling again—all of it pertaining to the play and how she'd failed to do one thing well or how she couldn't get the courage to go on.

I told Lana I'd be right over, which was obviously what she wanted in the first place. However, instead of rushing to the penthouse, I phoned the Palisades Patrol, the private armed patrol service wired to Lana's home in case of emergency. If anyone entered, an alarm would go off in the patrol's headquarters. They also had access to the penthouse, which was more important to me just then. The men were qualified to provide quick medical relief if it was needed, and they would be performing one other very vital service: their presence was sure to embarrass Lana so thoroughly that she'd never again try anything else of this nature. I instructed the crew to go right in and call me from Lana's bedside.

Within a half hour I was speaking with the medics, who said that while Lana had appeared to have taken some Seconal, they did not think she had overdosed sufficiently to require hospitalization. In the background, I could hear Lana surprisingly attentive and loudly refusing any medical attention. Her speech was decidedly less garbled than before, and as mean as it may sound, I had a private chuckle over the humiliation that Lana must feel having these strange men in her bedroom, seeing her without a trace of makeup, without *eyebrows* for Chrissakes! She'd brought it on herself, however, and nothing she could say or do would change that. In fact, I was surprised to find her less angry with me the following day than she'd been with Nolan. I defended my actions by stating that I was afraid it would have taken me too long to get to her in time, and Lana did not disagree. Her response was even uncharacteristically self-effacing. She said, "I feel like such a fool," and that was the end of the matter. It was also the last time Lana ever tried something of this type. Moreover, she was so humiliated that when the bill came for the relief team, Lana asked me to pay for it from her weekly allowance so that no one in Jess Morgan's office would know what had transpired.

The only way Lana could save face in light of these events and gain back her shaken self-respect was to press ahead with *Forty Carats*. She did so with previously untapped stores of determination, and I was both impressed and thankful. By the time we left for New York, she was at once radiant and scared as hell, but beneath it all, she was determined to conquer and *enjoy* the play.

We stayed at the Plaza Hotel in New York, ensconced in a luxury suite with a magnificent view of Central Park. The panorama was something on which Lana had insisted, due to equal measures of acute claustrophobia and fear of being spied upon by someone in a neighboring building. Lana was quite satisfied with our accommodations, though she was unusually oblivious to them as she fortified her spirit for the commencement of rehearsals.

Lana was able to get her mind off *Forty Carats* that first night. No sooner had we arrived than the William Morris office phoned with instructions for Lana to pick up reserved tickets for John Bowab and us at a play called *The Gingerbread Lady*. This seriocomic show was written by Neil Simon, the story of a has-been actress-singer who is attempting to conquer alcoholism and to salvage a decaying relationship with her daughter. A film version was being talked about, and though the wonderful Maureen Stapleton was starring in the show, the backers were thinking of Lana for the picture. We went; before the play was over, Lana had whispered to me, "No *way* would I do a film about this subject. It's too close to home." As it turned out, the play was not filmed until 1981. By then it had undergone changes including a new title, *Only When I Laugh*, and it starred Marsha Mason—Mrs. Neil Simon.

The show was funny to me, and things picked up even more when we went backstage to visit Miss Stapleton. She subsequently joined us for dinner and seemed genuinely awed at the presence of Lana Turner, flattered that we'd come to the play. I doubt she'd have felt as complimented had she known that Hollywood was planning to overlook her for the juicy film role. Though it wouldn't be the first time that a fine stage star has been snubbed in favor of a "name" star to help ensure a movie's success, it is not a practice well respected along the Great White Way. I remember Richard Kiley once telling me that when Peter O'Toole was named to play a part he had created on the stage, that of Don Quixote in the film version of *Man of La Mancha*, he went into his backyard, grabbed an ax, and splintered a row of orange crates. Though the film was not successful, O'Toole was paid in the neighborhood of $1,000,000 for so doing.

By the time we had dined and then dropped Miss Stapleton back at her apartment, she was full of wine and rather inebriated. John and our chauffeur had to help her up the stairs to her apartment. Despite the undignified nature of her parting, I was greatly impressed with the actress. She did, for one thing, have excellent taste in music. The restaurant to which we'd gone had a piano, and at one point John persuaded me to sing. When I returned to the table, Miss Stapleton told me that I had brought tears to her eyes. No doubt the white wine had helped her along, but it was still a kind thing for her to say. Lana agreed with our guest.

The following day, Lana had her first rehearsal with the cast of *Forty Carats*, a group of talented "unknowns" that included Anne Russel, Peter Coffield, and Kathleen Coyne. Naturally, Lana had assumed she'd have a limousine to take her to the rehearsal studio, which was four blocks away; when John showed up without one she was astonished.

"This is an *affront*," she wailed, "the most *un*professional indignity I have *ever* confronted in—"

John cut her short by saying, "You need the fresh air, Lana, and it's not very far to walk." He added, "This is a different world, it's not MGM, and we're not shooting *The Bad and the Beautiful*. This is regional theater."

Lana considered the veracity of what he'd said, and her rage subsided to mere miff. However, as she has always leaned heavily on the judgment of her directors, she agreed to go along with John in this matter. Standing between us like Dorothy off to see the Wizard and clinging tightly to John's arm, Lana walked to the rehearsal studio. She later realized that John had worked a very astute psychological maneuver.

Never mind the exercise, the walk had knocked her off her Hollywood high horse. It made Lana look at herself as an actress with a job to do rather than a superstar with an image to maintain. Unfortunately, without the buffer of her queenly cortege, Lana was even more frightened at the prospect of finally meeting these actors with their wealth of stage credentials. I told her not to worry, but she did just the same and was actually trembling when we reached the building and rode the elevator to the rehearsal studio. The doors opened, and John and I all but had to tug her slightly to get her into the small cavern of a room. She looked around, like a child inspecting her nursery school classroom, then she mustered her courage and strode in. That first step was, as the cliché goes, the most difficult; the rest was easy. John made the introductions, and I was pleased to see smiles and words of genuine admiration for Lana as each actor was presented. She relaxed visibly, and while the company engaged in some salutatory chitchat, John covertly took me aside.

"Taylor," he said, "I want you to go find something to do. Now that we've got her up here, it's important that she not have you to rely upon."

I couldn't have agreed more, and I immediately turned to go. Lana happened to look back just then and saw me head for the elevator. She asked if I'd be back for the lunch break; I told her I would, then I looked to John, who nodded quietly that it would be OK for me to do so.

After a bit of sight-seeing, I returned to the studio and found that Lana had undergone a wonderful transformation. She was laughing, outgoing, even touching her fellow performers—and, what's more astounding, allowing them to touch *her!* I realized her tension had been such that, in releasing it, she'd become almost giddy. Never before or after did I see her so very much off guard. Needless to say, a superlative rehearsal period followed—during which time I got to see a good deal of New York City and its environs.

One of the interesting nonevents of this period was the time I didn't meet Claudette Colbert. It was fascinating—and something I don't fully comprehend to this day. Lana, John, and I were having lunch in a Central Park café when we noticed Miss Colbert sitting at a table nearby. John explained that she was currently appearing on Broadway in a play with Rex Harrison, and while we were staring at her, Miss Colbert

chanced to look up. She obviously recognized Lana, but that
was as far as it went; it's unwritten law in any social situation
that the greater star will not come over to the lesser star. In
this case the ladies were of near-equal magnitude, so we
never got together. That sort of thing happened many times
over the years in my presence, most spectacularly at the
Harold Robbins New Year's party. Lucille Ball did not cross
the room to say hello to Lana, nor did Lana move to greet
Lucy—nor did Angela Lansbury greet either of them; nor I
noticed, on a lesser scale, did Barbara Eden rise to talk to
Jackie Bisset. Not that everyone has to be the best of friends,
but I thought this kind of behavior went out with the
Romanovs. I even heard Zsa Zsa Gabor remark once when
she and Lana were at just such a standoff, "You see, dahlings,
she doesn't want to be seen with me because I look so much
younger. . . ." Wishful thinking, honey. Nonetheless, there are
a lot of people I never got to meet in this fashion, although
I'd have gladly taken the hike across the room, restaurant, or
whatever, had I not been with Lana.

Forty Carats opened in Westbury, Long Island on June
29. We ran, a different city each week, through August 16,
during which time Lana got generally marvelous reviews and
more than justified her considerable expense by breaking
box-office records in most of these theaters. She ended up
enjoying the entire undertaking, though it utterly exhausted
her. Not that, for a minute, she didn't feel it had been worth
the effort. She returned to Los Angeles a conquering hero,
though neither of us was surprised when none of the people
who had predicted disaster called to congratulate her. I, on
the other hand, was proud of the lady and told her so over
and over. I was also as whipped as she was, having spent
nearly two months of seven-day weeks fussing over every
kind of detail imaginable. The one dark shadow that marred
the tour—and that was a harbinger of worse imbroglios—was
the occasional late curtains. These were caused by Lana's
vanity and willfulness—for example, her finding one real hair
sticking from under her wig and either returning to her
dressing room to snip it off or having the entire coiffure
redone. She never believed me when I said there were no
closeups; such is the seriousness with which she takes her
appearance. Even in film, where there *are* tight shots, Lana
resents looking bad, whether or not that's what the part

requires! The most striking example is *Madame X*, wherein Lana ages twenty-four years and sinks to the depths of depravity through drink and prostitution. She was so self-conscious about the old-age makeup that no visitors were allowed on the set. In fact, the film all but destroyed the relationship she had with her longtime makeup man Del Armstrong. Lana tried to prevent him from finishing the job on her face when she thought she looked sufficiently decrepit. Del did not agree and insisted on doing justice to the character, not to Lana Turner. She gave in, but she took to wearing a dark veil when traveling the short distance from her dressing room to the sound stage. However, the one concession she refused to make was clipping her fingernails, which remained handsomely manicured. How incongruous to be watching this film about a character who has been through hell, looking wan and impoverished and beaten, being tried for murder and lying on her deathbed, refusing to tell her attorney that she is his mother— watching all this *angst*—and being distracted by Lana's perfect nails!

Allowing, if one must, for that kind of anomalous behavior on a movie set, to have to deal with it on the stage is just plain absurd. Particularly when the by-product of Lana's behavior eventually was curtains rising over an hour late!

But these headaches were still in the future. For now, her intransigence was little more than a minor inconvenience. After seven weeks of overseeing a complex network of minutiae, making sure that our plane reservations were in order, keeping tabs on ticket sales, and writing ahead to each hotel to insist that our room be stocked with the likes of five gallons of distilled water, four quarts of unsweetened grapefruit juice, two six-packs of club soda, a half-dozen fresh lemons, four wastebaskets, one package of bacon substitute, diet margarine, one carton of egg substitute, *ad nauseam,* it was surprisingly refreshing to get back to a routine of unrelieved boredom in Los Angeles.

Chapter Seven

We spent a lot of time unwinding at Vince Pastere's home in Palm Springs, and it was during one of our visits that I was privileged to spend an evening with the man who is perhaps the world's greatest star.

I had awakened fairly early one morning and, slipping into a swimsuit, had gone out by the pool to lounge. Several hours later I noticed that Lana was up, and as I walked into the kitchen to greet her, the telephone rang. Feeling reckless, I did something I'd never done before—and, trust me, will never do again. Instead of answering the phone in a normal way, I snapped up the receiver and barked, "Mother's Saloon."

A distinctly familiar voice cut through my bullshit and said, "This is Mr. Sinatra. Is Miss Turner in?"

I was mortified, literally unable to speak. I turned a deep crimson and motioned spastically for Lana to take the offending instrument from my hand. She gave me a very strange look as she walked over.

"What's wrong, Taylor? Who *is* it?"

Still unable to speak, I thrust the receiver toward her. Lana took it and said hello; after a long moment she threw back her head and laughed. "Oh, that was my secretary being silly." A pause, accompanied by a stern look in my direction. "I'll bet he never does *that* again."

God, she was right.

Frank Sinatra had heard that Lana was in town and was calling to invite her to his home for dinner with some friends the following night. As a rule, Lana hems and haws for a few minutes before accepting invitations; this one she consented to at once.

Frank and Lana had a long, rocky history between them. They had been an "item" in the middle 1940s, when Frank's marriage to Nancy was on the rocks and he was dating numerous actresses. Lana turned to him in that futile effort to make Tyrone Power jealous; then in 1948 she turned from Frank to third husband Bob Topping. Frank finally settled down and married Ava Gardner in 1951, though less than a year later Lana was back in his life in a sensational way. The Sinatras and Lana both happened to be in Palm Springs, where Lana was recovering from her faltering romance with Fernando Lamas. Frank was out, so Ava invited Lana over to try and cheer her up. The women also ended up comparing notes on their mutual ex-husband Artie Shaw—and of course on Frank. Sinatra happened to stroll in while they were discussing him—"cutting him up" said a friend who had heard it from Frank—and in a rage he threw the two women out. Behind Sinatra's back Lana had dubbed him, "His I-Tralian Highness." Lana and Ava, themselves pretty strong-willed, up and went to Mexico, where they had a lively time. Naturally, the Hollywood gossips and tabloids alike began to hint about a lesbian relationship between the two, but that was untrue. A week later, Frank and Ava made up, although the marriage alternated between love and shambles until it was finally terminated in 1956. There was, the following year, a friendly reconciliation between Frank and Lana when he came to visit her immediately after the Stompanato murder, to offer any help she might need. Cheryl recalled to me that he sent her a phonograph and records while she was in jail. The relationship between the two superstars remained platonic, and in 1960 they even planned to coproduce and star in a few films together. These plans fell through, but Lana and Frank have remained in touch on and off ever since.

On the afternoon of Sinatra's dinner, Lana went into her dressing room at four o'clock to prepare for the evening. Doing some fast mental figuring, I determined that she *should* be finished by seven-thirty, which was when we were expected. It was going to be a casual affair, which meant that Lana needed ample time to get herself impeccably casual. We laid out a simple pair of gray slacks with matching sweater and a red plaid box vest trimmed with matching gray. The outfit was, of course, accessorized with matching boots and purse. We were actually making pretty good time until we came to the jewelry; Lana went through boxes upon boxes upon bags of rings, bracelets, broaches, earrings, pendants, and necklaces, finally discarding them all in favor of layers of gold chain and bracelets and a fifteen-carat pear-shaped diamond. My careful calculations aside, we were late leaving Vince's house by over an hour. Our host had called twice to find out how long we would be, since the eighteen other guests were getting hungry. I was mortified, as was becoming the norm, doubly so because Mr. Sinatra made these calls himself—a fact intended to hurry Lana along. I think that knowing he was "pursuing" her made Lana tarry all the more.

By the time we arrived at the sprawling Sinatra compound, we were ninety minutes behind schedule. Our car was admitted past the gate by security guards, and after we parked where the guards had instructed, in a lavish carport, we were ushered inside by the housekeeper. As we entered the living room, my eyes went instantly to the far end, which was dominated by an enormous restaurant-style bar. There, the guests were happily consuming predinner cocktails being prepared from behind the bar by none other than Mr. Sinatra himself.

"Ol' Blue Eyes" they call him, and blue eyes he has. Piercing eyes that are vibrant and alive. His silver hair seems almost to pick up that blue, framing a tanned face of extraordinary calm. He is not a tall man, but Frank Sinatra moves with a contradictory grace and toughness that make him seem tall.

When our host spotted us, he came immediately around the bar and greeted Lana with an affectionate kiss. Lana introduced me, and as he warmly shook my hand, I was even more completely enveloped by the man's charisma. He is truly one of the most electric personalities I've ever met: his eyes have a way of burning into you like lasers, though not in an intimidating way. He'd clearly prefer to be your pal rather than your enemy. He escorted us to the bar, where the other guests were clustered, each of them sizing Lana up one side and down the other. I'm not sure anyone even noticed me.

We had a drink at the bar while the buffet was being opened. I was alone with Mr. Sinatra, and as he's the kind of man you want to talk to, find yourself wanting to praise, I found myself overly effusive talking about an album of his that I'd recently heard on the radio. In it, he talked a bit about the history of each song before the music swelled in. I'm sure he's used to this kind of burbling, but he accepted my compliments with grace. When I remarked that, to my chagrin, the disc jockey had never mentioned the title and I had thus been unable to purchase a copy, he replied, "You mean *A Man and His Music*," then did me in by asking if I'd like a copy. I told him I would very much, whereupon he went off somewhere and returned with two specially jacketed pressings. Both were numbered and signed by him. Lana, who had just ambled over, graciously helped me thank him when words failed me.

No sooner had Lana and I finished our drinks than Frank led his guests into the dining area. As we entered, I saw to my right a long, overstocked serving table that was made of exquisite and highly polished teak, behind which two smiling Oriental servants stood dressed in immaculate white uniforms. The seating consisted of two large round dining tables made of the same gleaming wood, each with place settings for ten. I was not the least bit surprised that Frank had chosen to place Lana to his immediate left. I was, however, almost stricken when he indicated that I was to sit to his immediate right.

The Oriental dinner was superb, though I can't remember a word that was said before, during, or after—concentrating, as I was, on trying to look casual, as though I dined like this every night of the week. I *do* remember that at one point during the meal, Frank snapped his fingers and a white-uniformed servant appeared. "Bring some champagne," he ordered, and moments later, a large magnum was presented. He inspected the label, nodded, and while the servant opened the bottle, Frank asked if anyone wanted champagne. Much to my surprise, everyone at both tables declined. I had known that Lana would not want any, but I didn't understand how seventeen other people could *all* not like champagne. Personally, I loved it. I told myself that this must be some sort of custom, that nobody but Frank was supposed to drink the bubbly. But that didn't make any sense, so I decided to risk offending the host by gushing, "I'd *love* some."

As it turned out, the champagne had been refused simply because everyone but Frank had had their fill of alcohol while awaiting our arrival. Frank seemed, in fact, rather pleased that he wouldn't have to drink alone and, using his spoon, lifted some ice cubes from his tulip-shaped glass and transferred them to mine. The servant filled my long-stemmed glass, and as I toasted my newfound friend, then brought the topaz drink to my lips, I couldn't help being overwhelmed by one sudden, giddy thought: *My God, I'm drinking Frank Sinatra's ice cubes!*

After dinner, Frank pushed his chair from the table and said one word in Italian, which I didn't understand. It didn't matter; it meant that the meal was over. Everyone at both tables immediately rose, and we followed our host through sliding-glass doors that opened onto the enormous swimming pool. Like schoolchildren, we marched two by two until we reached a small auditorium. Inside was an array of sofas and overstuffed chairs, each with its own coffee table. There was a large stone fireplace on the right side of the room and a regulation billiard table toward the front. Beyond it was a high wall covered entirely in red velvet drapery. Toward the rear of the room was another bar, which I was able to examine closely when Lana requested that I make her a drink instead of having one of the servants mix it in the wrong proportions.

Once drinks had been served to the few who wanted them, everyone selected a sofa or chair. Frank sat toward the back of the room in a special chair with a built-in telephone system through which he could reach any part of the house. He picked up the white receiver and said a few muffled words. At once the lights began to dim, and the draperies opened to reveal a CinemaScope-sized movie screen. When the room was dark, George C. Scott walked into the frame. This was, I decided, the *only* way to see *Patton*!

After the movie, we returned to the main house for after-dinner drinks and an impromptu piano recital by one of the guests, Mr. Frederick Loewe of the legendary song-writing team Lerner and Loewe. Mr. Loewe prefaced his concert by requesting that no one speak while he was playing; he needn't have bothered with his entreaty, since his music effortlessly held the complete attention of everyone in the room.

Mr. Loewe's performance lasted for twenty minutes, after which we sat around in the yellow living room. All the while, Lana was poised comfortably on the arm of Frank's chair.

The conversation that followed was mostly about politics,

ranging from state to national. Politically, I found Frank one
of the most informed people I've ever met, and most of the
far-reaching predictions he made that night proved eerily on
target. I knew that Frank had been an intimate of JFK until
the president suddenly stopped calling—allegedly at the insistence of Attorney General Robert Kennedy, who feared a
public backlash from the singer's rumored connections with
organized crime. Frank supported Republicans thereafter,
and most recently, he was a highly visible advocate of Ronald
Reagan in his presidential campaign. Lana, incidentally, tried
to steer the conversation away from politics several times, but
that only seemed to annoy our host.

When the early hours of the morning were finally upon
us and it was time to leave, Frank walked Lana and me to our
car. As we strolled in the clear and beautiful desert night,
Lana held tightly to his right arm. Out of respect for their
privacy, I went ahead. I don't have any idea what Lana might
have said to him, but all of a sudden he angrily pushed her
away, and I heard him exclaim, "You crazy broad!" A moment
later he cooled, snickered, then continued to escort Lana to
the car. While she silently entered the car, Frank shook my
hand, said he'd enjoyed meeting me, and then walked briskly
back inside.

Knowing better than to ask Lana what all the shouting
had been about, I simply flicked on the stereo and drove back
to Vince's house. While Lana volunteered no information
regarding the tiff, I wondered if she had asked to stay the
night. Regardless, she spoke with Frank the following day,
and evidently all was forgiven. When she'd finished her
lengthy conversation, Lana relayed to me Frank's opinion
that I was a nice guy and one she should try to, in his words,
"keep around." My hat size increased proportionately.

In January of 1972, Lana's divorce from Ronald Dante
finally went before a judge in the Superior Court of Santa
Monica. Someone from Jess Morgan's office went to court in
her stead while she and I sat in her penthouse awaiting word
as to whether she would have to appear. In case her presence
was required, Lana had chosen her court wardrobe as carefully as though she were still on tour. As a matter of fact, she
elected to wear one of Nolan Miller's creations from *Forty
Carats*. She had decided that a limousine would also be

appropriate for the occasion, since there would probably be photographers present.

For three days we did nothing but sit by the telephone and wait. Then, on the afternoon of the third day, Lana was asked to appear before the judge. She had already been made up and coiffed, and we were chauffeured over; it took very little time for Lana to answer the few questions that were posed. The outcome was that Lana was granted her divorce and Dante was found sadly lacking in credibility. She was awarded a settlement of a few thousand dollars, which she never expected to see, nor did she ever seriously try to extract it. Someone from Jess Morgan's office routinely tried, however.

It is interesting and somewhat tragic to note the ways in which Dante's name would turn up from time to time. He was jailed on several occasions, once for allegedly having hired a professional hit man to do away with a rival nightclub hypnotist. We also heard that, more than once, he actually used as the introduction to his act, "Ladies and gentlemen: straight from the bedroom of Lana Turner, Dr. Dante!" Some kind soul even anonymously sent us a bottle of cheap beauty cream with Lana's name on it, which Dante was selling in whatever city he appeared. The beauty cream really made Lana furious, and she complained to her legions of lawyers. Unfortunately, no one was ever able to find Dante to order him to desist, and the issue was forgotten by all but Lana and me.

Forty Carats had been the only professional engagement for Lana in quite some time, and by March things were once more oppressively quiet. The one offer Lana did have was to take *Forty Carats* to other theaters. However, she had exhausted herself during the initial run and didn't want ever again to have to do an eight-performance week. The plan evaporated.

Because Lana wasn't earning anything beyond her residuals and the dividends from Jess Morgan's various investments, she was unable to give me even a cost-of-living increase. As a result, my cash reserves dwindled. Lana knew I was having a tough time staying afloat financially, and I was touched when she came to me one day and said, "Taylor, I know you're not making as much as you should be. If you'll bear with me, I'll make it up to you when the next project comes along." It was very thoughtful of her, and I appreciated

Lana's concern. I also knew that my creditors would be resoundingly unimpressed; so much for the prosperity of being a kept man. Thus, to get ahead financially, I took a job selling office supplies over the phone. I held that position for a couple of months, getting up at five in the morning and spending from six until noon calling all over the country, selling everything from staplers to bookshelves on a commission basis. I would still manage to be at Lana's condominium by one o'clock. It made her very uncomfortable when I'd try to talk about some funny incident that had happened at the office—as though the First Lady's press secretary shouldn't have to clean White House toilets on the side. But for a few months, that's exactly what I had to do to maintain a financial foothold. Holding both jobs left me bone tired, and it wasn't until Lana began digging into some of her considerable holdings that I could afford to work solely for her once more.

It was during this period that Lana first received an inquiry from a New York firm wanting to know if she would endorse a chain of health spas to be built across the United States. The offer came through Jess Morgan who, discriminating as ever when Lana's financial security was at stake, advised her that it was well worth looking into. The firm agreed that if she and I would fly to New York for a meeting, they would pay our expenses and put us up in our accustomed splendor at the Plaza. We accepted and on March 23 were on our way.

The people sponsoring this venture were the men behind the Jerry Lewis Cinemas, minitheaters that were popping up all over the place. They would eventually fade as quickly, though that catastrophe had not happened as yet. What the group had in mind was to use Lana's name and likeness, though not one penny of her money, to franchise and then attract customers to the spas. They had gone so far as to build a miniature mock-up of one of the proposed spas, and we were both very impressed by what we saw. Lana all but agreed on the spot, stipulating only that they allow her to be personally involved with the project, from selecting the color schemes to coming up with ideas—such as having a nursery in which exercising mothers could leave their children. The backers welcomed Lana's help, and we left New York with visions of Empire filling our heads. First, however, the work had to be done.

Our trip was followed by day after day of endless conference calls between New York and Jess Morgan, and Lana. When the details had finally been hammered out, it was decided that Lana should return to New York for a press conference to announce the opening of the Lana Turner Minispas. We flew east again on May 9, and the event was thoroughly covered by the local press. Lana even agreed to make rare television appearances, going on the "Mike Douglas Show" and others to promote the undertaking. In fact, the most successful television appearance that Lana has *ever* made occurred during this trip. At the time, David Frost was hosting his daily, ninety-minute program, and he asked Lana to be a guest. She was reluctant at first, due to David's reputation as a tough, forthright interviewer. However, she respected him for the intelligence of his interviews, and she was persuaded to do a twenty-minute segment. Privately, though, I'd made a deal with the producer for David to keep Lana on as long as he could. It would be invaluable publicity for the spas, and I thought the exposure would also do Lana's acting career some good. The producer and I agreed that if, while watching Lana, I felt she were becoming uncomfortable, he would signal David to terminate the interview.

For the Frost appearance, Lana wore a stunning turquoise jump suit with a gold brocade sleeveless vest that reached to the floor. That, plus her thirty-five-carat marquise diamond helped her to make a breathtaking impression when she came onstage.

To his credit, Frost was able to keep Lana interested and amused by asking questions that made her think, causing her to come up with answers that were not only to the point but often funny as well. Her remarkable native intelligence and wit were magnificently showcased, and it wasn't until after several commercials that Lana began to feel they must have used up their twenty minutes. Turning to her host, she asked how much more time they had. Lana was sincerely flabbergasted to learn that she had just taped the entire hour and a half. She felt embarrassed at having hogged the program, and she tried to apologize to the audience through the applause. Even the guests who had been bumped for Lana's sake appreciated the quality of the lady who had preempted them. It was the only television appearance of which Lana ever requested a copy.

The response to Frost's show was no less extraordinary and can best be summed up by a letter that arrived months later. It came from a Roman Catholic priest in Australia, who wrote to say that he had only known Lana from what the media had printed or broadcast about her over the years—and, frankly, he hadn't thought of her as a person of much depth. However, after seeing the "David Frost Show" he realized how wrong he had been. He was writing to explain that she had impressed him as a woman of great wisdom and warmth, someone who possessed a clear and very deep spirituality. The letter asked for nothing and gave her as much gratification as the written word possibly can. There were tears in Lana's eyes as I read it to her, and it's one of the few fan letters she ever chose to keep.

On the opposite end of the spectrum from David Frost was Johnny Carson. Lana's stints with Frost and Mike Douglas had gone over so well that she decided to give "Tonight" a try. The producers had said that it would be all right for Lana to come on and then leave, since, as she said to me, "No way am I going to move down the couch while other people come on." Yet, even that concession could not avert a disaster. David Frost and Mike Douglas are gentlemen who go out of their way to make guests comfortable. Johnny Carson is something else.

Lana appeared on Johnny's show looking stunning in a very sexy black evening gown. She won wild applause, then settled down to engage in the usual trivial banter. She mentioned the health spas, which after all was what Lana was there to plug, and at that point Johnny decided to get cute. "You have a reputation in this business for being something of a temperamental lady," he began. Lana gave him a bemused look and answered hesitantly but in a ladylike way that she was aware of her reputation. The manner in which she answered implied that she would prefer not to pursue that line of questioning. Johnny plunged ahead, however, eventually getting Ed McMahon involved. What evolved from this badgering was the two men urging Lana to pick up an ashtray and throw it as a demonstration of her rumored temperament. The audience, as it tends to do on that show, was shouting its encouragement.

Lana sat regally and smiled, even laughed, at their suggestion. Finally coming to realize that this ploy was not going to work, Johnny picked up the ashtray himself and, with a cry of "What the hell!" threw it over his shoulder. The audience cheered, and even Lana laughed politely. Moments later, quite unexpectedly, she shook his hand, expressed how delightful it had been to appear on his show, then stood and excused herself. She waved to the audience, blowing kisses as she made her way offstage. I left the green room to meet her, braced for a multimegaton outburst; I wasn't disappointed. As she passed through the curtain, Lana turned to me and growled, "Get me the fuck *out* of here."

We couldn't get to Lana's dressing room quickly enough. She hurriedly scooped up her cosmetics, and the instant she was changed, we left the NBC Burbank studio. All the way home, Lana ranted about how the man had tried to make a fool of her on national television and how she'd never again appear on his program. I tried to calm her, telling Lana that she had done extremely well under the circumstances. When we saw the show later that evening, I must say that my initial impression was quite conservative. Lana could not have handled the situation better. She came off looking like the Lady of the Camelias, while Johnny Carson looked foolish. Years later, Lana took vindictive pleasure in ignoring a request from the third Mrs. Carson for an autographed photo to give to a friend who was a Turner fan.

After so totally committing our energy and expectations to the Lana Turner Minispas, we were both sharply disappointed and more than slightly embarrassed when the project failed. During that summer a flood washed away the one model spa that had been built in Pennsylvania, and there were insufficient funds to rebuild. The telephone calls to and from New York began to dwindle, and within mere months of its inception, the whole project died a slow, pitifully quiet death.

Adding to these blighted hopes and Lana's professional inactivity was the fact that, in the space of a year, the penthouse had become a less desirable place in which to live. The building had deteriorated somewhat, and when the owners announced that Edgewater was going coop, neither Lana nor the ever-vigilant Mr. Morgan thought it a wise investment. Thus, with a keen sense of déjà vu, I took on the responsibility of finding a new place for Lana to live.

I was already an authority on luxury buildings in the

Beverly Hills/Westwood area, but a few new prospects had surfaced since my last hunt. One of these was the twenty-one-story Century Park East located just adjacent to Beverly Hills in the very fashionable Century City—the metropolis that had arisen on the grounds of what used to be the back lot of Twentieth Century-Fox. A number of movie stars already lived in the building, though the only ones I ever bumped into in my preliminary visits were Dennis Cole and Fay Wray.

When I contacted the Century Park East rental agent and explained what I needed, the young woman said that something had just opened up that would be perfect for Lana. The apartment had a one-hundred-eighty-degree view from the Hollywood Hills to Beverly Hills, then on to the Pacific Ocean, and continuing out to the Baldwin Hills, which lie just north of the Los Angeles International Airport. The rooms were not exactly large, but the sunsets would be glorious, and, best of all, the ceiling was nine feet high. It seemed too good to be true, not only the apartment but the fact that my search might mercifully begin and end with the very first stop.

Using the rental agent's telephone, I called Lana and told her to get out of bed, that I'd be there in half an hour to pick her up. We were back in Century City two hours later. As we explored the grounds, I could see that Lana liked the tennis courts, the giant swimming pool, and the openness of the putting greens. She was especially comfortable with having doormen on duty around the clock and with the elaborate security system. However, as we entered the apartment itself, I could see at once that she was disappointed with the size of the rooms. If she took the place, it would be the most constricted place in which she had lived since childhood. But Lana liked the view and the two large balconies, which could be filled with flowering plants of all kinds. She was extremely practical for a change, and, since the good outweighed the bad, she took the place on the spot.

Vince Pastere turned the apartment into a showplace, using only Lana's best pieces and getting rid of the rest. Lana moved in mid-August and quickly fell in love with the place. She even coined a name for it, her "Ivory Tower"—safe, clean, and secure. Lana lives there to this day.

Because of her concern for young people, Lana agreed to
fly to New York shortly after the move to participate in a fund
raiser for the drug rehabilitation program Phoenix House.
The theme of the affair was "A Tribute to the 1940s," and the
gala was held at the once-thriving showplace Roseland. The
roster of celebrities was one that, under ordinary circumstances,
would have precluded Lana's participation; it's difficult to be
the number-one star when you're sharing the roster with
Bette Davis, Jane Russell, Lena Horne, and many others.
But the cause was Lana's primary concern, so we were off
again to New York.

I'm convinced that people really do, subconsciously, dip
into private reserves of poise and energy when pressed, and
Lana did so the night of this gathering. Every ounce of the
legendary Turner style was there, more than I'd ever seen
before. As the limousine pulled up—characteristically ninety
minutes late and well after the other stars had arrived, the
still-thronging crowds outside started screaming, "It's Lana
Turner! It's Lana Turner!" It was like a scene from one of her
movies, complete with klieg lights and flashcubes. I climbed
from the limousine and felt just like Clark Gable or Robert
Taylor— until one woman grabbed me by the shoulder and
shrieked, "Get out the way, sonny, we want to see *her*!" Lana
milked the moment like the pro attention-getter she is,
waving and blowing kisses while some twenty-odd photographers backed their way into Roseland ahead of us.

Inside there was a crowd of two thousand people. Heads
everywhere turned as we were shown to our table, where
John Bowab was also seated. The photographers were still
there in force, and so crowded our table that we literally
could not get any air. The maître d' and I managed to
disburse all but photographer Ron Galella, famous for the
court order that bars him from coming any closer to Jackie
Onassis than twenty-five feet. Galella insistently handed Lana
a menu and said, "Here, put this in front of your face like you
don't want your picture taken." Lana just smiled and handed
it right back to him, and Galella hurried off as Lana was
announced to the crowd.

John escorted Lana to the stage—"That's OK, John," I
said as he jumped up before I could, anxious for one and all
to see that she was "his" date—and, taking the microphone,
Lana made a very nice speech about Phoenix House. She

added a wonderfully personal postscript, stating, "Being in such august company reminds me of the good old days when we looked after servicemen at the Hollywood Canteen—which, as you all know, was started by none other than our own Miss Bette Davis."

The crowd cheered, and Bette, who had been standing onstage talking to Joan Bennett, came up to the microphone and asked, "What did you say? I didn't hear you."

Lana didn't mind this teasing way Bette was fishing for a compliment, and she gushingly praised Bette's charitable work then and now. The interaction between both ladies was a real crowd pleaser, and Lana was in her glory.

The only uncomfortable incident of the evening was that four very tough-looking mugs came and sat at our table. They looked very intently at Lana, who politely tried to engage them in conversation. Meanwhile, John Bowab returned from the dance floor, his face creased with concern. Hustling me aside he said, "Get her out of here—those guys are Mafia."

With visions of Johnny Stompanato dancing through my head—along with imaginings of these hoods whipping out blackjacks as they paid Lana back for the killing—I smiled and said to Lana, "It's getting late, Seesha, we've really got to go." That word was our code for *danger*, and Lana wasted no time picking up on it and excusing herself from the thugs and the party. We never did find out what the men wanted.

Upon our return to the West Coast, a producer friend of mine invited me to the opening night festivities of the Shubert Theater in Century City. Since Lana didn't particularly want to go, I took actress Lois Nettleton. The play that was opening the theater was the Broadway hit *Follies*, starring the New York cast headed by Alexis Smith and Yvonne DeCarlo. Lois and I had a great time, highlighted by an introduction to the First Lady of the American stage, Miss Helen Hayes, who was the official hostess for the event. I was surprised to discover that she was such a tiny lady, though there is nothing small about her endurance. She stood in the courtyard after the performance and personally greeted every guest with a handshake and a few kind words of welcome. Gracious lady that she is, she welcomed me as though I were a long-lost relative, her eyes beautifully blue and bright, her smile warm and motherly. For Miss Hayes, I was just one of a sea of faces; for me, she was a moment frozen in time.

The following day I had nothing but praise for the show, and, naturally, now Lana wanted to see it. I was able to get tickets for the following week, and we went. After the curtain, Lana suggested that we go backstage and say hello to Alexis and Yvonne, both of whom she knew from her MGM days. We made our way to the stage door, and while an usher went to Alexis' dressing room to announce Lana, Yvonne saw us and came to the doorway of her dressing room. She was more plump than I'd remembered her in *The Ten Commandments,* and she was out of breath from having sung her heart out in the show's finale. But her smile was pure gold, and she seemed genuinely pleased to see Lana. The two of them chatted for a bit, then they laughed when Lana remarked that it was good to have seen Yvonne for a change without a desert backdrop and layers of veils.

Yvonne had to run and couldn't join us when we were called to Alexis' dressing room. Alexis, in an outfit by her favorite designer, Bill Blass, looked as if she'd just done a sitting for *Glamour.* She introduced her hairdresser, Joey Tubens, who had traveled with the company from New York, and after more small talk Alexis asked if we'd join them and a few of the cast members for a little aftertheater supper at the home of a good friend in Beverly Hills. Lana accepted, and the two women went together in Alexis' little sports car with Joey and me following in the Eldorado.

Everything started out well enough, Lana being quite sociable before settling down on the living room floor for some animated shoptalk with Joey. She had not had any real food all day and, as she was eternally watching her figure, had none now, subsisting entirely on vodka and tonic. As Joey later revealed, he was telling Lana the story of how, back in New York, he would do Alexis' hair every day for *Follies* and then, unknown to Alexis, would dash down the street to attend to another actress appearing in a different play—then race back to *Follies* just as Alexis came offstage for a touch-up. The anecdote played like a Polish joke in Warsaw, Joey's impish behavior greatly offending Lana. According to my pampered lady, a hairdresser can only be loyal to *one* star at a time. She informed Joey that he was wrong to have done

what he did, but Joey good-naturedly pooh-poohed the re-
buke. This infuriated Lana, and given the amount of alcohol
she had consumed, her voice climbed to the point where
everyone in the room stopped their conversation to listen.
Joey's voice and temper rose to the challenge, and Alexis
looked at me as if to say, "*Do* something." All I could do was
shake my head slowly, letting her know that there was
nothing *to* do when Lana got like this. The only sensible
course of action was to let it burn itself out. That had to
happen soon, I reasoned, looking at Lana, who was by now a
livid red. The more Joey tried to defend himself, the angrier
Lana became. Finally, she grew so frustrated that she silenced him by sheer force, screaming, "*Shut up!*" at the top
of her lungs.

The outburst had to have silenced everyone in Beverly
Hills. Certainly its impact on the dinner guests was considerable. Everyone was horrified, judging from their wide eyes
and dangling jaws, and terribly embarrassed since Lana didn't
stop with the scream but went on loudly lecturing Joey about
loyalty, about how the hairdresser had betrayed Miss Smith.
It was one of the few times I saw Lana completely lose
control, and no one dared to interfere. Joey finally had the
good sense to agree with Lana just to shut her up, then
excused himself and moved to another part of the house.
Lana found herself quite alone, still annoyed and muttering
into her glass. I was shocked and mortified by what she had
done and, frankly, didn't care to try and extricate her from
her faux pas. It was actor Gene Nelson who eventually took
pity on Lana, went over to her, sat on the floor, and talked
with her in a very subdued voice.

We left a half hour later, skipping the buffet. As we
drove off, Lana kept repeating over and over what a "little
prick" she thought Joey was. I didn't agree, but I didn't
argue, either. Lana *never* admits an error as, I've learned,
very few of moviedom's *grandes dames* will do. The one
exception who comes immediately to mind is the glorious
Bette Davis, a scrapper who can nevertheless face defeat with
grace when she's been bested.

The following day Lana asked me to send a flower
arrangement to Alexis Smith with a card that read, "Thank
you for a memorable evening." A week passed, and when the
flowers were not acknowledged, Lana asked me to phone the

florist to make sure delivery had been made. It had, indeed, and been signed for by Miss Smith's housekeeper. Lana was sincerely puzzled as to why Alexis never called or wrote. I was not.

Chapter Eight

It was during October of 1972 that negotiations began for a motion picture that Lana would make in England the following year. The original script was called *I Hate You, Cat,* a title that Lana never liked. She did, however, like the concept of the picture, and after we'd both read the screenplay, she remarked that she expected to get a lot of mail from moviegoers hating her for what her character does to twist the mind of her young son.

The part was an unusually nasty one for Lana, I had to admit. But then, her favorite roles have always been evil or sinister characters like Lady de Winter in *The Three Musketeers* and Cora in *The Postman Always Rings Twice.* That 1946 film is probably the finest picture Lana ever made; it had quality as well as controversy, the likes of which this new project couldn't hope to match. In the earlier film, Lana played a married woman who is seduced by a drifter (John Garfield) who persuades her to help him do away with her husband. Though they are tried and acquitted of the murder, Lana's character is killed in a car accident, for which, ironically, the drifter is executed. The quality came in equal measure from the talent of the filmmakers and also from the source material. It was based on a best-selling novel by James Cain, whose *Double Indemnity* and *Mildred Pierce* had already been made into enormously successful motion pictures. As for the controversy, co-star Hume Cronyn once told me, "That was due to the way the film seemed to give some seal of acceptance to the adulterous relationship between Lana and Johnny Garfield. I don't think either of them was particularly concerned about the film hurting their careers, though the producers softened the obvious by dressing Lana in white in virtually every shot, since white is generally associated with virginity. I seem to recall that the white wardrobe was the joint idea of Lana and the costume designer." That would have made sense from Lana's point of view for another, less artistic reason: the viewer's eye immediately goes to anyone who is wearing white on the screen.

I Hate You, Cat was not in the same league as *The Postman Always Rings Twice*. That was as true the day the script arrived as when the film was released. Lana and Garfield had crackled on screen, even though she insists they never had anything but a fine professional relationship; Ralph Bates, a solid but less compelling performer, did not help to ignite those kinds of sparks in the new picture. But then, few performers *ever* get a shot at the likes of a package such as *The Postman Always Rings Twice*, and Lana tries to be pragmatic where her career is concerned.

Another reason for Lana to accept *I Hate You, Cat* was that this was a time in Hollywood when all the *former* movie queens were making grim but classy horror epics, which is more or less what this film was. The craze had begun a decade before with *What Ever Happened to Baby Jane* starring Bette Davis and Joan Crawford, after which Bette went on to do *Dead Ringer* (1964), *The Nanny* (1965), *The Anniversary* (1968), and others, while Joan starred in *Strait-Jacket* (1964), *I Saw What You Did* (1965), and *Trog* (1970), to mention just a few. The shockers had a way of revitalizing careers by introducing the great ladies of the past to the young generation of moviegoers who frequented these films. In fact, Lana was one of the last holdouts, Olivia de Havilland having made *Lady in a Cage* (1964) and Tallulah Bankhead having starred in *Die! Die! My Darling!* (1965); even Yvonne DeCarlo had done the monster bit in "The Munsters" on television. Onetime American leading men were also getting a second wind with pictures of this type; Joseph Cotten, Nick Adams, and Russ Tamblyn had gone to Japan to collect big dollars to appear in fantasy and science fiction pictures. In theory, this movie could have been a good career move.

The irony about 1972 is that the wrong venture fell through. Instead of the health spas, it should have been this film that went gurgling downriver in a deluge. There were many difficulties on the British-made picture, not the least of which was the fact that its producer, Kevin Francis, was young and untried. He was the son of Freddie Francis, who was an industry legend for his well-made and enormously profitable horror films. Not until the contracts had been signed and we were in London in October of 1973 did we learn that prior to becoming a film producer, Kevin's previous experience consisted of having managed a fish-and-chips shop.

Nonetheless, Kevin managed to talk a good film when Lana was as yet unsigned. He was always *so* concerned with her image and well-being. A typical telephone conversation from Kevin would cover an eclectic range of subjects. Our first such gaggle of contradictions was typical. My notes show that Kevin wanted to make this a "Hitchcock" type of film; Lana agreed, but she did not want that exploited by the press since she didn't want to be compared to Grace Kelly. We would have a low budget, yet everything about the film would be first class. Kevin said, for instance, that he'd pay five times union scale to film scenes night-for-night rather than to film during the day, shooting through what an audience would obviously recognize as a night filter. Of *course* Lana's wardrobe could be designed in the United States—even though, Kevin admitted, he hadn't considered a wardrobe budget prior to talking with Lana. My notes also reveal that Kevin wanted to find an ideal director and suggested Don Sharp, whose previous film was *Psychomania;* Lana said she would screen that film before agreeing, but would welcome a few other names. Our producer concurred when Lana complained that the current title was a bad one, and we eventually settled on the infinitely better *Persecution* —though when the picture flopped under that moniker, it became the tacky *The Terror of Sheba*.

These and other details took one solid year to iron out and get on paper. Consider: more time was spent negotiating than shooting the damn thing! But Lana is an astute businesswoman who likes to have *all* her questions answered personally rather than through agents; it's safe to say that she is the opposite in business of what she is in love. In fact, she becomes furious if her personal bills are not attended to at once by her business office. By her own admission, Lana is "the fastest pay in town." As a result of these consultations and bargaining, the starting date for the film was constantly being changed, which prevented Lana from considering any interim projects and caused countless people to ask if she had, in truth, retired.

Apart from an occasional guest or infrequent outing, there was also unusually little social activity during this year. Lana liked to be on hand for Kevin's calls, so we spent a great deal of time at the Ivory Tower. The most interesting diversion during this period was when the unpredictable Mickey Rooney stopped by, one of the few celebrities ever to come calling. He brought with him a business associate, who was wearing a very expensive pair of sunglasses.

Lana had dated Mickey in 1936, the former Joe Yule having snatched her from the arms of Jackie Cooper while she was still a student at Hollywood High. Lana first worked with Mickey two years later on *Love Finds Andy Hardy,* the third and arguably the finest of the sixteen-picture Andy Hardy series and the film on which Lana met her longtime friend Judy Garland.

Lana and Judy had a curious relationship over the years. Lana was two years older, but during their early MGM days, she was also quite obviously the more sensual of the two. She had also won the affection of Artie Shaw and Tyrone Power, something Judy had tried and failed to do. Judy deeply resented what she came to view as her own "inadequacy" compared to Lana, which was ironic since she was easily much more sexually aware than her colleague. She also was hard pressed to understand why Lana drew so much more attention, seeing as how Judy was clearly the more versatile performer. She could act, she could sing, she could dance up a storm. The only "projecting" Lana did was between her neck and her waist. Ironically, when Judy and Lana teamed again in *Ziegfeld Girl* in 1941, though Judy once again had the starring role and exhibited a broad range of talent, Lana stole the show as a somewhat promiscuous showgirl. It was the film that made Lana a bona fide star and also was the first in which she appeared as a blond. *Ziegfeld Girl* was also an important stepping-stone for another actress. Though Lana describes Hedy Lamarr as "a sweet girl but not too smart," Lamarr surely gave Lana a run for the money in the beauty department in this and other films. Poor Judy, meanwhile, sang four great songs and acted her heart out but got the least attention of the three.

Despite their unspoken rivalry, Lana and Judy were seen

together in public, frequently on double dates. As time went on, maintaining objectivity proved more and more trying for Judy. Though both women were recognized as stars by MGM, no consideration was too excessive for Lana; she was even provided with someone to flip over the phonograph records in her dressing room. However, Judy let none of this interfere with their personal relationship or, later, with the friendship between their daughters. As an interesting footnote about a bygone era, they were also spied upon by an MGM publicist who reported their thoughts and doings to the studio brass.

Lana and Judy drifted apart after they left MGM and their careers diverged. Though there was genuine affection between the two, most friendships in Hollywood do not endure beyond the life of a film or a contract. Like marriages, they are strained by schedules and jealousies that neither party can for long control.

Mickey Rooney is an exception where friendships are concerned. He's ebullient and friendly and devoted and, yes, very short—but he makes up for the latter with towering reserves of energy. I could feel the advance guard of his effervescent personality as he scurried down the hallway after being announced. The *problem* with Mickey is that he never stops talking. He barely paused for breath during the entire afternoon, and I felt as though he would have held congress with a lampshade if everyone left the room. Lana, who had known what to expect, all but pushed Mickey toward me as I made everyone drinks, and I was hopelessly trapped behind the bar as he perched himself on one of the black leather stools and told me the story of his life. He recounted the saga of his many marriages, his luck good and bad, and went on about his strong belief in God. Through it all I tried to remain attentive, but he was just overwhelming. Lana, in the meantime, had engaged the other man in conversation, and I overheard her telling him how much she liked his sunglasses. By the end of the very long afternoon, she had them. By the end of the afternoon, *I* was beat.

Years later, when Lana was appearing in the play *Murder Among Friends* in Chicago, the producer and his wife invited Lana and me for dinner at their apartment; since Mickey was in town, they asked him up as well. As we were having cocktails, Mickey literally burst in with his current wife.

Once again he was a nonstop talking machine. At last, overstuffed with his gabbing, Lana screamed, "Mickey, for God's sake *shut up!*" But even Lana couldn't quiet him, and unnerved by his incessant voice, she had to excuse us from dinner. Mickey didn't understand what was happening, and as we walked out I heard him resume his conversation with our embarrassed hosts.

Visitors like Mickey—and even unlike Mickey—being rare, Lana and I were more or less our only mutual diversions. Though we both continued to "step out" as far as fidelity was concerned, our love for one another had grown to the point where outside relationships were becoming less and less frequent *or* necessary. We *wanted* to be faithful to tighten our bond.

It was during the preliminary arrangements for *Persecution* that the owners of Lana's building announced their intention of converting from an apartment to a condominium. In such a procedure, the present occupant is offered the chance to buy the apartment, or it is put on the block. The market price for Lana's Ivory Tower was $73,500—a steal by today's standards. Lana consulted with Jess Morgan who, although he'd never even seen the place, advised his client that it was not a good investment and suggested that she have me look for another apartment. I countered that that was, in fact, a rotten idea, since I knew from exhausting experience there was *no* building in Los Angeles more suitable than this one. Jess was unmoved, and in desperation, I pulled out the records of our move from the Edgewater. Including the cost of the custom draperies and the services of the interior designer, the sum was over ten thousand dollars. I suggested to Jess that he think of the moving expense and the down payment on the condominium as canceling each other out, thus reducing the cost to roughly $60,000. I played up the Ivory Tower as a good investment in a growing area, and I even reminded Jess how much Lana was saving in ever-rising gasoline costs by living in the heart of town, close to whatever meetings she had. I was pulling at every straw I could, hoping that Jess would see the sénse of it all. He resisted the badgering per se, but he came around and gave the purchase his qualified blessing. Something I said must have made sense, and I sighed mightily with relief. Lana breathed easier as well, since she really had not wanted to move again. To tell the truth, while Lana was pleased to have Jess's approval, I think she would have overruled him had he fought the acquisition. She complained bitterly many times that Jess would have seen her living in a motel if it meant that he would have more of her money to play with. Many times Lana told me about conversations she'd had with Jess wherein he talked about her money as if it were his own, saying, "I want to invest here," or "I don't think I want to buy that." Lana would let him go on for a while, then inevitably say, "But, Jess, dear, remember it's *my* money." He didn't take kindly to these rebukes, but there are the goddesses, and then there are the cherubim. Unfortunately, neither Lana nor Jess took the advice of *this* cherub that she also buy the one-bedroom unit across the hall. I felt like Patton pleading for permission to march on Moscow when I suggested that, after purchasing the second apartment, the two could be made into one very spacious dwelling. Lana came to regret turning a deaf ear to my suggestion, not only because her one objection to Century Park East had been the limited space but because her Ivory Tower alone is today worth $750,000.

Persecution was the first film Lana had made in over four years, and she was truly disappointed when it fell so far short of its potential. Lana's part was that of Carrie Masters, a wealthy American divorcée living in England. Crippled because of an accident that she blames on her son David, she torments him through a kindle of vile kittens—all of whom are named Sheba and who follow her murderous instructions. David's wife and baby are the first to die, the child being smothered to death by a fat cat and the mother falling to her death after being tripped by one of the feline fiends. In the end, the understandably deranged David attacks his mother, drowning her in a bowl of her cats' milk.

The film *could* have been a sick, gleefully horrific addition to the glut of Grand Guignol film products; it turned out unbearably stuffy and unintentionally silly. Making *Persecution* was itself alternately a pleasant and unbearable experience. The pleasant part arose primarily from being in London, which I was able to explore on weekends. I managed to cover a lot of ground in our chauffeured limousine; about the only place I didn't go was Buckingham Palace, and not because we weren't invited. The queen had sent a personal courier to request Lana's presence at a charity affair. Despite my unbecoming begging and fervent prayers, my employer declined, later remarking, "Who needs to meet another queen?" The *miserable* part of being in England involved the numerous gaffes and clashes of personality due to Mr. Francis's inexperience. To make matters worse, Lana was also frequently depressed because she had had so little communication with her mother and daughter. She received just one letter from home the entire time we were there, and that one came only because I phoned Cheryl and angrily informed her how distraught Lana was about not hearing from them. Cheryl's response to my outrage was a chatty, handwritten note that touched on such loving matters as the gas shortage and Gran considering going on food stamps. Whether she deserved it or not, I felt only sadness each time Lana went to that stone for water.

The first several weeks in England consisted of costume and wig fittings as well as marathon script conferences. As shooting neared, we moved from a suite at the Dorchester to a lovely, 250-year-old rustic inn called the Burnham Beeches. The one-hour drive from London to the studio was not one that Lana cared to make each morning and night; though Burnham Beeches was less luxurious, it was only twenty minutes from the studio. Once the actual shooting had begun, our schedule was incredibly taxing. We opened with a bang, having to shoot in one day every scene featuring actor Trevor Howard. He had flown in from another film he was making in Spain, and we shot his scenes with Lana at the London Zoo from dawn literally until dusk, finishing just as the sun went down.

The most noteworthy confrontation with Kevin Francis was one of the first, and it made bitter foes of Lana and her producer for the duration of filming. Without asking permission, Kevin had sent Lana's chauffeur on an errand into London. Although the producer *was* paying for the car, Lana likes to have an automobile available to her around the clock, as indeed is the practice in the film industry. When she learned what Kevin had done, she expressed her displeasure. He didn't take to it kindly, but he had the presence of mind not to further intimidate his star. Thereafter, they bickered in small tit-for-tat fashion, Kevin upsetting Lana with some discourtesy or inconvenience, though never pushing her far enough so that it got out of hand. However, as soon as he could strike back he did so with a vengeance, suspending Lana (because of a cold she was fighting) the instant her scenes had been completed. That meant she couldn't do her own dubbing in long shots—which had been filmed silent, since the microphones would have been visible—and on location, where extraneous noises would have proven distracting. Kevin rescinded his decision, but only after canceling several meetings with us and with the William Morris representative in London. Even then Kevin had not finished with Lana. When it came time to review the photographs taken on the set, we found them, in a word, to be awful. Only sixteen of the hundreds of photographs featuring Lana were even remotely acceptable, the others being technically bad or unflattering. Contractually, she had the right to reject any shots she chose, but rather than leave Kevin with nothing, she reluctantly approved several borderline photos. We found ourselves wondering if the photos were intentionally bad though Kevin was not so much of a lunatic to sabotage his own film.

All things considered, it was not with regret that we left England on December 23. Nor were we surprised when the picture failed to get many bookings in the United States, although it actually turned out better than it deserved to. Our director was Don Chaffey, an experienced hand at fantasy filmmaking, who had gotten some good performances from his players and had created a fine visual texture. However, the picture we saw made much less sense than the script we first read, many scenes critical to the mood and exposition inexplicably missing. Neither of us was surprised to discover that after Don handed over his cut of the film and went to Africa on another movie, Kevin decided he could "improve" the picture with some editing of his own. What he did was to butcher the film, though Lana was and remained quite good in both versions. For her efforts she won the prestigious Silver Carnation for Best Actress at the Sitges Festival of Horror Films in Spain.

When it rains it pours, as they say, though in Lana's case it was mostly acid raindrops falling upon her head. Fresh from one intransigent producer, Lana found herself very briefly up against another January of 1974, when she was offered the juicy role of Dee in the film version of Jacqueline Susann's best-selling novel *Once is Not Enough*. Kirk Douglas, George Hamilton, and David Janssen would be her co-stars, as prestigious a lineup as one could hope for. We had both read the novel while in England and enjoyed it very much; Lana was naturally quite pleased to be asked to do the part. However, upon reading the script she had one small objection. There is a lesbian side to Dee's character, and while Lana was not uncomfortable with that, what *did* bother her was a specific scene wherein Dee has a rendezvous with her female lover and the camera dollies in for a lingering shot of the two women kissing on the lips. Lana felt that such a scene would be offensive to an audience as well as embarrassing to the actresses who played it. She felt that the women's love could be implied in a number of ways, and she wanted to leave the details to the viewers' imagination.

At the suggestion of producer Howard Koch, he, director Guy Green, and Lana's William Morris representative came to the Ivory Tower late one afternoon for a meeting about the film. Lana had dressed very carefully, selecting a form-fitting gray sweater with matching slacks and shoes, accenting the outfit with simple gold jewelry. It was calculated to help Lana win her point by showing them they would be getting their money's worth if they gave in on this one matter and hired her.

Lana had a wonderful way of taking command at business meetings, pseudo-tyrannical behavior she learned from the moguls. She boasted of being one of the few stars on the MGM lot who was never intimidated by the very formidable Louis B. Mayer, refusing to think of him as anything but a damn tough audience. Lana would play out scenes for me of her going into the Little King's office. As he watched impassively from behind his massive desk, she would get her way through petulance, pouting, wheedling, cajoling, foot stomping, tantrums, and, as a last resort, tears. Sometimes all of the above. Not that her methods *always* worked. For example, Lana coveted the role of Amber in *Forever Amber*, which Twentieth Century-Fox's Darryl Zanuck produced in 1947. Director Otto Preminger wanted Lana for the part, and as he told me once over lunch in New York when I'd applied for a job with him, to help persuade Zanuck that she was ideal casting, he invited the two to a dinner party. There, Lana did everything she could to soften Zanuck, flirting with him and even on one occasion planting herself in the mogul's lap. Linda Darnell got the part, Darryl perhaps having decided to repay Lana for the hard times she "gave" his star Tyrone Power. Regardless, if Lana doesn't always win, she never fails to fight the good fight. She maintains that determination is more important to an actor than talent, and one of her favorite illustrations of this fact is Diane Varsi. Miss Varsi was the very talented actress who played her daughter Allison in *Peyton Place*. According to Lana, she had the talent to succeed but not the stomach for the power games one needs to play to get to the top in Hollywood. Movies are *not* a vocation for the wishy-washy. If you don't want it badly enough, if you aren't willing to go on countless auditions *and* put up with the politics as well, this is not the industry for you.

After the usual how-are-yous were out of the way with Messrs. Koch and Green, Lana began the meeting by saying, "Well, now, gentlemen, I think we should put *all* our cards on the table." Presuming that her own bluntness would inspire the same, Lana told the three men in no uncertain terms that she really wanted to play the role but that the offending scene would have to be rewritten in a more tasteful way. The meeting took exactly three minutes. The producer advised Lana that the scene would not be changed; she regretfully declined, and the trio departed. The filmmakers then went directly to Alexis Smith—a fitting inspiration!—who agreed to do the sequence as written with Greek actress Melina Mercouri.

Lana was a trifle stunned by her own expendability in this matter, but as it turned out, her judgment had not been wrong. The film was not a big box-office hit, and it could certainly have used some of the old Turner magic. I went to see it without Lana, who hadn't the desire or even the curiosity, and the audience *did* squirm in its seat and laugh nervously when the camera lingered on the kiss shared by Alexis and Melina.

February of 1974 was a busy month for us as Lana abandoned one medium for another, consenting to give an exclusive, quite extensive interview to *The Ladies' Home Journal*. It was decided that reporter Jane Ardmore would

"ghost" the story under Lana's own byline. Jane lived in Los
Angeles and had known Lana for many years, so the two
women were quite comfortable together. When the article
was completed, I was surprised to find myself a part of
it—though in a less than flattering context. In speaking of the
evils of the press, Lana said, "Case in point: my secretary
Taylor Pero. He is my closest friend outside my family. . . . But
the press snidely derides him as my 'confidant,' 'companion,'
'consort,' or what have you. So rotten—trying to make us
lovers. Taylor's private life is his own; this type of publicity
hurts him and hurts me." It was not a truthful statement, and
what *really* hurt was to be given this public brush-off. Over
seven years later, after our incredible parting, Lana would do
it again, telling reporters at the Deauville Film Festival in
France—and being so quoted by *Newsweek*—that she has
been "celibate by choice since 1969." Lana felt she had to
protect that old devil "public image," which is something I
encouraged where the movie queen persona was concerned.
MGM used to do that all the time, lying outright about her
life—describing her father as an actor-hoofer, for example, or
tracing Lana's theatrical ambitions to mythical childhood
performances—and Lana was blindly carrying on the tradition. Romantically, however, I'm not sure exactly what image
there was to protect. *The Ladies' Home Journal* article also
contained many other inaccuracies regarding her private life,
in particular describing her relationship with Cheryl and
Gran. They were, said she, oh-so-close and ever-so-loving. I
wish she'd have told the truth; the real Lana Turner is a far
more fascinating person than the saccharine shell she manu-
factures for the press.

The real Lana Turner. I wonder how the world would
have reacted over the years if Lana had appeared before them
unadorned and psychologically naked? What would people
have thought if they could have seen Lana in action? I'm sure
they'd have reacted not very differently than I did, astonished
by Lana's possessiveness and scheming; astounded not only
by the fact of it but by how small-minded her thinking could
sometimes be. An incident of which I was really an objective
third party involved a hairdresser named Kenneth, an able
young man who decided to move to New York to better
himself. Lana was shocked when he broke the news to us,
since she knew she'd never find anyone else to make a house

call for only twenty-five dollars. I was not unaware of Lana's real concern, though she played the scene as though she were worried about Kenneth.

"You can't *do* this," she told him. "It will ruin your life! Think about your lovely apartment and car and all that you have here in Los Angeles."

Lana resorted to every trick she knew to make him change his mind, and she was very near convincing Kenneth not to go when I took him aside. I told him he was an ass if he changed his mind because of Lana. "She's only worried about Lana Turner," I said. "If you and I were to drop dead right now and Lana absolutely had to go somewhere, she'd say 'Tsk-tsk,' step right over our bodies, and worry about burying us later." Kenneth did indeed go to New York, and eight years later, he is still living there, very happy. As much as I loved Lana and as much as I still care for her, she is, above all, a vain woman. Vanity dominates her, guides her thoughts and actions, overrules every other consideration in her life. Businesswise, you can always take her at her word: she lives by her slogan, "The truth is like surgery, it cuts, but it cures." When her face or figure are involved, you're wise to keep a saltshaker handy. I suppose I shouldn't be surprised that in interviews, articles, and books about herself, she has been unwilling to confront the woman she really is.

The story she tells about her first face-lift is equally typical. According to Lana, she did not intend to undergo a major operation; she only wanted her upper eyelids prevented from sagging "ever so slightly," as she recalls. She consulted Dr. Mac, who recommended an ear, nose, and throat specialist. The doctor's eventual ambition was to enter the field of cosmetic surgery, and, in fact, the best cosmetic surgeons are those with a background in this area. It affords them a fuller knowledge of that portion of the anatomy, something one should obviously have before tampering with it. Lana had confidence in the doctor's ability to correct the drooping eyelids, and in 1966 she went in for cosmetic surgery. She says she was *astounded* to come from under the anesthetic and find that the doctor had gotten "knife happy," turning it into a radical face-lift. The cost of malpractice being what it is, I cannot help looking askance at her claim that he was unauthorized to proceed. But Lana would never admit either having needed or sought a complete facial overhaul—just as she would never admit having argued with Kenneth for any but the most selfless reasons. Regardless, the operation proved traumatic to Lana. As a result of the surgery, her upper lip was narrowed ever so slightly, taking away forever the lush, full mouth that had made men yearn to kiss her. It also left a permanent, white V scar running down the front of each ear. Never again would she be able to wear her hair pulled back from her face. Many, many times over our years together I would see Lana sitting in front of her mirror, examining those scars and crying. Her various hairdressers would treat them as if they were the most natural thing in the world, which they *were* in Beverly Hills, where hardly a woman over the age of forty hadn't had something done. Lana, who never viewed herself as being part of the milieu of ordinary women, would not be consoled. She's a fool, for she was and *is* something special—but nonetheless human for it.

A face-lift, of course, is like a passport, something you have to renew every five years or so. The metaphor goes deeper in Lana's case, since she regards her appearance as her ticket to survival. By March of 1974, we both felt that it was time for another operation; even though she was still quite lovely by ordinary standards, the motion picture camera is not an ordinary standard. After all the horror stories I'd heard about the first operation, I was surprised when Lana went back to the same doctor. When I questioned this, she explained that by this time he'd become a full-fledged plastic surgeon, had even done his wife's face. The truth of the matter was that, the doctor's ability notwithstanding, Lana was embarrassed to go to a stranger. *She'd rather stick with someone who is imperfect but familiar.* Lana checked into Doctor's Hospital in Beverly Hills under the assumed name of Jean Barron—"Jean" for her childhood name and "Barron" for my own last name before I was legally adopted by my stepfather—and this second time around the doctor did a job that was nothing short of miraculous. Even Lana was pleased with the results. Though he could not entirely rid her of the V scars, he did manage to make them considerably smaller, though as time and gravity have a go at them, they will once again become rather prominent. Sort of like Pinocchio's nose; for in this and all other unpleasant truths, Lana would go on disguising, adorning, or obscuring the facts. She is, I must say, an extraordinary "surgeon" herself.

*   *   *

Carmen took a brief vacation toward the end of March, during which time I moved back in with Lana to play housekeeper. Whatever ill feelings I may have begun to harbor toward Lana on many subjects, she will *always* have my respect for the care she took of Carmen. I won't bother to examine her motives; the bottom line was extreme generosity on Lana's part. Representative of Lana's attitude is that while we were in England, that sentinel of finance Jess Morgan had sent her a letter that read, in part, "We were reviewing some of your fixed expenses which are still being incurred while you are in England. We were wondering whether there was any possibility of having Carmen work on a minimum basis and be paid accordingly. Certainly the work needed in your apartment is minimal. She could find other work and still be available to you full time when you return." Without bothering to think about it, Lana told Jess exactly what he could do with that idea.

I distinguished myself as quite an acceptable housekeeper, and I suspect now that it was the job I should have held all along. No doubt Lana and I would still be together. As chef I was especially formidable, one of Lana's favorite dishes being my recipe for sole. She has ordered fillet in the finest restaurants in the world, including Maxim's of Paris, but it had never tasted as good as mine—said she. If *that* was a line of bull, I relished it all the same.

Since there was literally nothing cooking but my fillet and since Lana was pleased with her new face-lift, she felt this was a good time to have new publicity pictures taken. I made an appointment with her favorite photographer, John Engstead. Unlike many contemporary actresses who don't care much about portraiture, Lana directs her own photo sessions. In fact, she is so distressed seeing other actresses looking old or just plain sloppy that she is inspired to go out of her way to show them up. Lana usually pulls it off for, as they say, an ounce of cure is better than no prevention. To assist her in choreographing sessions like these, Lana insists that there be a floor-length mirror beside the camera so that she can check every detail of her person before the shutter begins to click. She also requires soft romantic music to help her mood, and she admits no one into the studio except her party plus the photographer and his/her assistant. As a rule Lana prefers male photographers, feeling that they have the capacity to *interpret* women, with an instinct for their most alluring or provocative assets.

We were late arriving at Engstead's studio, Lana having dallied as usual and burdened us with several changes of wardrobe and her new hairdresser—a young man who'd accepted her absurdly low fee for the privilege of being able to list Lana as a client. We found Engstead and his assistant wringing their hands as we came through the door and established a beachhead in his studio; Engstead was on a tight schedule with successive sittings for, ironically, Dick Van Dyke and Mary Tyler Moore. Nor were Engstead's worries ended once we'd arrived. Lana required another half hour to make last-minute adjustments on her makeup and hair; Engstead just gritted his teeth, not only because of the additional delay but because he always gently fought with Lana about her coiffure. He preferred a loose, just-out-of-bed look, something that Lana would rather die than condone—this, in spite of Engstead's unarguably fine reputation. Lana would sit by that mirror and all but glue every hair into place with hair spray, deliberateness that amounted to another power play. However, Engstead let her work her way since, by the end of a session, he always got what he wanted. It wasn't so much a matter of wearing Lana down or convincing her that he was right, as catching her when she wasn't quite ready. He would wait until the hot lights and perspiration had helplessly eroded Lana's work, then he'd snap a few pictures of his suddenly *very* sultry subject. To the surprise of no one but Lana, Engstead's final shot of this sitting, with several locks askew, proved to be the sexiest shot of the bunch and remains Lana's favorite.

The fall of 1974 was even more depressing than the summer, and Lana was in a rut. There was talk of a Broadway play, *Mother Goddam*, but Lana turned it down because she would have been required to play an Oriental madam of a whorehouse. I pleaded with her to reconsider, to think of what Broadway would mean to her stymied career. But true to form Lana wouldn't budge, and not because of the seedy nature of the part. "Everybody coming to see the play would be expecting to see Lana Turner," she explained, "and there I'd be, hidden beneath a black wig." I tried to entice her with the exotic possibilities inherent in the costuming, but though intrigued, Lana was intransigent. Next came an offer to guest-star on an episode of "Marcus Welby, M.D." for the very reasonable sum of $10,000 for less than a week's work. I urged Lana to take it but was once again stonewalled. She'd been burned too badly on "The Survivors," she said. No more television. I pointed out that "The Survivors" really had been an unfortunate exception, that many stars including Bette Davis, Cliff Robertson, Elizabeth Taylor, Gloria Swanson, and others were successfully jumping between media with no loss of prestige. No, said Lana, the public should go to the mountain, not the mountain to the public. I rejoined that that theory is well and good when you've the draw of a Robert Redford or Barbra Streisand, but Lana was adamant. Such is the clout of a personal manager.

Chapter Nine

Lana began 1975 with no work on the horizon, and though I was restless as hell, it didn't even cross my mind to look for other employment. I knew that I was going nowhere professionally, and I knew that the prospects for improvement were not good. But Lana and I were so close as friends and as lovers that I could no sooner up and leave her employ than up and leave her side. Looking back, I see that the entire relationship was like a Rubik's Cube, every face of it entangled.

Because of the abysmal state of affairs, by the end of January I had upgraded Lana's bleach to an Event in my calendar. Even though she'd come down with a miserable cold, Lana did not cancel her hair appointments—though she did restrict them to just a wash and set despite the fact that her dark roots were really showing. To Lana, a natural brunette, there is nothing on earth more important than maintaining her blond hair. It's one of her most famous attributes, and the only one that is artificial. Every fourteen days she *must* have that bleach, no matter where she is or what she's doing; between bleaches, usually two times a week, Lana snuggles up to her custom-built shampoo bowl and has her hairdresser give her a set and comb-out even if she isn't going anywhere or seeing anyone. Entire production schedules have always been organized around this ritual, something that had gnawed at Kevin Francis, though he was far from the first. The most outstanding "victim" of Lana's fixation was her longtime stand-in Alyce May. Alyce revealed that she would get calls in the middle of the night whenever the fancy struck Lana to change her hair color. The following morning, Alyce would have to be up extra-early to pick up a lock of Lana's hair, head for the salon, and have her own hair dyed to match. This did not happen during the making of a movie, when Lana's color had to remain consistent from shot to shot; between films, however, or shortly before a new picture was to go into production, Alyce had to mime the star's look in case she was needed. How Alyce put up with this for thirty years, I'll never understand. A fine actress in her own right, she was, like Diane Varsi, too sweet to make a sizable dent in the business.

The hairdresser and the girl who gave Lana a weekly manicure were virtually her only social outlets during the early months of the year. From these people Lana received briefings on all the local gossip, concise reports not unlike those the president receives from his advisers. Lana reveled in these summaries, for they enabled her to stay on top of the news without, as she was fond of saying, "having to go out and play in the traffic." The telephone was Lana's other link to the outside world, and she spent hours alternately commiserating and laughing with her closest friend, actress Virginia Grey.

Lana and Virginia have a very interesting relationship, one that alternately warmed and depressed me over the years. The two first met on the set of the film *Dramatic School* in 1939, although their careers thereafter went in decidedly different directions. Virginia has always represented the tougher, foulmouthed woman that Lana refused to be in public, and the fact that they *are* so opposite is one binding tie, a hook that transcends other considerations. There is also a love-hate facet to their friendship, or more accurately a pity-contempt attraction due to the fact that one became a star and the other did not. Lana made sure that Virginia worked in as many of her pictures as possible, shepherding that Virginia accepted but ultimately resented. Today, she's a hardened, embittered woman—her welcome mat is cynically inscribed "Go Away"—though this is due less to her unrealized ambitions as an actress than to her own edition of Lana's ill-fated Tyrone Power romance.

Virginia dated Clark Gable for a long time. In fact, she was not the only person in Hollywood who was surprised when Gable married Carole Lombard instead of her in March of 1939. As Lana neatly assessed the snub, "Clark was really very naughty to Virginia." That was uncharacteristic of him, since Lana recalls that Gable was usually overly kind to everyone. In her own case, he helped her through many awkward, stumbling moments on her first starring vehicle, *Honky Tonk*, made in 1941, and the first of four films they made together. She was nervous enough as it was, though playing against the King was devastating. Lana said that to put her at ease he'd tease her in a very friendly way, and that whenever she'd fumble a line he'd do the same in the next take as if to show her that it happened to the best of them. The worst time she ever had with Gable was when his bride of a year came to the set of *Honky Tonk*. Lana recalls, "Carole had heard of this hot little blond on the lot and decided to come over and check me out. If you think I was nervous about working with Clark Gable, how do you think I felt when I looked up and saw the Queen watching us shoot a scene where I had to kiss her husband?" Lana was too shy to say anything about how unnerved she was by Mrs. Gable's presence, but director Jack Conway sensed that something was distracting her. He took her aside, and she confessed her apprehensions, after which Conway conferred with Gable. He was most understanding, going over to his wife and explaining the situation. Lana reports that Carole smiled good-naturedly and left the set. Other reports have stated that Miss Lombard was slightly more jealous than that, but Lana says that if that's so, she failed to feel the daggers as Carole walked away or during any subsequent meetings.

Lana was also with Gable when tragedy struck. The following year they were shooting *Somewhere I'll Find You* when, three days into filming, Miss Lombard was killed when her plane plowed into a mountain outside of Las Vegas. She had been on a tour selling war bonds.

Lana told me that after Miss Lombard's death, Virginia tried to win Gable back, going so far as to imitate the fast-talking actress. But her efforts proved fruitless. Gable tried to forget his grief by becoming a machine gunner on a bomber and fighting in World War II; after the war, he married Lady Sylvia Ashley. Virginia never married and carries a torch for the actor to this day, two decades after his death. It's a ghoulish fact of life, but wives inevitably fare much better than mistresses when a man dies. Kay Gable is comparatively well off, as is another of Lana's widowed acquaintances, Sandra Dee, whose husband Bobby Darin left her enough money so that she and her son can live comfortably. Not so Virginia. She moved into a small apartment in the San Fernando Valley and could not help being very sour-tempered about the change.

Despite their deep, very old friendship, Lana and Virginia actually see each other no more than once per year. When they get together, they are mutual proof that time and fortunes have changed for them both—and in neither case for the better. But when they *do* meet, Virginia is no less blunt and Lana no less motherly than I'm sure they were over four decades before.

Lana's lingering cold lasted into March, a month sparked by a welcome call from New York-based publicist John Springer. The call was to ask Lana to consider a tribute Springer wished to organize for her at New York's Town Hall. Lana seemed embarrassed by the thought and was inclined to refuse; I couldn't allow that to happen. What she needed now was attention, never mind publicity. I couldn't help but think of how debilitating the solitude was for her, particularly compared to what she had known before. I was reminded of something Vic Damone had said when he spotted Lana in the audience during one of our trips to Las Vegas. After introducing her to the showgoers—who gave her a standing ovation— Damone related how, years before, he was at the MGM lot and, seeing her walk across the street, was so smitten that he drove his car into a wall. We were lucky, nowadays, if someone honked while we waited at a light. Working in tandem over the next few days, John Springer and I prevailed upon Lana to accept the New York tribute.

John's brainchild was realized on April 13, and we were able to attend only when "The Mike Douglas Show" generously agreed to pay our fares east in exchange for Lana's appearance on the Philadelphia-based program. The tribute was attended by over two thousand people, including SROs; there wasn't even enough room for additional standees. The program opened with two hours of clips from Lana's greatest films and culminated with the automobile flight in *The Bad and the Beautiful* and Lana's dramatic appearance onstage.

Unwilling to refute her reputation for tardiness, Lana arrived at Town Hall mere minutes before she was scheduled to appear—although I suppose I should be thankful that we were in the ballpark at all, timewise.

As a result of the enormous amount of publicity generated by the tribute, all three television networks expressed strong interest in having Lana star in a made-for-television movie. Lana said she would be interested in a one-shot, very classy package, and the networks said God, no, they'd never consider her for anything else. But like so many good intentions in Hollywood, this one dwindled after months of meetings and the submission of several subpar scripts. It was one of the few times I found myself really hating the industry, since Lana had been the epitome of cooperation reading the scenarios and making intelligent comments about them. *This* dead end belongs to the networks alone. A lesser washout *was* Lana's fault, however, as she dashed John Springer's plans to take the tribute on the road. "I now have commitments to present the show in the British Isles, South Africa, and in the States and Canada," he wrote after the Town Hall triumph. "There are several other stars who are willing and eager to tour, but I'd like to present you as soon as possible on the heels of the worldwide excitement that was generated by our show in New York." Unfortunately, Lana had peaked too early with Town Hall, and she lost interest with the very real prospect of lesser receptions in other cities. She did not extend herself to accept any other tributes, even for the sake of John Springer. John and I were both disappointed, needless to say, but I was powerless to change Lana's mind.

One briefly interesting offshoot of the Town Hall appearance was an interview Lana had given to reporter Lisa Connolly of *The New York Times*. The interview had gone very well we thought, but when the article appeared, it proved to be something of a hatchet job. Particularly distressing was the way Connolly had categorized most of Lana's fans as aging homosexuals. Lana decided that she wanted "to get that bitch Connolly," and she issued retaliatory remarks in *The Advocate*, the largest of all the gay publications. Lana was hoping to make this a national issue, and she was disappointed when her comments in defense of her fans and of gays were not snapped up by every wire service and mainstream newspaper in the world. I tried to convince her that the issue simply wasn't sufficiently inflammatory, but she took the apathetic response very personally as a sign of her fading influence. I suppose it *was* an equal measure of both.

Much more pleasant than futile tilts with the press was a futile dinner with producer Albert "Cubby" Broccoli, one of the most powerful figures in world cinema. Lana had first met Cubby when he palled around with Frank Sinatra in the 1950s. Now he was a giant in his own right, wealthy and influential due to his role as producer of the James Bond adventures. As Roger Moore once remarked when I met him in London, "He's the kind of man whom conglomerates don't buy out, he takes *them* over." (On that occasion, the astonishingly young-looking, fifty-three-year-old Moore also revealed some of his much-renowned wit. He had co-starred with Lana in an overlooked costume drama called *Diane,* made in 1956 and written for the screen by Christopher Isherwood. In the film, Moore played Prince Henri of France and complained to me bitterly of the fact that he had had to wear his hair longer than Lana's. He added, "I never thought that wearing a lounge suit and tie would ever be uncomfortable after wearing period costumes."

Cubby invited Lana and me to dinner to talk about Lana's career. The power of a Cubby Broccoli behind us was *exactly* what Lana needed. We drove to Cubby's home, which was notorious for having belonged to actor William Powell when he was busy making headlines with sex-bomb Jean Harlow. The curving driveway was fronted by a black iron gate; I announced our arrival to a little black box, and the gates parted without visible human assistance. It was quite a nice touch for the producer of the 007 adventures.

The house itself was colossal, larger than any home I'd ever seen. The endless driveway led us to the mansion's stately portals, and as I parked, our host came out to greet us. Cubby does not look like a millionaire, at least not like a Beverly Hills millionaire. He's round and seraphic, a little gruff but completely without pretension. He reminded me of Lou Costello, only slightly more intense. He was also without a doubt the youngest over-sixty-year-old I'd ever met. Cubby welcomed Lana very warmly, and he shook my hand with no less sincerity.

The interior of the house was even more impressive than the outside. Through a central hallway as wide as a two-lane highway, we were shown into the family room, where Dana Broccoli was seated in a sofa made of black ranch mink. A beautiful woman with raven hair, Dana couldn't wait to embrace Lana, whom she had known for many years. While the women discussed old times, Cubby invited me to help myself to some hors d'oeuvres, which were arranged on a coffee table the size of a dance floor.

After a few moments of chic palaver, Dana announced that, regrettably, she couldn't join us for dinner because of a charity function she had to attend. Well aware of Dana's devotion to a variety of causes, Lana willingly excused her while she, Cubby, and I departed for Matteo's Restaurant in Westwood.

Much of the dinner conversation centered around Lana's desire to be in a top-drawer production, and Cubby gave her some brotherly advice on how to go about soliciting a picture of that sort: more parties, optioning a few novels and trying to put together the financing herself, getting out on the tennis court where so many of Hollywood's deals are made. I remember thinking as he spoke, *This is what Lana should do more of, cultivating friendships with people in high places who can help her.* I know that seems terribly opportunistic, but only a fool stands on principle in Hollywood. As long as no one is hurt, there's nothing wrong with incurring a favor now and then. God knows people did that sort of thing to Lana throughout her career.

Apart from doling out advice, I felt certain that Cubby had an ace up his sleeve, a plum part for Lana in some upcoming production. He had tried diversifying once before, producing *Chitty Chitty Bang Bang* in 1968; though that picture had been a flop, maybe he was going to try again. Or maybe he wanted Lana for a Bond film, inspiring visions of flying off to exotic places for the shoot. Why *not* have a female villain, thought I? Or maybe they needed a new, more glamorous Moneypenny—who, after all, was supposed to be the true love of Bond's life. But, it was not to be. All I can report of substance is that the food at Matteo's was excellent, as always; that I was thoroughly impressed with Cubby's life-style, one that I felt Lana deserved to be living instead of worrying whether or not she could afford to keep Carmen on full time. As they say talk is cheap, which is maybe why there are so many wealthy people in Hollywood.

The problem of Lana's career was put on the back burner for a week thereafter because, quite suddenly and much to our delight, she was offered $4,000 plus expenses to appear on a top-rated English talk show called "The Russell Harty Show." She accepted, and we flew to London on August 31, staying in a gorgeous two-bedroom suite at the Savoy Hotel, overlooking the Thames. Since it was unusually hot for England at that time of year and as there is no air conditioning in all of the United Kingdom—that and perked coffee are sorely needed over there—we kept our windows open to catch the breeze from the river. The smell that accompanied it was old and fresh and invigorating, overall a soothing and unpressured environment, the very distraction we both needed.

Because she was so relaxed, Lana was very loving from the day we arrived. She sought my hand, and we cuddled more than usual; I realized then that we probably belonged in a cottage somewhere, away from the madness of the movie business. We were a perfect match when Lana was at ease, and we needed nothing more than each other's company. How I wished we could uproot and do something else, even if it were herding sheep in the Highlands. There would have been time for a lot more affection, more laughter, less aggravation, and best of all no fucking *image* for Lana to coddle and protect like some frail china cup. I'm convinced we both would have been better off and would still be together to this day.

But—no such luck. Worse, we moved right from the pleasure of that cool Thames breeze into yet another bout of getting ready for showtime. We were late for the Russell Harty taping—love or no love, I was growing to *hate* Lana's lack of punctuality—and when we arrived, we found the program's staff drastically pressed for time. But Lana came up with one of her typical excuses, claiming "flutter-bys," a nauseatingly coy hybrid that nonetheless charmed the pants off the British. In truth, we had been delayed yet again by Lana's tresses. To prepare for the show, we had requested the hairdresser who had worked with us on *Persecution*. Unfortunately, that woman was on another film, and a different girl was brought in. Lana instructed her every step of the way, as if the young lady were as stupid as she was patient. Lana also demanded that only the utensils we had brought with us be used, Carmen having packed her usual hot rollers, curling iron, miniature hair dryer, and the like— not to mention culinary necessities such as Lana's MBT broth, her favorite spices, Lawry's seasoned salt, packets of dried soups, and more. She'd also carted along a portable electric fan, which I had to hold to keep her face cool lest her makeup spoil from perspiration. Yes, I minded *very much* holding that fan like some eunuch slave before Cleopatra; however, it was preferable to the delays to which we'd have been subjected had anything happened to Lana's war paint.

The show was aired the following night, and as if in homage to Lana's own tardiness, it came on an hour later than scheduled. However, an unusually large number of the early-to-bed English stayed up to watch the show, and it received an excellent rating. Not only had "The Russell Harty Show" earned its keep, but Lana was encouraged by the fact that the Turner Mystique could still pack 'em in. Notwithstanding, television of this type is a one-time thing and a convenient way for an audience to stargaze from the comfort of their living rooms. Lana needed deeper reassurance of her marketability, which is why upon returning to Los Angeles she agreed to appear in her second play, *The Pleasure of His Company*. There was no tour, just a three-week stint in Arlington Heights, Illinois. The play is good if lightweight, the story of a divorced, middle-aged couple who attend their daughter's wedding and discover they still care for one another. Lana was the perfect choice to play the remarried Katharine Dougherty; no less ideal was the selection of Louis Jourdan to star as her roué husband.

To find a new designer to work with Lana on her stage wardrobe, we launched an investigation worthy of the FBI. It was June Lockhart who came to our rescue by recommending a brilliant young man named Jean Pierre Dorleac. Jean Pierre had done June's clothes for years, and she graciously offered to set up a meeting and make introductions all around. Lana accepted, and she was impressed enough with Dorleac to commission the young man on the first meeting.

As was her custom, Lana did all the actual design work on the wardrobe, leaving the surprised Jean Pierre little more to do than suggest fabrics and colors. Given his limited participation in these preparations, Jean Pierre and I were both taken aback when Lana was presented with the wardrobe and announced her dissatisfaction with the work. She began requesting an inordinate number of changes, which the designer grudgingly made. Lana was still dissatisfied, and as the date neared for our departure, Lana and Jean Pierre were barely speaking. He was finally relieved of his duties, the finishing touches being done upon our arrival at the theater by their wardrobe mistress. She even had a falling-out with June Lockhart for having recommended him. Once again, everyone was to blame except Lana, even though she was hours late for each fitting and rarely took any suggestion the designer dared to make. Seven years later, Jean Pierre has become one of the most successful designers in the industry, the winner of numerous awards including an Oscar nomination in 1980 for the film *Somewhere in Time*.

The Pleasure of His Company opened on November 21, 1975, and was enormously well-received. John Bowab did an excellent job handling both his superstars, and audience reaction was so overwhelming that the engagement was extended to a full seven weeks.

One of the joys of spending nearly two months in the Midwest was the pleasure of the company of Mr. Louis Jourdan. Louis is the same charming, very debonair man he plays onscreen, lacking only the sense of humor that is written into many of his scripts. I don't mean this in a derogatory way; like every European actor I've ever met—with the exception of Roger Moore—he is very intense and takes himself *very* seriously.

I first met the French actor during preliminary rehearsals, which were held in Lana's suite at the Hilton Hotel. Lana had known him and his wife Kique for years and thought Louis a trifle formal; I found him, rather, a man of unusual discipline. For example, during one rehearsal he very politely asked if there was anything cold to drink. I reached into our ample supply of beverages and poured him an icy 7-Up. He thanked me, then asked for a spoon.

"You drink 7-Up with a spoon?" I asked, wondering if this were some quaint European custom that ought to be explored.

"No," he replied, "I use the spoon to stir out the carbonation."

Barely more enlightened, I asked why.

"Because the carbonation is gas, and gas will make you bloat unless it's stirred out."

As I said, a very controlled man. He is, in fact, the most constrained actor I've ever met. Every night before the play, and then between scenes, I'd find him pacing up and down the hallway outside the dressing rooms, murmuring his lines over and over. Amazingly, he did this on opening night as well as on the last night of his performance. What I found even more fascinating was that he told me that he thinks only in French, translating to English as he speaks. The same is true of his lines in the play, which were written in English though they registered in his brain as French. Being a hopeless monolinguist, I have an almost supernatural regard for that kind of ability. Louis is also very strict about liquor and cigarettes; he doesn't smoke, and allows himself nothing more potent than a half-bottle of wine per day. Generally Louis actively *seeks* tranquillity: I overheard him tell Lana one day that he selects projects that will subject him to a minimum of pressure. "I have done many plays in this theater," he explained, "and one reason I return every year is because there is absolutely nothing else to do here. I make it a sabbatical, bring my books and record albums, and when I am not performing, I remain in my room listening to music and reading good novels." I knew that Lana related to this—though in her case she watches television and gabs on the phone.

The fact that Lana knew the Jourdans quite well led me to believe that we might be in for a fascinating time, getting together for fun little dinners, discussing the latest Hollywood gossip, and exchanging interesting stories. Once again, my expectations were dashed. Louis was always a gentleman and as pleasant toward Lana as she was to him, but we had little social contact. Still, Louis was a chatterbox compared to his wife. Kique once asked me if she could borrow a particular hair conditioner she noticed I was using. I gladly obliged, but she returned it the next day, coolly reporting that she didn't care for it. That was the extent of our conversation during the entire run of the play.

One of the innovations that Lana had decided upon for this, her second, play was that she was going to do her own makeup, thus sparing herself the expense of having a professional makeup person in tow. Accordingly, before leaving Los Angeles, she had called Jack Freeman and enlisted his aid in selecting all the appropriate products. Unfortunately, Lana hadn't had time to experiment with her makeup kit before leaving, and she didn't do so until the day of the technical rehearsal—when the actors are expected to appear onstage exactly as they will on opening night so the necessary lighting and sound adjustments can be made and noted.

On the morning of this technical rehearsal, Lana seated herself before her custom-built three-sided mirror in the bedroom of our suite and went to work. Stage makeup is much thicker than street makeup, applied with sponges and brushes and then meticulously blended. Lana toiled long and hard until she was satisfied with the results, at which time it was my task to apply her eyelashes. This, to Lana, was as important as the Second Coming. There couldn't be one drop too much glue on them, and they had to begin at a precise spot on the inner lid and sweep up and across her black eyeliner until they extended one-sixteenth of an inch above the edge of the eye, well beyond the eye itself. Once they were positioned, the false lashes were cemented to Lana's own lashes with layers of heavy mascara.

It was always a challenge to apply the lashes to Lana's satisfaction. If I failed, they would have to be taken off, the glue cleaned away, reapplied, and the entire process repeated—this, whether or not the curtain was ready to go up. Many times I pleaded with her that even people in the front row wouldn't notice if her lashes were a fraction of a bloody millimeter off, but Lana wouldn't allow such "shoddiness." "*I'll* know," was her ever-ready reply.

After all our laborious work, Lana was ready for the stage. I thought the makeup a little heavy, but I said nothing to Lana lest she decide on wiping it all off and starting from scratch. Besides, it was up to the director to make such decisions.

Louis expressed it best when Lana stepped under the pink lights of the stage, which further intensified the pastiness of her application. "She looks like a corpse," he said casually.

Agreeing with Louis in principle but employing vastly
more diplomacy, John Bowab told Lana that the theater was
rather small and that what she was wearing might do better
in Yankee Stadium. He advised her to return to the hotel,
take the makeup off, and just apply a light daytime base.
Lana, always able to draw upon her wonderful sense of humor
in the most embarrassing situations, said, "Well, I told you
guys I didn't know what I was doing!" Throughout the run of
the play, Lana wore only a simple Etherea peach base and
looked like a dream onstage.

Quite naturally, the management of the Arlington Park
Theater wanted Lana to plug the show in the Chicago area.
Louis was a good steady draw, but the owners wanted a
sellout. Lana wasn't averse to doing a few interviews, and the
theater publicist was willing to waive every other publicity
chore if Lana would agree to appear on just one program, a
popular local show, which had not yet gone nationwide. It
was called "The Phil Donahue Show," and the publicist
explained that Donahue had a very easy format, with an
audience comprised mostly of middle-aged ladies who would
be thrilled to see her. Lana agreed to appear sight unseen,
although I made it a point to catch the show the following
morning.

There's no denying the quality and intelligence of the
show Donahue does, but I nearly fell out of bed when I
realized the format to which Lana would be subjected. All I
could see was this handsome, gray-haired man running back
and forth through his audience, shoving a microphone at
these "middle-aged ladies." The audience hounded the guest
like bargain hunters at a street sale, and while ordinarily I'd
have found the program enjoyable, all I could see was Lana
sitting alone, in front of all these *National Enquirer* and Bible
readers, who would finally have the opportunity to ask questions they may have wondered about for years—things like
"Why have you been married so many times?" or "Who
really killed Johnny Stompanato?" It was a nightmare, made
worse even as I watched, since it was announced to thunder-
ous applause that Lana Turner would be on later that week.
Adding potential injury to embarrassment, we just happened
to be in Stompanato's home town. Unlike other cities we had
visited, Lana utterly avoided the public while we were in
Chicago, and she relied upon a police escort when we went

anywhere. We hadn't *really* expected trouble, but to taunt Stompanato's friends and family by possibly having to discuss the affair in their midst—that was insanity!

At noon, after I had awakened Lana in my usual gentle fashion, I cut short the massage and demanded to talk to her at once. Alarmed, she sat right up, hair in disarray, face without a trace of makeup, looking remarkably innocent. I sat on the edge of the bed and recounted what I'd seen that morning. When I made a point about the Stompanato killing, his name caused her to recoil, as if I'd tapped a private well of fear and sadness. We had discussed the murder, of course, but only when Lana was more in control of her emotions than she was upon awaking from a deep slumber. As I went on to describe the circular set and format, Lana's eyes slowly widened with terror.

"Oh, my God, Taylor!" she gasped at last. "I can't appear on a show like that!"

I told her I already knew that; the problem was getting out of it.

"But it's already set!" she continued. "What am I going to do?"

Damned if I knew. We were both frantic, and after running the gamut of excuses, we reluctantly agreed that there was only one out: the truth. And it was Lana who decided just *how* to break it to the producer of the play; in times like these, she found it *very* convenient to have a personal manager. I was to call the producer and explain that Lana had neglected to consult with me before committing to the show, a decision that (enter the heavy) was in my estimation a bad one. If the producer phoned Lana, she would simply hide behind the dodge that my word was law.

Fortifying myself with a belt of scotch in my orange juice, I placed the call and told the simultaneously angry and bewildered producer why Lana could not go on the program. Since I'd left no option, he had no recourse but to cancel the engagement. He had nothing to do with me for the remainder of the run of *The Pleasure of His Company*, nor did he like me any better for a battle that spoiled the closing days of our run. Lana was piqued to the extreme when informed that Louis was being allowed to depart the show before the end of its extended schedule because he was leaving to shoot a film in Europe. Lana refused to go on with an unknown co-star and I saw her standing by her open hotel window gulping down lungfuls of cold air. She came down with bronchitis, and I was the one who had to tell the manager that now he had to find *two* unknowns for the remainder of his all-star play, neither of whom justified the expense of the added performances—which, paradoxically, had been the *reason* Louis had left in the first place. This wasn't the last time I'd take a pie in the face on Lana's behalf. However, the more she worked the more my winsome boss and playmate was being replaced by the resurging MGM star. While I was perfectly willing to intercede on the behalf of one, the other was far too self-centered for my taste. My holding the portable fan, her self-inflicted illness; these were minor league inconveniences compared to what lay in store. Had I been a seer, I might have advised myself then to gather up the Seconal Lana left behind and gulp them down before heading back to Los Angeles. Surviving the next few years would have been easier had I been blissfully insensate. . . .

Chapter Ten

Lana's refusal to participate in the Donahue show was not so much the act of an egotistical or pampered woman, though Lana can be both, as it was the self-defense mechanism of a beautiful icon taking control, seeking to perpetuate the fading aura that the studio system created for her. This was vividly brought home one day when, after years of proudly declaring that she had *never* tried out for the part of Scarlett O'Hara in *Gone With the Wind*—implying that if she *had*, Vivien Leigh would never have become a star—Lana and I were watching "The Mike Douglas Show." A film historian came on with screen tests of the actresses who had sought the role. We watched one clip after another until there she was—little Judy Turner. She happened to have been superb, but that's beside the point; I could feel Lana's embarrassment as she was caught in her own tiny fib. She watched the short clip and, realizing that she could no longer deny having sought the role, said simply, "Oops!"

Image before truth, façade rather than fact, pride over all—that was Louis B. Mayer's and Hollywood's legacy to Lana Turner. When she was divorced from show business, she was able to let her hair down and be a real person as she was in Hawaii or in Palm Springs. Otherwise, she was becoming increasingly an anachronistic pain in the neck. I once fell to discussing this fact at a party hosted by Bette Davis in her West Hollywood apartment, a party intended to show the Hollywood community that she *could*, against all predictions, be happy in an apartment. In typical Davis fashion, the actress offered a history not just of Lana Turner but of the origin of Hollywood glamour. By this time I had taken to carrying around one of those handy pocket tape recorders to make notes to myself, and I captured Bette's words for posterity.

"When sound came to the movies," she began, "and they brought many of us from New York, from the theater, that created two groups of actors out here. The ones who really made this town were the so-called glamour personalities. Gary Cooper. Joan Crawford. Clark Gable. Lana Turner. Errol Flynn. They had no theatrical background, none of them. What they *did* have was something to offer films, something that was sensational, personality-wise. That overcame everything else. In fact, I think Lana ended up turning into a very good actress. *The Bad and the Beautiful* was a damn good film, and she's never been better—except maybe in *The Postman Always Rings Twice*. And she was very good with Spence in *Cass Timberlane*, which was a fine picture. But what they had, the thing which made this town, was more than the rest of us had who went in solely for acting. My basic interest was the performance, not the offscreen image. Lana was different. She consciously perpetuated the glamour thing. But that was a large, large, large part of the industry back then. *I* felt that I had no obligation to anybody when I wasn't working, at first. But I was criticized by my peers who said, 'You must realize that this is different from the theater. The offscreen impression is just as important.' That's how you came to be preoccupied with your appearance. You realized that you owed the public something. People like Lana never appeared in public any way but *put together*. I think that the public still wants that, because film stars are the only royalty this country has ever had. Look at what's happened today. There's nothing to copy about an actress's hair or makeup or dress any more. Actors go around looking like little bums, and that's wrong! They disappoint people like mad. Look the way you want to at home, live your own life, but give the American people their kings and queens."

After being assaulted by Bette's incisive monologue, I remember thinking, how true that was and how tolerant it made me feel toward Lana. I left Bette feeling genuinely repentant for the anger and unbounded frustration I'd experienced over Lana's deliberateness pertaining to her appearance. Dear Lana, selflessly saving Hollywood from decline!

A few days later, still at the height of my forbearance, I bumped into Keir Dullea, whom I mentioned earlier. Though the star of such classic films as *David and Lisa* and *2001: A Space Odyssey* is himself quite a natty fellow, he did not agree with what Bette had said, being of the opinion that appearance has little to do with star quality. "It's self-esteem and confidence that make a star," he said confidently. "You can't develop that by dressing up. When I was a young actor, one of the other unknowns who was always going to the same readings was Robert Redford. We became quite friendly, and what he had then—the same quality that he obviously has today—is that he *believed* in himself. Warren Beatty is the same. Lana Turner is different."

I had always realized that Lana wasn't the most confident personality in Hollywood, though I'd been so close to her for so many years that I didn't realize how out of touch she was. It didn't *matter* how actors dressed on Dinah Shore or whether they wore makeup to interviews. That really *was* her whole world, and it wasn't what audiences were buying en masse. That's why talented players like Bette and Katharine Hepburn were always working and Lana was not. On top of being more tolerant, I now began to feel sorry for Lana. She *couldn't* save Hollywood from its decline; in the minds of moviegoers and the new generations of actors, Lana's ways were old hat! However, Keir did say one very kind thing about Lana, something I wish he'd have said on "The Tonight Show" for Johnny Carson to hear. "Professionally," he assured me, "Lana was very giving to me as an actor. I've found that a lot of the reputations, like hers, aren't deserved. I'm not trying to pretend there aren't damaged people out there, but I find actors as a whole quiet, introspective people. Some of them can flare up, but that's because they're very emotional people who become annoyed when they don't get what they want *from themselves*. I've only seen actors get mad at others when insensitive people try to dominate them. Take Otto Preminger, though he isn't the worst, really, because he's too overt. As much as I really despise him—we worked together on *Bunny Lake is Missing*—he doesn't knife you in the back. He knifes you in the front. But there are a lot more monsters on that side of the desk."

(Parenthetically, it's appropriate that Keir mentioned Otto while discoursing about Lana. Though the two were allies in the pursuit of *Forever Amber,* one of her most famous battles just happened to be with that most tyrannical of individuals. In 1959, when the director was powerful enough to cast his own films, he personally selected Lana to play the part of a rape victim in *Anatomy of a Murder.* As was his practice, Preminger and his wife personally made the rounds of the Beverly Hills clothing stores to select the wardrobe for his picture. He hadn't told Lana he was going to do this, simply phoned her to meet them at such-and-such a shop to try on the selections they had made. When Lana failed to show up, Preminger called her agent—who informed the director that Lana only wore clothes created by the well-known designer Jean Louis. Preminger was annoyed, and he explained that since Lana was to play the wife of a second lieutenant, off-the-rack clothes were quite appropriate; and besides, no one told Otto Preminger how to prepare his films. The director's edict was repeated to Lana, who didn't go for it at all. In a highly publicized move, Lana told Preminger that if he didn't take Jean Louis, he couldn't have her. Preminger released her from the film and hired Lee Remick, whose career sky-rocketed along with that of co-star George C. Scott. Lana later told me that she would never even *consider* working for Preminger again, no matter *what* part was offered.)

As it happened, shortly after I met Keir Dullea, I was invited by a friend to attend a book publishing party for author Roald Dahl, the noted fantasy-mystery author. Dahl also happens to be the husband of one of my favorite actresses, Patricia Neal. As Miss Neal was present at the party, I monopolized her attention more than I'm sure she would have liked. I'm glad I did; she's a marvel of insight and courage. She's also Hollywood's most famous survivor. Shortly after winning an Oscar for *Hud* ("and just after I'd been offered the *greatest* amount of money for another film,") she was felled by what she refers to as "my ghastly stroke." She recovered through the most painstaking kind of perseverance and is acting up a storm in films like *Ghost Story.*

Not surprisingly, my employer sneaked like a thundercloud into the conversation, and, shooting for a triple crown of amateur psychoanalysis, I asked Miss Neal how *she* managed to overcome the glamour typecasting, whereas Lana never really was able to. She smiled and replied, "You'll think

I'm bragging, and I don't intend to. But I am not, like Lana or like Rita Hayworth and others, a *film* star. They were not brought up or trained on the stage. Lana has gone into it, I know, but if you really want to be an actress, you have to *start* on the stage. If you're a good actress with no stage experience, you can learn to act well on film in time, as Lana did. But it takes much, much longer. And by the time a lot of these screen actresses have mastered their craft, they are past their so-called prime and don't get a second chance. There are many actresses who fit into that category and who are not doing well professionally."

That, in a one-line nutshell, is Lana—though there's a brief postscript. Several years after leaving Lana's employ, I was introduced to Dr. Joyce Brothers on the set of the film *The King of Comedy*. We spoke while the crew was preparing a shot in which she was to appear. At first we talked about how this serious role was going to obliterate the impression that star Jerry Lewis could only play fumbling clowns. "All it takes is one great role to reverse an entire career," she said.

I considered this for a moment, then I had to disagree. "What about Lana Turner?" I asked. "Rave notices never saved her from the impression of being little more than a sex symbol or a glamour queen."

"You're right," Dr. Brothers admitted, "but that's because even in later years, with films like *Peyton Place*, there was sex, even if she were not playing a sex symbol per se." Dr. Brothers added that another part of the problem with Lana was that she had not only her screen image with which to contend, but her sensational offscreen life as well. Other love goddesses hadn't quite that volume of press to overcome, so they could play a variety of roles. Beyond the sex-and-glamour sphere, Lana was in deep trouble.

In essence, all of these considerations defined the complex professional bind in which Lana found herself. And as if her faltering career were not trouble enough, personal problems reared their familiar little heads. Shortly after we had finished with *The Pleasure of His Company*, Lana had her annual checkup with Dr. Mac. He found suspicious material in the area of her cervix, and, while not wanting to alarm her, he recognized that this must be attended to immediately and suggested that Lana make an appointment with one Dr. J. Nolan of the Southern California Cancer Center. Lana was naturally extremely upset as was I, though she seemed to fret equally about her physical well-being as about what the news of possible cancer might do to her career. We enlisted the help of Dr. Mac and his nurse to devise a cover-up worthy of the CIA. Lana would go to see Dr. Nolan using the assumed name of Mary Bowen, a widow, whose home address was my own. We purchased a black wig, and Lana wore as little makeup as vanity would allow, also leaving home all of her jewelry. Of course, Dr. Mac would have to tell Dr. Nolan who the nondescript Mary Bowen really was, but he promised the information would be kept utterly confidential; not even Lana's mother and daughter were told. Lana did not want to worry them, and she also believes that no one can repeat something they aren't told.

Lana's hands were trembling a few days later when we went for her first appointment. She was holding my hand very tightly, and because of her tension and slight disorientation being in a place she never wanted to see, her fear was something I could actually *feel*. I felt hopelessly inadequate, unable to take this burden from her. I'm sure that at this moment, Lana felt pitifully alone.

Lana Turner did not get any special privileges at the center. Dr. Nolan confirmed that she had symptoms and what might well be the beginning of cancer, but it was nothing that couldn't be checked at this very early stage. She continued to visit Dr. Nolan until the symptoms were cleared, weeks during which we lived with mutual, but largely unspoken, fears. I came to appreciate the torment through which victims of any kind of serious illness must go. In light of this, I must say that Lana was quite brave once the initial shock had worn off. She was even able to serve up vignettes about death, in the self-assuring manner of one who, afraid of the dark, starts to whistle. Death had fortunately not touched our lives in recent years, though Lana had seen enough of it in the person of her father, in Johnny Stompanato, her beloved coworkers from Clark Gable to John Garfield, even lovers like Tyrone Power and two ex-husbands. However, I was surprised to learn after all these years that Lana refuses to attend funerals and has stated in her will that she is not to have one. She said she wants to be cremated, her ashes scattered by plane over the Pacific Ocean. Lana told me that it is nearly impossible for her even to *film* a funeral scene. During the shooting of *Imitation of Life*, Lana grew very fond of Juanita Moore, the black actress who played her maid, Annie, in the film. Annie dies toward the end of the picture, and there is a funeral scene which was staged at a church in Hollywood. Even though she knew the casket did not contain the body of Miss Moore, Lana became hysterical as co-star Mahalia Jackson began singing her gospel farewell. Lana had to be helped by her makeup man and other crew members to her trailer outside the church, where she remained until she could control herself to go on with the scene.

After what seemed interminable visits to the cancer center, Dr. Nolan declared at last that Mary Bowen need not return for further treatment. Only then did Lana and I relax. Lana regained her good humor and returned to her old unhealthful habits, though the possibility of a recurrence has probably haunted her. She used to *say* so with every puff she took on a cigarette, with every ounce of diet soda she downed. Lana Turner will, I am sure, outlive *me!*

Hard on the heels of her treatment, Lana was rocked even further when Cheryl declared that she was going to sell the Calabassas home and move to Hawaii. Lana was deeply upset, though in equal part by her daughter's decision to move and indecision over what to do with Gran. Lana didn't want her mother moving into the Ivory Tower, that was for certain. For one thing, Lana was away enough, and Gran's health poor enough, that she would have to hire a nurse. There was barely enough room in the apartment for one other person, let alone a third. For another, Lana's feeling about living with her mother was unchanged from the time this problem first arose. Under the circumstances, she and I both agreed that the best thing to do was to investigate a retirement hotel. I called a friend of mine, whose mother was living in just such a place, and he assured me the home was an excellent one. I drove out to see it, then I checked out a few others. I reported to Lana that the one my friend had suggested seemed the best such housing available. It was equipped with a swimming pool, game rooms, a beautifully appointed dining room, and a small coffee shop. The rooms themselves were small but bright and pleasant.

Lana was not entirely happy with this arrangement, though she knew there was no alternative. Here, at least,

Gran would be surrounded by a competent staff and far more friends than she had had in Calabassas. In fact, on the day Gran made the move, we were all cracking jokes about the possibility of her meeting some nice, retired millionaire. However, as we drove away, Lana started sobbing about how terrible she felt leaving her mother "all alone in that one little room." Not terrible enough to have her stay at the Ivory Tower, but Lana had made her decision and would have to live with it.

Happily, Gran eventually came to enjoy not only her little place but also not having to provide for herself quite so much. However, in March of 1981 she decided to seek out a fresher, balmier climate—as she had when she made the fateful move to Los Angeles nearly a half century before—and moved to Hawaii. With Lana's reluctant blessings, she rented a two-bedroom apartment and shared it with a female companion hired by Lana. The two women are now the best of pals. I went to visit Gran just before that move, after Lana and I had not spoken to one another for over a year. During my brief stay, Lana phoned her mother, as she did once every day. When Gran told her I was there, Lana simply informed her to say hello for her, then she hung up. As always, Gran did not argue with her lofty daughter. Gran and Cheryl remain quite close; Cheryl and Josh are doing very well selling real estate on the islands.

There is a wonderful New Yorker by the name of Harold Kennedy, a man who is one of the nicest and funniest men I have ever met. And probably one of the canniest. Harold has been associated with the theater all his life, but he is most noted for coercing movie queens and other stars to appear on the summer circuit in stage productions that are produced and directed by a man who is also one of the co-stars: himself.

Harold has managed to get some of the greatest names in Hollywood onto the stage in sometimes exhausting tours, from Tallulah Bankhead to Gloria Swanson, from John Travolta to Charlton Heston to the late Robert Ryan. I'm sure he learned a lot about friendly persuasion from Orson Welles, who gave him his first stage work.

Harold wrote several letters to Lana outlining in detail what he had done in the past and what a spectacular future he thought she had "touring the provinces," as he phrased it.

Harold even suggested that Lana telephone Gloria Swanson
to verify his credentials, which Lana promptly did. As always,
she asked me to get on the other extension and listen in and
make notes. After a few rings, the unmistakable voice of
Gloria Swanson made "Hello?" sound majestic.

Lana said, "Hello, Gloria?"

Gloria said, "Yes?"

Lana said, "This is Lana Turner."

Either unmoved or suspicious, Gloria said, "Yes."

Lana said gamely, "Dear, I'm calling at the suggestion of
a Mr. Harold Kennedy who—"

"Yes," she cut in, "the man who *tricked* me into going
on the stage!"

Clearly apprehensive, Lana said, "He tricked you?"

Gloria replied, "Yes. Years ago, I was at a party in New
York after I had agreed to do a play for someone else. I had
no stage experience whatsoever, and Mr. Kennedy came up
to me and said, 'Miss Swanson, I understand that you're
going to appear in a somewhat challenging play.' I looked at
him rather queer, as though he were a critic. I said nothing,
and he continued, 'Don't you think you should get your feet
wet in summer stock before you undertake something so
vast?' I thought about that for a moment and said, presuming
the query had been rhetorical, 'I guess I should.' It just so
happened that he had a play for me, and after talking it over
with him, I agreed to do it before tackling the other one.
Well, I did his show as if to the manner born, no problems
whatsoever—as he confessed he knew I would. *That's* how he
tricked me."

Gloria went on to rave about Harold, and bolstered by
my urging, Lana concurred that we should hear just what this
aggressive fellow had to offer.

What Harold had to offer was a tour of *Bell, Book and
Candle*, a play written in the early 1950s and subsequently
made into a motion picture starring Kim Novak, James
Stewart, and Hermione Gingold. Although we had been
looking for an original play so that Lana could finally *create* a
stage role, there was none to be found; and among existing
works, there are very few good vehicles for, as Harold would
discreetly say it, "an actress of a certain age." A diverting
comedy about a coven of New York witches, *Bell, Book and
Candle* was the most suitable one being offered, and Lana

said she'd do it. It is a credit to her that she'd be playing the same part played by the younger, though certainly not more youthful, Miss Novak twenty years earlier!

Unlike the previous plays Lana had done, she undertook several successful tours with *Bell, Book and Candle*. She enjoyed the play tremendously, and the part fit her like a proverbial glove: each time the curtain rose on Lana in her long, black gown, a black cat cradled in her arms, I found it impossible to imagine anyone else playing Gillian Holroyd. Harold was a glorious director for her, in some ways better than John Bowab. Though John had a firmer directorial hand, fitting player to part, Harold gave Lana rein to explore the role. He didn't fill her head with intellectual marching orders, background about her character and her motivation that some actors find interesting but that Lana does not. If Harold's work was not as good as John's in terms of drama, it was better theater; if it was not quite art, it was a lot more fun. And because Lana was serving the audience rather than the playwright, she earned first-rate notices—a fact that was at once thrilling and finally disturbing. By this, Lana's third play, she was confident enough to have blossomed into a full-fledged, cold-as-ice, swellheaded prima donna. She was worse than in any of the stories I'd heard about her MGM days and worse than she'd ever been with me. I suspect that because she could *see* her audiences and *hear* their applause, she felt as if she could do no wrong. In short, success on the stage had gone to Lana's head. Accustomed to breaking box-office records, she became "ill" whenever a house was half full; if the saintly, patient Harold insisted on having a doctor examine her, Lana would repeat what she had tried in Arlington Heights, literally *making* herself ill with gusts of cold air.

If this was the bad side, the plus side of the tour each week was going to dinner with Harold and the other cast members between the Sunday matinee and evening performance. Harold would have only one cocktail but needed even less to regale us with fascinating anecdotes about the legends with whom he had worked over the years. Harold is also a devilish tease and got away with murder when it came to ribbing Lana. He would often turn to me and, loud enough for her to hear, say something like, "Taylor, would you tell that aging ingenue you run around with to try and stay *out* of my light when I'm onstage?" Lana would pretend to be insulted, then return with a line like, "But I'm doing you a *favor*, Harold dear. At your age you look *better* in the dark." Lana likes nothing so much as someone who can make her laugh or get her mind working, and Harold was more than a match on both counts. It was only during these meals that Lana was her pleasant, old self.

Immediately after the 1976 winter tour of *Bell, Book and Candle*, Lana was approached to star in a film called *And Jill Came Tumbling After*. The script was based on a true story about two young people who fall in love and, only after being married, discover that they are half brother and sister. We both liked the script very much, especially for its mature and sensitive approach to a most delicate subject. Lana signed to do the film, which would be released as *Bittersweet Love*—a commitment that would net her fifty thousand dollars for nine days' work. She would play the part of the wealthy mother of Meredith Baxter-Birney, who was cast as the ill-starred young girl. Meredith was very professional, although she gave the impression of being rather unfriendly. I quickly discovered that this wasn't the case at all. She happens to be extremely nearsighted, and without her glasses she can't see her hand in front of her face. This accounted for the many times Meredith walked right past us without saying hello, since when we *did* call to her, she'd stop and squint all around in an effort to locate the speaker.

The cast also included Robert Lansing, an eagle-browed, very intense actor who is best known for his portrayal of Brigadier General Frank Savage on the television series "Twelve O'Clock High." Lansing had actually been brought in at the last minute as a replacement for Gig Young, who had worked on the picture for three days. Whether because of drugs, pills, or booze, he was incapable of remembering his lines and was forced to leave the production. Less than a year later, Gig took his life.

Rounding out the cast was Celeste Holm, whom I was looking forward to meeting. But, alas, she and Lana had no scenes together, and never the twain did meet.

The picture was made quickly, efficiently, and largely without incident. It was scheduled to open October 27, and just prior to its release, Lana helped to promote the film. The most tactically complex of the interviews was her appearance on "The Dinah Shore Show." Lana actually came off quite well, although the best story was the one the audience never saw. Dinah's show taped at one o'clock in the afternoon, which is an early call by Lana's timetable. Not only did it mean getting up before noon, it would limit the time she had to do her own makeup before going to the studio. I had several conferences with Dinah's staff about scheduling Lana as the last guest, the program personnel having a difficult time comprehending why Lana couldn't simply begin her day earlier. I can't blame them. Nonetheless, contradictory to policy they had regarding stars of Lana's stature, they agreed to let her come on last. Even so, Lana was late on the day of the taping. Dinah exhausted every guest on her panel while waiting for Lana to arrive, and when we finally drove up to the gate at CBS, a guard alerted the staff. Two associate producers came running out and told me to put the car *anywhere*, then they rushed us through the cavernous building and into a dressing room. Acting as though she had all the time in creation, Lana patiently explained that she needed to touch up her makeup and hair and had to change into another outfit. The staff members were outwardly polite, though I knew they must be boiling inside—as I was. Disregarding the obvious tension and inconsiderate of the lateness of the hour, Milady planted herself before a mirror and asked that the show's writer be brought over to review the questions Dinah would be asking. By now the air was thicker than blood; finally, briefed about the spot and assured that she looked as gorgeous as she was going to get, Lana went to the set. Dinah played it perfectly. Seeing Lana in the wings, she rose from the couch and greeted her congenially, as if there had been no delay whatsoever. Mercifully, the interview went well, thanks to Dinah and her warm Southern charm. Lana was so pleased when it was aired that she sent Dinah a beautiful rose tree for her home, along with a handwritten card thanking her hostess for everything. Dinah's response was as gracious as the lady herself.

Conversely, on the bottom of our *Bittersweet Love* hit parade was an interview Lana gave to columnist Marilyn Beck. Ms. Beck is syndicated in a slew of newspapers, a fact that has caused me to lose a great deal of respect for same. The columnist had broken her foot in an accident and could not leave her Coldwater Canyon home. Lana balked at going up there for the interview because it reminded her of the old days when one had to pay homage to Louella Parsons and Hedda Hopper. She eventually went only for the good of the picture, and we both thought the interview had gone well—that is, until we read it. Ms. Beck took off after Lana, making her sound far more vicious, self-centered, and inconsiderate than she really is. Typical of the unfair remarks she made was one that said, in essence, that in days of yore the very presence of Lana Turner would have been sufficient to pull a huge crowd, while today she traveled alone. Reading this, Lana crumpled the paper in disgust and I sarcastically asked, "What did she expect us to do? Call central casting and have them send two hundred cheering people over to her cul-de-sac?" For nearly a year thereafter, at my suggestion, Lana refused to talk to any journalists *period*.

Bittersweet Love opened to lukewarm reviews that saluted the cast but damned the film itself. To the surprise of no one, the picture did not perform well at the box office. Apart from the mixed reviews, it was hurt when Avco Embassy Pictures threw it into the marketplace with virtually no promotional campaign. There is no way a film can carve out an audience if theatergoers don't know it's playing, if there are no advance posters, theatrical previews, or eye-catching newspaper advertisements. Even film buffs are oftentimes ignorant of the release of more important pictures than hers, such as Elizabeth Taylor and Richard Burton in *Under Milkwood* or Lord Laurence Olivier's *The Entertainer*, to name just two. Though Lana did everything she could to help *Bittersweet Love*, she was Don Quixote fighting windmills against the likes of *Rocky, The Omen, Network, All the President's Men,* and *Taxi Driver*. It was a time when even commercial films like the football thriller *Two-Minute Warning* were getting creamed; we didn't stand a chance. I don't even think the producer's very earnest solution would have helped: "If only I could have gotten Meredith to do a nude scene in the film. . . ."

It all added up to yet another crushing disappointment, *Bittersweet Love* being an ironically apt description of Lana's relationship with the motion picture industry.

Chapter Eleven

As unpleasant as 1976 was for us professionally and personally, socially, for me, it was a riot. Lana was still her stay-at-home self, but I wasn't about to stay in the Ivory Tower and watch television each night until we went to bed and fell asleep, played pool and fell asleep, or just plain fell asleep in front of the tube. While I loved Lana more than I did when I dutifully hovered by her side in the early days, I needed fellowship. We may well have been husband and wife in every respect but my mailing address, but I liked being with people. In fact, I think the deeper I got in my relationship with Lana the *more* I needed people. I was fearful of being dragged into the same very lonely life-style that she had come to prefer. Lana had been active once; now, afraid of being measured unfavorably against the woman she was thirty years before, scarred by failures beyond her control, she avoided even the *prospect* of comparison. She partied when we were somewhere new, where people would be speechless and awed by the legend. Otherwise, like Miss Haversham of *Great Expectations*, she sat, unstirring, as I tried to entertain her. But I just couldn't sit and hold her hand every night lest we *both* suffer the depression brought on by a decaying constitution.

I went to parties and banquets whenever I could, wanting to drink in festiveness and *life* like a camel slurping up water before returning to its trek through the desert. My favorite of these was a mammoth carnival held annually by Debbie Reynolds at a private club called Pips.

Debbie is an absolute no-nonsense lady who loves and knows Lana probably as well as Lana does herself. We ran into one another quite often over the years. The first time was impressionist Jim Bailey's opening at the Dorothy Chandler Pavilion in Los Angeles. He was a mutual friend of Lana's and mine, and over more than one dinner he complained to me that neither he nor any other female impersonator had ever been able to master Lana's walk, capturing the way her shoulders sway from left to right while her hips swing right to left, all garnished with a mixture of raw sensuality and femininity. Nonetheless, Jim does everyone *else* to perfection, from Judy Garland to Barbra Streisand. During the intermission of Jim's show, Debbie took it upon herself to introduce the audience to all the celebrities who were present. When she came to us, she introduced Lana as "the greatest star of them all." Lana was flattered, but between blowing kisses to the theatergoers she hissed at Debbie to dampen the clowning and go back to her seat. Need I say that Lana's protests merely inspired Debbie to repeat and embellish her praise. This sort of wonderfully loony behavior is typical of Debbie, as I was soon to discover. We met soon thereafter at a party held by a prominent attorney, where for a time Debbie played the part of a starlet hoping to be discovered, buzzing from star to star. At one point she pretended that I was a producer and plopped herself on my lap so hard that I thought she had broken one of my balls.

Beyond the flamboyance and the ribbing, Debbie is very sensitive to people's wants and needs. She telephoned Lana for days preceding the Pips gala, feeling that it would be good for her to attend and making sure that she would do so. Debbie understood Lana's attitude toward parties, and it was Debbie's plan to lavish so much attention on Lana prior to the bash that she'd be ashamed not to show up. Yet, when the night of the party arrived Lana said she simply didn't feel like getting all decked out. I felt slightly self-conscious as I walked in the front door of Pips by my lonesome; I was not surprised, only mortified, when Debbie spotted me and yelled from across the jam-packed room, "I knew she wouldn't come! I *knew* it!"

Though Debbie was openly annoyed with Lana, she was very kind to me, introducing me to some of the celebrities who were present. I say "some," since there was a familiar face everywhere I looked. I moved to the bar when suddenly a voice assailed my ears. I looked along the counter and

spotted my favorite comedienne surrounded by a group of
her friends. I had been impersonating Phyllis Diller for years,
using lines from her albums in my singing act. In her own
queer fashion, Phyllis looked great. Her hair had been pulled
up and knotted around a hard-boiled egg, which had an eye
painted on its forward end. Above the eye, like an awning,
was a half pair of rather overpowering lashes, which I noticed
were barely longer than Phyllis's own.

Emboldened by my intake of alcohol, I elbowed my way
to Phyllis's side and gently took her hand in mine, Hollywood
style: gently, with feeling. I said in earnest, "Miss Diller, I
want to thank you for all the fundraisers, supper clubs,
cocktail parties, bar mitzvahs, and dinners to which I've been
invited because of you."

"Me?" she exclaimed. "Why me?"

It was a perfect setup and imitating her unmistakable
nasal roar, I said, "I want to thank you all for coming here
tonight, because it takes a *lot* of courage to come to a joint
that's this filthy."

Phyllis immediately recognized the line from one of her
albums and broke into her lusty laugh screaming, "This man
is doing my *act!*" We proceeded to do the routine together
and had a wonderful time. I must have done something right,
since later in the evening Phyllis asked ten other people,
including me, to come to her Brentwood home for more
drinks. Phyllis has a lovely home, at once elegant and, as one
might expect, just a trifle unusual. As we were given a
minitour, she explained that every room is named for a
different celebrity. The living room is the Bob Hope Room,
complete with a life-sized oil painting of Mr. Hope. Phyllis
said that he was thus honored for having been very helpful at
the beginning of her career. Then she led us through a large
chamber that used to be a bedroom but now housed only her
costumes. Our next stop was what she called the "Après-Fuck
Boudoir," after which we went to her combination library,
family room, and screening room. "This one *used* to be the
Doris Day Room," she told us, "until I met her." Although
Phyllis didn't go into specifics, she had admired Doris's
movies sufficiently to dedicate a room to her, but she reneged
when she finally met the woman. Phyllis hinted that she did
not like Doris *at all*, but she would not elaborate.

Phyllis reinforced my estimation of her as one of the

funniest people alive. She is fast, and she can be both broad
and subtle. I particularly liked her quip about an actor who
was so proud of his golden Oscar statuette that he had it
bronzed. But Phyllis is also a charming hostess who exudes a
surprisingly matronly air and who cares about everyone in a
motherly way. She would pause in the tour to run to the
kitchen or to the bar for one of us and was very attentive to
our comfort. It was very early in the morning before I left her
home, one of the most enjoyable times I've ever spent
anywhere.

Another interesting outing came just after New Year's,
1977. Since Lana didn't even want to attend private dinners
as a rule, I went alone. A friend of mine, director John
Erman, invited me to have dinner with him, Bernadette
Peters, and her manager at the manager's home. John knew
that I admired Bernadette and thought I'd enjoy spending an
evening with her—which I did. I'd been smitten with her
when she was appearing at nightclubs in Los Angeles, impressed
not only with her talent, which is extraordinary, but by her
dynamite figure and alluring manner. She possessed a com-
posite beauty that reminded me of the sexy innocence Lana
had when she was very young, before she lost what she calls
"the baby fat" in her face. Nor was I disappointed in Bernadette
as a person. She is not only witty and pleasant, but cooked up
one helluva lasagna. Only after the meal did she reveal that it
was a strictly vegetarian recipe. I was doubly impressed,
though I remain omnivorous.

There were other parties, including one very memorable
one at the home of Natalie Wood and Robert Wagner on
North Canon Drive. I don't recall how the pert Natalie and I
got onto the subject of our respective daughters, but I was
rather shocked when this very homey lady said that she hoped
her two daughters would live with their prospective husbands
before they got married. "It's not that easy to choose the
perfect mate," she said, "and to expect that it would happen
without knowing each other well enough, without living
together for a period of time, just doesn't seem sensible." I
couldn't help thinking that if this were one of the notoriously
good and upstanding mothers talking, imagine what goes on
in the *real* Hollywood Babylon! Not that I was a prude; I
suspected my daughter Maylo *would* one day live with someone. But with girls, I think very many fathers have a difficult

time not thinking of them as perennial babies to be protected and kept locked in a high tower for Prince Charming.

All in all, I enjoyed these parties. What I came to realize after several months, however, was that I really would have enjoyed them more had Lana been with me. Discounting the few fights in which she may have become embroiled when we stirred amongst the public, I sorely missed her running commentaries on her peers. She can be quite amusing when discussing the film industry, and I would have *loved* to have heard Lana's homilies as Valerie Perrine plucked ticks from her German shepherd's penis or a very, *very* short Mel Brooks argued with a very tall scientist that the only value of the Viking Mars Lander was that the lower gravity on the Red Planet would enable humankind to manufacture a light-as-a-feather matzo ball. What irked me more is that, as Cubby Broccoli had hinted, staying out of circulation meant that Lana was also missing the movers and the shakers in Hollywood. At best, Lana was also missing a few good laughs, which she could have used to boost her spirits.

Why Lana's mood was baleful harks back to the inescapable reality of her unemployment. The only career movement was an aborted lurch, the suggestion that Lana tour in John Bowab's production of *A Little Night Music*. The producers flew Lana and me to Phoenix, Arizona, so that we could see John's local version of the musical. Lana enjoyed it a great deal, but she was mortally afraid of having to sing, even though she would be crooning a guaranteed crowd-pleaser, the hit song "Send in the Clowns." I urged her to give it a try, but Lana was adamant in her refusal. When I informed John of her decision, he resolved to try and change her mind on the return flight to Los Angeles. However, he never got the chance. *Pro forma*, Lana and I missed the flight. We caught the next plane out, but because Lana didn't want John making jokes about her lateness, she made up a lie and swore me to secrecy. When we returned to Century City, John phoned. "I saw them put your luggage on board," he cried. "What happened? I've been worried sick!"

"Well," Lana began, "Taylor and I were just about to board the plane when these two dear little nuns came up to the desk. They were desperate to get back to Los Angeles because their mother superior had taken very ill. Since everyone had already gotten on the plane, Taylor and I decided to give our seats to them and catch another flight."

Lana told the story so convincingly that not only did John buy it, I heard him retell it at cocktail parties to illustrate what a wonderful humanitarian Lana is. It was the only worthwhile fallout from our short trip.

With the exception of her brush with cancer, Lana has generally been very fortunate healthwise. She seldom gets anything more serious than a cold, and half the time those are self-inflicted. Whenever she'd tell me I was remembered in her will, I'd laugh and reply earnestly that she would doubtless outlive me. She probably will, too. Unfortunately, luck was about to desert her for the second time in too short a period. We were driving to the dressmaker's salon when Lana began to hiccup. By the time we reached Mary Rose's shop in the Valley, Lana was experiencing sharp pains in her chest. I called Mary Rose to the car, and Lana explained that she wasn't up for the fitting. We left, and glancing to my right, I could see that Lana was in severe pain. I suggested that we go directly to the doctor's office, but all Lana wanted to do was take some Gelusil and climb into bed. I was quiet for a moment while she continued to groan, then I said, "Forget it. You're going to see Dr. Mac."

Lana protested at first, but by the time we reached the Beverly Hills medical building, her skin had a yellow-green tinge to it. I practically carried her to the elevator, and when we reached Dr. Mac's office, his nurse took one look at Lana and hurried her to an examination room. A half hour later, the nurse came out to tell me that Lana would have to be hospitalized at once. Dr. Mac wasn't sure what the problem was, though he suspected a liver ailment.

Though Lana was in considerable pain, we decided against calling an ambulance. The ride is terribly frightening for a patient who's conscious, and as Lana pointed out through gnashed teeth, she wanted to avoid the publicity. So we bundled her into the backseat of the Eldorado, and I drove her as quickly as possible to St. John's Hospital. The staff had been alerted, and Lana was taken directly to intensive care.

Thanks to medication and careful monitoring, Lana's color improved considerably, and when I came to visit, she thanked me for not having allowed her to go home. While I was there, Dr. Mac came to see her, and I left them alone; when he called me back into the room some time later, Lana was in tears. Dr. Mac was gently patting her hand, and softly, as though he were addressing a child, was saying, "There, there, Lana. You know what you have to do." Lana nodded, at which point Dr. Mac turned to me and said ominously, "And I'm putting *you* in charge of making sure that she does it."

I had no idea what he was talking about, and though Lana's best interests were both my job and my pleasure, I could not help thinking, *Christ, what do I have to be responsible for now?* But my iniquitous thoughts passed when the physician explained that Lana's liver was near collapse, her natural constitution crumbling because of her considerable intake of vodka and poor dietary habits. Dr. Mac warned us that, in particular, if she did not restrict her intake of alcohol, Lana would literally finish off her liver and thus herself. His pronouncement sobered Lana—at least, for a while. Upon leaving the hospital four days later, she became a teetotaler until the flush of health returned. For a short time thereafter, she acceded to my insisting that she remain on the wagon, but we both knew that my goal-line stand was doomed. Lana chose to view moderation as no less healthful than abstinence—possibly more so, since cold turkey had made her edgy and unusually short-tempered. Thus, after a few weeks of nothing but plain juice, Lana returned to a limited consumption of alcohol. That meant she diluted her vodka with Ocean Spray Cranberry Juice, the mixture fast becoming severely imbalanced on the side of the vodka. Eventually, she shifted to vodka and papaya juice as a public relations ploy, one that I had inspired: in trying to soften Lana's image as a boozer, I lied to a reporter and said that she was a devotee of health food beverages, something that helped to keep her figure trim. Nutrition proved to be a topical subject, and my remarks earned Lana a good deal of (for once!) favorable press. I realized that by actually switching to papaya she would be able to expound upon her masquerade as a kissin' cousin to Adelle Davis—though in truth, each jar of papaya was filled with equal portions of vodka. If anyone ever wanted to sample the stuff, Lana would protest, "Oh, you wouldn't like it. I've added things like brewer's yeast, liver powder, and lecithin." Unless I tutored her before each interview, she could never remember the *names* of the additives, much less what they were exactly. The irony, of course, is that Lana wouldn't go near "foul-tasting" health foods to save her life, which was in this case more a fact than a figure of speech. She prefers starvation as a method of losing weight, and when informed during a bleach that her hair was falling out due to poor nutrition, she still refused to improve her eating habits.

Through luck and her own awesome metabolic resilience, Lana not only recovered from her liver problems but undertook a summer tour of *Bell, Book and Candle*. We were both still beating back the lingering shadows of her illness. It was a problem that transcended the comparatively trivial problems of the play and a bond that forced us to stay together, eat together, be in close physical proximity—I to keep her in line, she to lean on me when she became troubled by this tangible evidence of her vulnerability. Death frightened her enormously; not that she's alone in her fear, but it didn't seem so far on the horizon as it had before. Though Lana would occasionally channel small bursts of anger at other members of the cast and crew, I was able to defuse these efficiently. In every way, physically and emotionally, this was the most delightful and loving period Lana and I ever spent together; the calm before the storm, as it were.

As a result of the uncustomary lack of tension, the summer tour of *Bell, Book and Candle* was also filled with more levity than usual. Lana and I were constantly slinging bad puns back and forth, and as if by kismet we were involved in more outrageous incidents than in previous journeys. The most outstanding of these happened while we were in transit from the home rented for us in Cape Cod to our next stop, which was Corning, New York. We were at Logan Airport in Boston, Lana seated in a wheelchair, her carry-on luggage stacked on her lap. Just as we were cleared through security and heading toward the boarding area, I saw a photographer jump from behind a column and swing his telephoto lens in our direction. I recognized him as a fellow who had been dogging us all over Massachusetts trying to get a good shot of Lana. Needless to say, the last thing I wanted was someone publishing a picture of Lana in a wheelchair with some absurd caption about her being too infirm to walk. I knew I had two choices: one was to hurl myself at the shutterbug who, mercifully, was smaller than I; the other was to spin the wheelchair round and dash for the gate. Deciding that retreat was the saner course, I did a wheelie and sped down the corridor. Unfortunately, I hadn't had time to warn Lana, who had been sitting serenely behind the pile of luggage when I apparently went crazy, pitching the chair first to the left, then rolling it to the right as I kept looking over my shoulder. She screamed and demanded to know what the hell I was doing, but I had only enough breath to bark, "Just sit still and hold on," as the photographer orbited in eccentric circles to get his damned picture while I sought to avoid him and at the same time not run over innocent bystanders.

Cast member Louise Kirtland happened to be with us, and within moments of my frenzied flight, she understood exactly what was going on. Running ahead to the airline counter, she breathlessly demanded a hiding place for us until take-off while I remained in the middle of the airport, spinning Lana in circles as she loudly voiced her objections. At last I saw Louise gesture wildly toward the employees' lounge, which the airline had opened for us. Steadying the wheelchair, I made a beeline for the sanctuary with the photographer in hot pursuit. I beat him to the door by seconds, and with flashcubes bursting at our back, we were locked inside. Lana was ripping mad, and as I was too busy catching my breath, Louise offered the explanation on my behalf. Lana quickly forgave me for making her seasick, while the airline employees looked at the three of us rather oddly. As a postscript, the photographer *did* manage to get a picture of us as we both *walked* toward the plane, and the shot appeared on the inside page of a story in the *National Enquirer* under the banner headline, "Lana Turner Romance: She Captures the Heart of a Man 20 Years Younger." The quotes in the article itself were really rib-ticklers, since Lana nor I had ever uttered a word of it. Typical was, "I love her—she's a joy to be with," which I was supposed to have said. As it turns out the first half of the line *was* true, and for the *National Enquirer* a fifty percent record for accuracy isn't bad.

We wound up the tour just before Labor Day, and Lana took the months of September, October, and November to recuperate from exhaustion. Lana got more of a rest than she bargained for when she stepped onto her balcony and a particularly strong wind literally blew her off her feet. She came crashing down on her tailbone and injured her back, which left her bedridden and in awful pain for days. She was subsequently forced to visit a chiropractor three times a week for several months.

Shortly after her accident, Lana received an invitation from the tenacious Debbie Reynolds to attend the Thalians' Ball at the Century Plaza Hotel. The gathering was to honor Rita Hayworth, and while Lana avoids sharing the spotlight with anyone, she decided to make an exception. In a scenario that only her complex mind can have conceived, she feared that her absence might be mistaken as jealousy or resentment toward her onetime rival. That was important to her as, with rare exceptions—such as Dante or, later, myself—Lana does not hold grudges. Whether that's because she wants to like people or to have them like her is difficult to say.

Perhaps because they *were* similar in so many ways, Lana honestly never feared or disliked the former Margarita Cansino, ex-dancer and the sex goddess of Columbia Pictures. Their marriages and their divorces roused the same public fascination, and though Lana scored in terms of numbers, Rita had a classier stable with the likes of Orson Welles, Prince Aly Khan, and actor-singer Dick Haymes. The competition did not emerge fully blown: that is, neither actress was initially touted as one studio's version of the other. Rita had been appearing in motion pictures for two years longer than Lana, though she didn't become a star until 1941, by which time Lana had emerged as the glamour girl to beat. Rita came closer than anyone, and in fact the lead changed hands more than once. I feel that it was fate more than any other factor that dictated which lady was in the fore. In their first films, for example, both actresses did nothing more than move sensuously across the screen, Lana in *They Won't Forget* and Rita as a tormented soul in *Dante's Inferno*. Lana got the greater attention strictly for her sweater and sashay; had the roles been reversed, the women may well have exchanged careers. When there was parity in terms of star magnitude, that's when the horse race started. Whether by coincidence or studio hijinks, the two were at times virtual *doppelgängers*. The two actresses earned their first serious notices within two years of one another, Lana in 1946 for *The Postman Always Rings Twice* and Rita in 1948 for *The Lady from Shanghai;* each flopped in concurrent Biblical epics, Rita as *Salome* and Lana in *The Prodigal*. Each revitalized her sagging career with a literate, glossy soap opera, Lana in *Peyton Place* and Rita in *Separate Tables* one year later; each tried the same ploy with a British horror film in the early 1970s, though Rita wisely walked off *her* Freddie Francis production, *Tales that Witness Madness*, after a few days.

Regardless of Lana's reasons for attending, she was going to go first class. Since there was no time to have a gown made for the event, nor was Lana up to standing for a lengthy fitting because of her injury, we went through the endless collection that hung in a closet in my office. Lana selected a fabulous white evening gown made years before by Jean Louis, one which clung to her as though it were sprayed on.

The dinner was scheduled for 7:45 P.M., but we didn't arrive at the hotel until nine o'clock, just in time for the entertainment portion of the program. The photographers went wild when they saw Lana, and she paused in the lobby to pose for them. Moments later, an usherette came from the ballroom to show us to our table. As we entered Lana stopped to say hello to her good friend June Allyson, then she sidled to the next table to greet Rita. Rita was there with Princess Yasmin, her daughter by Aly Kahn and a beautiful young woman at that. I wish I could be as complimentary about her mother. I had never met Rita before, but in all candor the years had not treated her as kindly as they had Lana. Though no one could take away the character inherent in her magnificent bone structure, she looked puffy; her once sinfully tempting smile was lackluster, her famous red hair was a mousey blond. At fifty-nine, she seemed more matronly than classy; the difficult times to which she has since succumbed reinforce the impression I had that we were witnessing the frail serenity before the fall. I wished that I had never met her, preferring to recall the wonderful way she looked in *Gilda, Blood and Sand* with Tyrone Power, and *Miss Sadie Thompson*.

We were seated at the next table over from Rita, and it was painful to overhear people around us comparing the two former sex goddesses. The consensus, unfortunately, was that there could *be* no comparison. I wondered, fleetingly, if Lana could have *known* that would be the case and had elected to attend for that reason—but I dismissed the thought as unworthy of her. I felt bad for Rita but at the same time proud of Lana. It was the same kind of pride I had enjoyed the night Bette Davis went on about the obligations a star has to the public. Lana *could* have let herself go to ruin, and everyone would have understood. But she hadn't, she had pride and she had a sense of courtliness. Maintaining these were often hell for us both, but at moments like these the anguish seemed worth it.

Since I couldn't bring myself to look at Rita, yet couldn't really avoid her, I was pleased to notice that none other than Phyllis Diller was directly to my left. I greeted her like an old chum, only to find that she didn't remember who the hell I was. So much for friends in high places. I preserved my shattered self-respect by reminding myself that entertainers' lives move so fast it's impossible for them to remember all the people they meet. I consoled myself by warming up to actress Anne Jeffreys, who was sitting across from me and looking just as beautiful and chic as she had on the "Topper" television show.

Lana and I somehow managed to sit through the evening's "festivities." In a film "tribute" to Rita, someone had dug up vintage film clips of the walk-on parts she'd had in terrible films like *Blondie*. Not one clip was screened from any of her more noteworthy pictures. But the worst was still to come, as the lights came back on and a troupe of male dancers ran down the aisle to escort—*drag* is a more accurate description—the dazed Rita onto the stage. The applause was tepid, and I couldn't help recalling the cheering for Lana at Town Hall, when John Springer couldn't turn the cheering off, when Lana wore with such elegance the age that had so ravaged her colleague. After Rita's squires had departed— how *awkward* she was, even allowing for age, this woman who had been so graceful and so light on her feet as the Terpsichore, the Greek goddess of dance in *Down to Earth*— Debbie and Ruta Lee presented her with an award. Rita accepted the honor simply by waving to the audience and returning to her seat. Debbie stood uncomfortably alone at the microphone for several seconds before reminding everyone how shy the actress was, which was why there would be no acceptance speech. I later learned that, in her private little vacuum, Rita had simply forgotten to deliver one.

There was a party afterward, but Lana was too dispirited to attend. I couldn't blame her, and we drove to the Ivory Tower in silence. After I helped her from her gown, we spent the rest of the evening discussing the event. Lana was not so heartless as to come right out and state that Rita should have taken better care of herself, although I knew she was thinking that. Rather, she seemed annoyed with Debbie for having subjected the woman to such a public flogging. I pointed out that Rita had seemed oblivious to the goings-on, which was a blessing, but that didn't assuage the discomfort we felt for her. As usual, Lana was able to cap the conversation with a bitter but wry observation: "If the Thalians or anyone else ever want to make *me* the guest of honor at an event like this," she said, "and if I am stupid enough to accept—*shoot* me."

Toward the end of December we went to the Brown Derby for yet another meeting concerning yet another project that would die aborning. We selected the Brown Derby because of its amber lighting, which was quite flattering to Lana, a valuable asset when discussing a new film. The meeting was about a movie to be made for television based on the life of tennis great Maureen Connolly. The script for *Little Mo* was ambitious and moving, and Lana was anxious to play Mo's mother. We met with the producer, Jack Webb, the onetime Detective Friday of "Dragnet." Jack was a very quiet, very intelligent man, who was obviously impressed with Lana. He agreed that while the role would be a challenge for her, beyond any role in her repertoire, he thought she could rise to the occasion. But there was one stipulation. In order to provide her daughter with tennis lessons, Mrs. Connolly had lived on the verge of poverty all of her life. Accordingly, the character *must* wear off-the-rack clothing from the studio wardrobe department. To say that that did not appeal to Lana is an understatement. Not that she wouldn't be compensated for her inconvenience: playing Jessmyn Connolly in the three-hour film would net Lana $50,000, including $2,500 prepayment for the first rerun in the United States and the distinction of having her name above the title. Lana reluctantly agreed, and the next day she and I went to the old Samuel Goldwyn Studios to see what the wardrobe mistress had gathered together. It took several hours to go through the selection and for the necessary alterations to be marked. Lana clearly was uncomfortable with clothes that had been worn by God-only-knew-who previously, even though everything had been cleaned. As perverse as it sounds, I admired Lana's professionalism in putting up with this inconvenience.

One hurdle overcome, the second we faced was transforming Lana's beautiful blond tresses to the dark brown required by the part. Her hairdresser experimented with several different dyes over a week's time. The first made Lana's hair too green, the second too red. The third, as they say in the saga of Goldilocks, was just right. Lana was generally miserable through it all, and the lonely Christmas away from mother and daughter both did not help to cheer her.

Because of her involvement with *Little Mo*, Lana was obliged to postpone a Dallas run of *Bell, Book and Candle* until April. She was unhappy having to disappoint Harold Kennedy that way, but the television movie had come to mean a lot to her. Harold could not disagree that that was the more important project, and he actually seemed pleased that Lana would finally have a meaty film role to play. Rehearsals and fittings continued through the early part of 1978, Lana having to cut back on readings with the other actors when she came down with the flu. However, she pressed on with the fittings, holding them in her living room to help expedite the project.

When shooting was only a few days off, Dr. Mac reluctantly informed Lana that in his estimation the producers should pencil in shots that did not feature her for the first day. He felt it would give her that much more time to regain her full strength, something that would only benefit the rather cumbersome shooting schedule in the long run. Lana passed his suggestion on to the producers, and they seemed amenable. Then, much to our dismay, one of Jack Webb's people called back to say that if Lana could not begin on time, she would be replaced. Lana was stunned, but her hurt shaded to indignation as she paced about the Ivory Tower announcing, "I'm *not* going to endanger my health just because of their damned schedule! They can *wait* one more day." That was absolutely true; movies are shot a piece at a time, and the producers could just as easily have filmed actors reacting to

Lana's dialogue, saving her scenes for the following day. I recommended to Lana that a call from Dr. Mac might ameliorate the situation, and she agreed. Well, the call certainly *did* accomplish something. Within hours, I received a call from Webb's office informing me that Lana had been replaced by Anne Baxter. It seems the producers had had Miss Baxter warming up in the wings all along; they were never really convinced that Lana would put up with the very unglamorous requirements of the part. Too, Miss Baxter came cheaper for what was essentially a supporting role and, best of all, just "happened" to be the same dress size as Lana. The substitution was made without the producers or the cast missing a step.

The replacement came as a severe blow to Lana's flagging professional ego. Still, the following day she bravely dictated a telegram to Anne Baxter, wishing her well with the project. As I've said, Lana is not one to hold a grudge; any telegram *I'd* have sent would have contained directions to the nearest cliff. Her adrenaline drained, Lana took to bed for several days of rest and depression.

Chapter Twelve

When Lana finally stirred, I noticed her loitering before every mirror she happened to pass, gazing at her dark brown hair and feeling bad over the opportunity she had lost. I felt abjectly sorry for her and sick over the fact that the best I could do was to phone her hairdresser to hurry over and turn Lana back into a blond. It proved to be just the right medicine, for as the brown was rinsed away, with it went Lana's depression. *Little Mo* was behind her; though less exciting, ahead lay *Bell, Book and Candle* in Dallas.

The month before the play opened passed slowly, uneventfully. Once we walked out the door for the airport, however, things changed swiftly. Since we were late reaching the airport, our first-class seats had been sold. We were forced to ride in the rear of the plane, though Lana was every inch the hooded Nagaina as she wound toward these endmost seats hissing, "*Sooooo*, now I have to travel steerage!"

Our seats were right in front of the lavatories, and once we were airborne, there was a never-dwindling line of passengers who had to go to the bathroom. Each member of the queue stared openly at Lana, who was swathed in mink and wearing her customary shower of gold and bracelets. She ignored everyone, busying herself by relieving the nearby rolling server of its supply of alcoholic beverages. Whenever no one was looking, a diamond-encrusted hand would dart out, grab as many miniature bottles as it could, then stuff them into the pockets of her mink coat. Soon, my own jacket pockets, attaché case, and even my *socks* were similarly bulging. It was like a fraternity prank, and the two of us sat there giggling like kids. We never enjoyed a flight quite so much as that one, for as I've always said Lana is at her best when playing the little girl. Too bad it didn't happen more often!

During our four weeks in Dallas, Lana and I became very friendly with Kennedy's assistant director Ron Nash, a bright and eager young man. One night, Lana confided to him over dinner something she and I had already discussed at length, that she was growing tired of *Bell, Book and Candle* and wanted a fresh vehicle. Not one to shy from a gift horse, the ambitious Ron announced that he would *find* her a play, the *ideal* play, provided that he be allowed to direct it himself. I could see Lana squirm slightly. As much as she desired a new plateau, she had come to love Harold Kennedy as a person, a director, a fellow actor, and a stage mentor. To snub him like this and, worse, to employ the services of a man he had helped to train—it was a sticky situation at best, especially because Lana knew that Harold would not hold her back. However, having just been betrayed herself, she was particularly sensitive about stabbing other people in the back. Ron and I had to explain that there is a difference between firing someone and simply working with someone else on your next project. This matter of putting deals before friendship is one aspect of show business that still makes many people uneasy. Some three years later, when business brought me to the headquarters of Lucasfilms in North Hollywood, I bumped into actor Harrison Ford, who had just scored a monster-sized hit in *Raiders of the Lost Ark*. We ended up having coffee in the cavernous egg factory that George Lucas had converted into a lovely office building across from Universal Studios—ironically, one of the studios that had turned down Lucas's *Star Wars*. I found Harrison one of the most modest people I had ever met in the entertainment industry. He is six-foot-two but looks shorter simply because he hasn't got an ego the size of the forecourt at Mann's Chinese. I was surprised to learn that after playing the lead in George Lucas's *Star Wars* and *The Empire Strikes Back*—respectively the first and second most popular films of all time—he was *not* the first choice for Lucas's *Raiders of the Lost Ark*. He got the part only after actor Tom Selleck had to turn it down, since he was already committed to the television series "Magnum, P.I." I asked Harrison how he could not help being bitter about that, and he told me he's come to expect all of his rewards right there on the film set, anticipating nothing more than that moment of professional gratification. It struck me as a sound philosophy.

Incidentally, I myself learned the hard way how friendship and business are often incompatible. I had written a film project for Adam West, the actor who played television's "Batman." A producer wanted very much to make the picture but insisted on using another performer in the lead role. He wanted someone who was a "movie actor" not a "television actor." I've never subscribed to that distinction, but that's beside the point: I had to choose between backing Adam, a friend of many years, or selling him down the sewer. I wanted the money, and I wanted the movie, but I had to back Adam. One thing I learned when Lana ultimately cashed *me* in is to treasure and defend my true friendships above all.

Getting back to Lana and Ron, it would be sometime before the budding director presented Lana with an ideal vehicle. In the meantime, I happened across a new play entitled *Divorce Me, Darling,* a lightweight by Broadway standards but perfect for the smaller theaters that were clamoring for Lana to appear. I kept the play under my hat during the Dallas run, since Lana doesn't like to be distracted by extraneous concerns while she's working. The Dallas stay was followed by one in Hartford, Connecticut, after which we returned to Los Angeles. Lana did not want to go right into another play, so I put *Divorce Me, Darling* on the shelf. But there was another project to consider, an offer from ex-actor Marty Ingels—the husband of singer-actress Shirley Jones— to star Lana in some sort of very lucrative endorsement. Marty runs Ingels, Incorporated, an enormously successful agency that places celebrities in various promotions and television commercials; his own "Eliminate bullshit from your campaign" magazine ads are still much talked about in Hollywood. Lana had not done any kind of advertisements for decades, not since MGM forced her to sponsor the likes of Lux Toilet Soap. *(Is this the world's most beautiful complexion? "Gracious no!" says this lovely star modestly. "I've found this gentle Lux Soap care really makes skin lovelier.")* Nor would she endorse anything bourgeois like roach motels, floor waxes, or toilet bowl fresheners. I was encouraged, therefore, when I spoke with Marty on the phone. He was one hundred percent in accord with our thinking and repeated several times, "Do you mean to tell me that Lana Turner will consider doing a *commercial?*"

Marty and I had a very long conversation, during which I listened to him extol Lana, calling her the last glamorous star in Hollywood, saying that Raquel Welch and her ilk could never be what Lana was. We finally got around to discussing the high-caliber stars he had placed in blue-chip promotions, and agreeing that Marty's firm would be ideal to represent Lana, he and I decided to get together for a meeting the following day.

Lana had been asleep while these preliminary negotiations were going on, and bubbling with glee, I went to wake her in the usual fashion. I squeezed her feet, attending to each toe individually, then worked my way up each leg. Usually I'd have kept on kneading until she gasped with pleasure, but I couldn't contain my enthusiasm. Drawing open the blackout curtain, I sat on the edge of the bed and informed her of my talk with Ingels. Lana was delighted, saying, "Who the hell needs an agent when I have you around?" Naturally, I was pleased by such uncustomary flattery.

The following day I did not, unfortunately, meet with Marty. He had been called to a taping, so I sat down with a young lady who seemed no less enthusiastic than he about finding a proper enterprise for Lana. Lana had asked me specifically to request something dignified and in keeping with her image. I fully expected the account executive's enthusiastic nod accompanied by, "I hope she won't mind if we look into a beauty product or diet program account." I concurred absolutely and left the meeting feeling that we would see some action very soon.

When I told Lana about our discussion, she was so happy that she immediately called Jess Morgan and told him what had transpired. Jolly Jess was probably more pleased than either of us, thrilled with the prospect of having big bucks flowing into Lana's coffers. He even tendered a rare commendation for the way I had managed the affair. Now I *knew* I was doing something right.

It's amazing how not only the best-laid plans of mice, men, and personal managers often go astray, but how damn *fast* it sometimes happens. Within a matter of days, we received a call from Marty's office to inquire if Lana would make an all-expenses-paid appearance at the opening of a

country club in Phoenix. Lana refused, frankly surprised by
the lack of prestige attached to this first offer. I tried very
politely to impress upon the Ingels representative that we
were interested in *commercials*, the kinds with residual
payments—not *travel*. The agent said of course, no problem,
she understood and would get back to us real soon. Quiet
weeks passed before we received another request for a personal appearance and then another, both of which were firmly
refused. I repeated with impatience our original concept and
had it explained to me that these were just "let's-get-to-know-
each-other" assignments, not an end-all. I replied that if
people didn't know Lana by now, a trip to some stupid golf
course wasn't going to help. I told the girl as politely as
possible that, further, her spiel was beginning to sound more
and more like the subject of Ingels' no-bullshit credo. She
grew a little formal with me and promised to see what she
could do. Through all of this never once did Marty himself
phone. As often happens with talent agencies, the clients are
wooed and snared by the chief operating officer and then
shuttled down to an underling who doesn't have quite the
same grasp of what is desired. Not surprisingly, the calls
became increasingly sparse until, within a matter of weeks,
the phone stopped ringing altogether. No one on Lana's side
of the undertaking ever said an unkind word about the way
I'd handled the whole affair. Still, it was a deep disappointment to me.

Seeking distraction from the sputtering crash of my
project, I upped my intake of parties, the most memorable of
which was a dinner party hosted by a friend of mine in the
Hollywood Hills. While I was there, I met two stars who
impressed me tremendously: Rock Hudson and George Maharis.
A year later Rock and I would meet again in Chicago and I
would have the opportunity to get to know him better, but it
was George who impressed me the more that night. He had
not worked a great deal since a severe case of hepatitis forced
him to leave the popular television series "Route 66" in 1963.
There was a short-lived detective series called "The Most
Deadly Game" in 1970 and a supporting role in "Rich Man,
Poor Man" in 1977. George is a better actor than his record
indicates, but he just doesn't seem *anxious* to work all that
much. I found him to be quite introverted at first, merely
terse later on; however, I learned a lot about him just by

looking into his eyes. There was a peacefulness to them, a quality unusual in Hollywood. The closest most people come is a drug-induced glaze. I suspected, and later learned for a fact, that George had discovered contentment with life's simple pleasures, and he simply did not require an abundance of work. Somewhere along the line most of us lose that capacity, thanks to the pressures of ambition or the need to compete.

In the waning days of 1978, Lana received a film script for a movie entitled *Witches Brew*. It played like *Star Wars Meets The Exorcist;* the story was about a union of arcane, occult incantations with computer technology, a marriage to provide a sorceress with awesome power. The movie would be filmed in and around Los Angeles by producer Jack Bean, the husband of singer-dancer Mitzi Gaynor. Lana respected Jack's good reputation, and if the film sounded a bit fruity, she liked the idea of playing the wealthy head of a witches' coven. What was even more appealing was the chance to create *two* roles. In the script, the witch utilized the ancient power to transfer her spirit into the body of a younger woman, simultaneously drawing the woman's soul into her own terminally ill body. Lana would get to play the witch in the bulk of the film, and the trapped young woman in the ending. And there was a clever twist that Lana and I really fancied; before the transfer, Lana's character revises her will to leave her money to the younger woman she will soon become.

Despite the film's modest budget, Jack had managed to round up some top-notch stars. Actress Teri Garr of *Young Frankenstein* and *Close Encounters of the Third Kind* was to play the young woman, with Richard Benjamin on hand as an involved third party. Lana approved of the cast and signed to do the film for $25,000 up front. Also in Lana's contract was the provision that Mary Rose be placed on the payroll to create her wardrobe. The designer came up with some stunning gowns that, as ever, became part of Lana's personal wardrobe; Lana reciprocated by wearing without charge her own forty-thousand-dollar royal crown sable coat as well as some of her own jewelry, adding about a million dollars to the look of the finished picture. One other stipulation that Lana had insisted upon in *all* her films was that no close-ups be shot after six in the evening. Her left eye tended to get puffy as she became fatigued as the day wore on. The puff was a lifelong obsession *not* because it was eminently visible but because it was a flaw about which she could do nothing. To have removed it surgically could possibly have left Lana with her lower lid paralyzed. As with anything Lana could not have, she dwelt upon it compulsively and "beat" it by writing it out of existence in her contract. When I dared suggest early in our relationship that she simply not drink while filming, Lana looked at me condescendingly and said, "Taylor, dear, anyone who can survive some of these directors and *not* drink is either a saint or a fool. I am neither." As it turned out, even a steady flow of vodka, provided intravenously, would have been barely sufficient to keep any actor contented on the set of this film. Even a supernatural agency would have been hard pressed to make our director a palatable figure. That's a shame, because we really *did* have a good script and a great cast. Richard proved to be a surprisingly serious, very fine and cooperative actor, and he and Lana worked very well together. As for Teri, I think that she and Lana could have become closer friends if shooting hadn't been limited to just a few weeks. But the director—

He was on an ego trip, working the actors as if this were *Hamlet*, throwing fits and being difficult when he didn't get what he wanted. This wouldn't have been so bad if he'd had an iota of talent. In actuality, he didn't know much about directing and had evidently been hired because he came cheap. More than once Jack Bean had to take him aside and lecture him on his manners and the inconsistent timbre of the performances that were emerging under his vacillating hand. Thankfully, the worst blowup of all came on the final day of shooting. The temperature was one hundred five degrees, and Lana had to play a scene with Teri in the backseat of a Mercedes stretch limousine. The camera operator was positioned in the front seat, beside the driver; on the rear floor of the limousine lay the sound technician with all of his equipment. So that the sounds of traffic would not drown out the dialogue, the windows were all shut; nor could the air conditioner be used for the same reason. As a result, it was well over one hundred twenty degrees in the car, and, to top things off, the sequence called for Lana to wear her fur coat.

Since there was no room in the car for the director, he

instructed his actresses how to play the scene and then settled himself in the shade of a tree. He sent the car around the block, and when it returned, he suggested a second way to handle the exchange. Then a third. Between each take Teri had to come out for air, while Lana had her makeup blotted of perspiration. During one such break I heard her grumble, "Ladies are supposed to *glow,* this is sweat!"

When the car pulled up for the third time and the director strolled over to prepare for a fourth take, Lana stepped up to him and complained, "You've more footage than you *need* for that scene. No *way* am I getting back into that limousine."

Teri concurred and walked off, while the director looked from one to the other of the actresses and screamed, "Oh, *yes,* you are!"

Lana smiled sweetly. "No," she said firmly, "that's enough." When Lana puts her foot down, it *stays* down; with her hairdresser and me in tow, she strode confidently toward her air-conditioned trailer. Filming on *Witches Brew* was most definitely finished.

It's amazing to me how critical it is for directors and co-stars to be compatible in making a motion picture. The results are seldom good if a movie is shot under the strain of an adversary relationship, since the creative process is such a collaborative one. The performers and directors must be open, compassionate, sensitive, emotive, and undiverted from the needs of the film. When there are jealousies, petty or large, the finished product cannot help being undermined. A perfect example was the trouble on *Witches Brew,* though it was not the first time Lana had had difficulty with a director. One of the most memorable conflicts, she once told me, occurred when Lana played a Nazi spy opposite John Wayne in *The Sea Chase* in 1955. The director was John Farrow, father of Mia. Lana had just finished *The Prodigal* and was ordered by Farrow to leave at once for Hawaii, where the exterior scenes were going to be shot. Upon arrival, however, Lana discovered that Farrow had wanted her there not for filming but to log some time with her in bed. She let him know up front and without mincing words that she was not interested, and as a result, he was unpleasant and often downright cruel to her throughout filming. Particularly annoying was the way Farrow made Lana come to the ship on which they were filming, whether she was in a scene or not, leaving her to broil in the hot Hawaiian sun. The picture was, not surprisingly, uninspired and not particularly well acted.

One of the few joys of making *Witches Brew* was the chance to spend some time with Richard Benjamin's wife, actress Paula Prentiss. She had worked with Lana on *Bachelor in Paradise* and made a special trip to the set just to say hello. Paula is a tall, friendly, sultry woman, whose keen sense of humor raised spirits when our mad director happened to have them quite down. I noticed that when she wasn't on the set, Richard would telephone her at every opportunity, inquiring about the doings of their son, four-year-old Ross, and telling her about the latest showdown with the director. I did not wonder that the couple has one of the most enduring marriages in Hollywood.

Witches Brew has never been released, due to legal battles that erupted immediately after the film's completion between Jack Bean and his accursed director. Luckily, there was no time for Lana to ponder this cinematic fiasco, since she went directly from *Witches Brew* into a new play. Entrepreneur Tony De Santis wanted her to appear in a play of our choice at one of a trio of theaters he owned in Chicago. Lana said she was interested—because she could select the play—and Tony turned us over to Jim Pappas, the managing director of the Drury Lane McCormick Theater. I immediately suggested *Divorce Me, Darling* and sent Jim a copy. He called the day it arrived to say that it was a *perfect* show for their audience. He explained that theatergoers in the Midwest do not go in for heavy drama. They want to see a star and at the same time be entertained by something very light. Certainly our experience with *The Pleasure of His Company* corroborated Jim's standards.

The moment the rights to the play had been obtained, and the deal consummated, Lana and I sat down and put *Divorce Me, Darling* on tape. As we were due to leave for Chicago in less than three weeks, Lana simultaneously went into a whirlwind of costume fittings with Mary Rose. Somehow the wardrobe was completed and the play learned when we left for the Windy City. Lana even had time amidst this tempest of activity to wreak hell against Dreyer's Ice Cream for *daring* to use her name in an ad. "Like Lana at Schwab's" was the slogan they had used, intending to summon up the old ice-cream parlor image. What it summoned up was outrage from Lana that someone was making money from her name and fame. Marshaling her legal retinue, Lana pounced. She came away with a written apology and an invitation to visit their factory.

Tony De Santis has a reputation for spoiling stars with his generosity, a reputation he well deserves. We were met at O'Hare International Airport by Tony's private limousine, and its telephone immediately rang so that our host could welcome Lana to Chicago. We were chauffeured to the very spacious and luxurious two-bedroom guest condominium that Tony maintains on the forty-fifth floor of the Lakepoint Towers— at seventy stories tall, the largest such building in the world. The rooms offered a spectacular view of Lake Michigan and the Chicago skyline. Lakepoint Tower was to be our home for several months, as Lana spent the remainder of the year doing sellout business in *Divorce Me, Darling*. Nor did she waste any time personalizing her new abode. She had a dead bolt installed on the door of the master bedroom the day after we arrived. Lana wanted to know that her jewels and furs were safe while we were at the theater. The lock was in violation of the building's fire code, but as was the case with *everything* during our stay in Chicago, Lana just didn't care.

True to form, after we arrived Lana decided she wouldn't have anything to do with any hairdresser but her own. There were certainly qualified beauticians in Chicago, and Jim Pappas knew several who had pleased the likes of Claudette Colbert and Ginger Rogers. Lana, however, didn't care for any of his people. She insisted on flying her personal hairdresser to Chicago every fourteen days for a bleach and wash, which meant putting him up for the night as well. She paid for these expenses. Flushed with star treatment and what was to prove yet another triumph on the stage, Lana was beginning to regress again to her glory days at MGM. As it turned out, with the exception of our accommodations, very little in Chicago was good enough for Miss Lana Turner. In the nine years we had been together, I had seen nothing to match this behavior. Lana was perpetually finding fault with the lighting or with the way the other actors hit their marks, and she even admonished the propmaster for not putting enough water in an ashtray, thus leaving one of her cigarettes to smoke onstage for a few minutes. Furthermore, each day Lana ordered me to make certain that distilled water was being used in the fake cocktails she drank onstage. Distilled water is the only kind Lana will drink, convinced that it will prevent calcium buildup in her joints and by its lack of minerals contribute to the smoothness of her complexion. I reminded her after several weeks that the propman knew what he was doing; she became irritated and told me to continue checking each performance all the same. Thank God virtually every show was a sellout, since Tony didn't seem the type of theater owner to have tolerated very many "sick" calls because of small audiences.

That Lana finally allowed her short temper to touch me was the harbinger of what I'll oversimplify by calling a change in our relationship. I let the matter of the distilled water slide, allowing for Lana's eccentricity. But something like it was always coming up. A few nights later, Jim Pappas was using me as the brunt of "kept man" jokes. In the past, Lana would have told him to go suck pond water; instead, she laughed along with everyone else. When I mentioned this to her in private, she said that I was just being overly sensitive. No doubt I was. But her own *in*sensitivity marked the beginning of a new set of signals from Lana. She began treating me like a serf, with the aloof discourtesy of the snob I'd expected but did not find when I went to work for her. Lana's manner with me became imperious and affected, her voice too frequently harsh or impersonal, her criticisms quick and unforgiving. She rarely looked me in the eyes when we spoke. I was hurt, I was upset, and I was angry. In the end, I suffered in silence because I convinced myself that Lana was only human, that she had earned the right to strut a bit. She'd been down for so many years that to be at the top of *anything*, even a regional theater, was a heady, inflating, disorienting experience. I told myself that all of this would pass. It was the first and by far the smallest of the miscalculations I would make in what turned out to be my tumultuous, damn-near-fatal last year with Lana Turner.

Chapter Thirteen

Despite the backstage shenanigans, *Divorce Me, Darling*
did such hefty business that Tony De Santis wanted Lana
back in Chicago as soon as possible. Coincidentally, while
she'd been doing that play, Ron Nash had been working in
New York and managed to find that perfect play he had
promised to deliver. The play was *Murder Among Friends*,
and it had actually been on Broadway for a disastrous run of
twenty-three performances. Upon reading the play, both
Lana and I were so impressed that we had to call Ron to ask
just *why* the play had failed. He explained that star Janet
Leigh had just not been a strong enough actress for the part
of the fifteenth-richest woman in the world, nor was she a big
enough name to pull jaded New Yorkers into the theater. Her
co-star, the late Jack Cassidy, though an inordinately gifted
singer-actor, had likewise been little help in terms of marquee value.

Murder Among Friends was the finest and certainly the
most tailor-made play with which we were to be involved. In
addition to being rich, Lana's character, Angie Schweppes, is
unhappily married, in this case to a pompous Broadway actor,
whose career is on the decline. Unknown to her husband,
Angie has been plotting with his agent Ted, her lover, to kill
him; unknown to Angie, Ted and her husband are themselves
lovers and actually conspiring to murder *her* for her money.
The entire play takes place over a single night, New Year's
Eve, and to quote one reviewer, "has so many plot twists it
makes *Death Trap* look like a Sunday-school pageant."

Tony De Santis booked *Murder Among Friends* to play
another of his Drury Lane Theaters and, though it took quite

a bit of conniving, Lana was also able to have Ron Nash hired as director instead of one of Tony's local talents. It was another example of the way he bent over backward for his stars—although shortly after opening night, Tony became as disenchanted with Lana as I had.

Though I thought it impossible, Lana was even more overbearing than she had been during *Divorce Me, Darling*. To begin with, she was constantly taking my diet pills, which made her more irritable than usual. Moreover, her manner far exceeded the flush of box-office victory. The months of her run were the *only* real power she'd have for perhaps a year; it was as though she were preparing for the drought by drinking deep at the expense of everyone else. She complained about people individually, as before, and she found the ideal way to badger and subjugate the company as well as the audience in one mighty blow: through late curtains. There is a rule of thumb in the theater that for every minute past curtain time you keep an audience waiting, it will take you that long to win them back once the play has begun. If that's true, winning the audience *should* have been a lost cause. It was not unusual for a curtain to be more than a half-hour late. Many times I stood silently in the dressing room as I listened to the angry chatter and frequent foot stomping of a restless audience while Lana applied yet another coat of lipstick. She never seemed to care that these people had planned an evening around the play. In her mind they were subjects of the queen, baby-sitters and dinner reservations be damned. Miraculously, through the synergy of star quality and a good performance, Lana managed to recapture her audience and always left them screaming for more. That only made things worse, of course, since she saw that she could get away with anything. She began to feel invincible. The only saving grace is that these accolades left Lana in high spirits and caused her to be comparatively loving for the rest of the evening. She was still haughty, but the vindictive edge was blunted by the applause. Like an ass, I put up with those mood shifts—for then. More critical was that Tony also forgave her since she was making him bundles of money—for then.

As Lana felt more and more at home in the role of Angie, Ron and I tried to forget about her flashes of animosity. We tried to look ahead, to formulate some serious career plans for Lana, which meant for Ron and me as well. Our plan, which we presented to Lana over lunch one day, was to bring *Murder Among Friends* back to Broadway. We'd thought her ego would compel Lana to jump at the opportunity, but much to our surprise, Lana could not have been more thoroughly *against* the idea. She was able to play relatively short, unpressured runs of plays and make a minimum of five thousand dollars a week; Broadway was a long-term commitment and more pressure than she cared to handle. Ron and I immediately sought to convince Lana that Broadway was not just the next reasonable step in her lustrous career, it was the *only* step. Whereas Lana was no longer an asset to motion pictures, a medium whose primary audience was the teen market, her glamour and fame among the older theatergoers would draw crowds to any stage. Nor had Ron come without ammunition: he'd already canvassed theater managers and was able to recite chapter and verse as to the many who were more than anxious to have Lana on their marquee. Ron had also anticipated Lana's inevitable question of fee. He had scouted around to find out who was making the largest salary on Broadway, which at the time was Yul Brynner in the revival of *The King and I*. His wage was twenty thousand dollars per week plus a hefty percentage of the box office. Ron assured Lana that she'd make no less.

Lana retaliated, as only she could, that money and rekindled fame aside, she did not want to live in New York. But this was the last gasp of a dying argument. The temptation of glory on the Great White Way was a difficult one to ignore. Though Lana is not a person who makes snap decisions, my final argument was the clincher, as I'd intended for it to be: if we were a success, Lana would be a shoo-in for the motion picture version of *Murder Among Friends*, which was sure to follow. Lana perked up visibly, and the three of us shook hands, one for all and all for one like the Musketeers. It would be ridiculous to say that I didn't entertain visions of grandeur. The plan was to have Lana do a one-year run of *Murder Among Friends* in New York. Having established the play as a hit, she would leave the show and return to her Ivory Tower. I would in the meantime have found a replacement, someone like Anne Baxter, to carry on at a lesser salary. That would inflate the producers' profits, guaranteeing Lana, Ron, and me a weekly income of several thousand dollars. If the play was a *huge* hit, Ron and I would form road companies for London, Australia, and wherever else, sharing equally large proceeds from these endeavors. It seemed as if all my years of hard work were finally going to pay off in a big way. I had never dreamed of being a Broadway producer, but here it was being offered on a silver platter.

To say that Ron and I were excited is like calling the space shuttle just another airplane. The two of us held strategy conferences whenever possible, some dealing with finances, others focusing on creative problems. For example, we knew that Lana's Angie was playing well to a suburban Chicago audience, but Ron knew the performance would have to be burnished to the height of haute couture to guarantee acceptance in New York. Neither of us was worried; if anyone could polish an apple like that, it was Lana Turner. No problem seemed insurmountable, not even raising the million-plus dollars we'd need. Lana would be our collateral. I was frankly thrilled with the prospect of at last riding rather than carrying Lana's coattails.

Murder Among Friends was so successful that a few short months after it closed we were back with the show in Chicago playing the Drury Lane Watertower, the third and most prestigious of Tony De Santis's theaters. Not only was it the largest and best equipped, the Watertower was the only house frequented by Chicago's major critics. That made it a do-or-die prelude to our hopes of reaching Broadway. Although New York critics are not swayed by the reviews of out-of-town journalists, a play's reputation works subliminally on any viewer. Few shows are lauded on the road and then panned in New York; conversely, virtually no play that flops on the road will find a Broadway theater willing to light it with a sixty-watt bulb. It was, accordingly, of vital importance that Lana not miss a single curtain. This was the one thing the Broadway operators had told Ron they would not tolerate. They had heard the stories about Lana's tardiness on the road, and they would sooner lose a star than lose an audience. A quick check with Actors Equity would be all they'd need to do us in, since the stage manager is required to file a daily report on exactly what time the curtain goes up and comes down. Hell, I wasn't even certain that *Tony* would continue to put up with Lana's chronic lateness, not in his preeminent theater. I patiently explained this to Lana, explained it more than once, and each time she doggedly replied that she wouldn't be late.

Our summer run opened to extremely strong box office, and the Chicago critics praised Lana's performance, though the play less so. Ron and I were not perturbed by this lopsided reaction. Our plan had always been to sell Lana Turner rather than *Murder Among Friends,* something that would have been impossible had the material been over-powering. The greatest successes by film actresses on Broadway have been with merely serviceable plays: Debbie Reynolds in *Irene,* Lauren Bacall in *Applause,* Katharine Hepburn in *Coco,* and so on. We felt as confident as ever about Broadway—until Lana began behaving once more like Louis B. Mayer's china doll.

Despite the excellent reviews, Ron wanted Lana to begin toning down her performance, exercising the control she would need for Broadway. But Lana was lazy and pre-ferred a broad, almost burlesque parody of the chic sophisti-cate, a characterization that is best described as Martha Raye without the comic flair. Lana listened to Ron and tried to follow suggestions, but I frequently found him sitting back-stage, quite beaten, helplessly rolling his eyes heavenward as he listened to her clumsy delivery. I tried to understand how this woman who was so reliant on directors could be so suddenly thick-skulled; I finally came to realize that she was viewing the play as a movie, something to be rerun precisely, each night, as it was the night before. Once she had mastered the scenes with the director's help, he became less impor-tant. Lana did not seem to see the stage as a liquid medium, one in which an interpretation can change and evolve over the course of time. Exploring these crannies helps to keep the performance fresh, as any seasoned stage actor will tell you; Lana tried to comprehend that, but she was cheating her audience and cheating her own growth as an actress, and she didn't fully realize it. Ron wanted Broadway so badly that he was willing to put up with Lana's fumbling performances. I, however, was not.

Incidentally, I don't believe that Lana would have been quite so insensitive with another director, a John Bowab or a Vincente Minnelli. Ron didn't have their credentials, and as creative as he was, he also didn't have their battle-honed instincts. Few people realize that a director must not only be an artist but a psychologist as well. Lana has done her best work for men of this type, those who inspire her to take chances and at the same time assure her that he and the rest of the cast is rooting for her. Lorne Greene, who played the prosecutor in *Peyton Place*, once described to me over a game of gin rummy the kind of director who could wring a classic performance from Lana.

"Someone like Mark Robson on *Peyton Place*," he said, "a man who would discuss with all his actors not only each role, but the role within the context of each scene, and every scene within the context of the picture. He would stage each scene with meticulous care and run through it once or twice, then film it from so many different angles that you'd think you were making ten complete pictures. We shot it from above and below, from north, south, east, and west. It was a lot of work, but when he intercut all that coverage, the results were exquisite. He also understood the people who worked for him as well as the people he was trying to create on celluloid. An actor can't help but benefit working for a director who cared so much for his coworkers and the film. As a result, he was not a man of confrontation. Even a temperamental actor wouldn't have had a problem with him. If you were doing a bad job, he had a way of telling you that was inoffensive. 'You know,' he'd say, 'that wasn't very good, and I think we can do it better. Let's try.' He'd never tell you something was terrible and take you to task. Or if he *did* have something strong to say, he'd take you aside and do it very quietly. Yet, even though he was a man of decision, he always listened to reason. And if you disagreed with him for a good motive, if there were voracity to your thinking, he'd change his mind. He loved actors and actresses, and that's the best way to get them to work well for you."

The late Mark Robson was a rarity in that way. He certainly had Ron Nash beat in the coddling department. Nevertheless, Ron had damn good ideas and was surely worth listening to, but Lana simply wasn't able to master the character of Angie. Her vision was limited to one perception, and one perception only: that audiences came to gawk at her, not to see a play or revel in the nuances of characterization.

As for her chilly attitude overall, I was able to tolerate that because the people around me were so fine and so

giving. I missed volleying ideas back and forth with her, but
she wasn't the only intellectual partner in town. No, what
irked me was Lana's selfishness where third parties were
concerned, in particular her fellow actors and her audience.
We had been suffering late curtains since day one of this
engagement, and every night Lana would go into an agony of
detail to the company about how she was definitely going to
be up early the next morning and definitely going to be at the
theater a half hour before curtain, as per Equity rules. Come
the following day, every one of her promises was broken. The
curtains became later with each and every performance, and
every delay left Ron and me less hopeful about the prospects
of bringing "Stomach" Turner to Broadway. Fueled by this
looming disappointment, I realized that there was nothing to
lose by playing hardball with Lana, warning her that if she
didn't mend her ways, *Murder Among Friends* would be her
swan song to the stage—as, indeed, it has proven to be.

Our next show was a matinee, and Lana kept the audience waiting for one hour and seven minutes. That is doubtless a record in the annals of live theater. The fact that it was
a matinee made her sin even worse, since these audiences
are primarily senior citizens who come into town on chartered
buses. Only an idiot could fail to recognize that these theatergoers will leave in the face of a considerable delay, since
their buses are due at other functions later in the day. That
Lana is not an idiot made her actions that much more
detestable.

We were in Lana's suite at the Ritz-Carlton Hotel, which
is located in the same complex as the theater. Lana was
calmly applying inconsequential finishing touches to her makeup while the minutes accrued like the links of Jacob Marley's
chain. Despite our *very* early start, despite my entreaties for
greater haste as curtain time approached, Lana played the
game by her self-centered, deliberate rules. I could do
nothing but pace the floor in angry silence, not wanting to
intimidate her to the point of refusing to go on, yet aware
that something had to be done. Every fifteen minutes the
stage manager would phone from the theater, very upset and
justifiably wanting to know when the hell Lana would arrive.
I tried to be diplomatic, but it was a lost cause. Mrs. O'Leary
was more popular in Chicago than Lana at that point.

On this particular day we were finally in the home

stretch, fifteen minutes past curtain but ready to get Lana into her wig. The telephone rang for the fifth or sixth time, and she calmly ordered me not to answer it.

"I think I'd better," I replied. "They deserve as much."

"Don't *answer* it," she repeated, stopping her preparations to stare at me as though I were an imbecile.

I came very close to throwing the damned wig at her and sweeping my arm across the makeup, which was spread out on the table. Instead, without a word, I set the wig aside and answered the phone. The understandably nettled stage manager advised me that two busloads of people had already been given refunds and departed and that no one remaining in the theater was buying the old bromide, "Due to technical difficulties there has been a slight delay. . . ." I suggested that he announce instead, "The performance will be delayed until the bitch who's starring in this play can get her makeup on right." I'm sure he'd have done it if what remained of the theater's reputation were not at stake.

When I returned to the dressing table, Lana didn't say a word to me, nor I to her. We got the wig in place, and well aware of the lateness of the hour, Lana still took time to examine herself in the mirror, back, side, and front. She found to her horror a single strand of her own hair was sticking from beneath the wig, and she reached for the scissors to cut it. She tried the scissors once or twice, snipping away at the air as though trying to annoy the ass off me, before cutting away the offending hair.

My vision was a swirl of red as she rose and we walked to the elevator. We were mute all the while, Lana finally breaking the silence by rasping, "When I tell you *not* to answer a telephone, you *don't* answer it."

Teeth clenched, I growled right back, "In *that* case, you'd better consider getting someone else *not* to answer your phone."

The doors slid open just then, and we rode the crowded elevator without speaking. I was so overwrought and not at all looking forward to facing the cast and management that I had to summon what professionalism remained to keep from trashing my duties and boarding the next plane out of Chicago. Instead, I swallowed my self-respect and set myself up for her final word in the matter. In front of this group of total strangers in the elevator, Lana actually fisted her right hand

and punched me in the chest. It didn't hurt, except in the pride; everyone looked at me as if I were some kind of dog the mistress had decided then and there to housebreak.

The other actors were understandably embarrassed to go on the stage and nervous about the waves of rancor that were sure to radiate through the half-empty house. But they went out and did a wonderful job, for which they were *almost* rewarded at the conclusion of the play when a little old lady sitting in the front row shouted out, loud enough for Lana to hear, "Next time be here when you're supposed to be!"

I felt like shouting, "Hear, hear!" but Lana was not fazed. Assuming the manner of a school marm, she asked the elderly woman to repeat what she had said, loud enough so that everyone could hear. The lady obliged, and Lana smiled, filled with humility and charm. "Yes," she addressed the audience, "I was late, and I apologize. But there are times, ladies and gentlemen, when we *all* have our tummy problems. Today, unfortunately, was one of those days for me. I was having a difficult time getting away from my *commode* to be with you."

The lavatory reference did exactly what Lana had intended it to do, embarrassing the audience into laughter followed by appreciative applause. I could all but hear them thinking, *Despite her suffering she came and did the show. What a trouper!* Lana bowed deeply to the old woman, who was by this time actually being booed by members of the audience.

So much for our rewards in this life.

That afternoon, still incensed and in a quandary about what to do next, I happened to bump into Tony De Santis. Since I was Lana's personal manager, and in essence responsible for "delivering" her on time, I was not spared Tony's dander. He told me that he was considering bringing up Lana on charges with Actors Equity. I couldn't have given him more encouragement if I'd placed the call myself, but my support did not assuage him. He had done everything humanly possible to make our job as easy as it could be. In return, Lana was ungovernable, I was more blow than go, and Tony couldn't even collect insurance on the loss of revenue since Lana hadn't been ill. He didn't bother listening to my apology, and I realized then how Lana was managing to ruin my reputation along with her own. Forget about Broadway;

some day *I* might want to entertain in Chicago, and Tony De
Santis was a guy to have in your corner, not against you. I
went directly upstairs and tried to explain all of this to Lana.
I didn't ask her why she lied to the audience; she'd slathered
the bullshit so thick that to start spooning it away would take
hours. Instead, I simply started spending less and less time
with Lana and more with the other cast members. I did not
quit; that was the easy way out. One way or another I would
find a way to catch Lana red-handed in a lie. It had, sad to
say, reached the point where I really wanted to be there to
say, "I told you so."

Choosing "sides" against Lana was not a simple decision after nine years, regardless of the circumstances that had propelled
me into it. However, each time I found myself softening, each
time the old lovable Lana would briefly surface and my sup-
pressed love for her would struggle against common sense, she'd
manage to do something new to stir me into a frenzy. Her
pièce de résistance came a few days after our matinee row. In
any play or film Lana did, I noted that she singled out one person to dislike for the duration of their working relationship. The
selection was almost arbitrary at first, based on first impression
or some mild offense. However, once she'd made her choice,
she undermined that person with a vengeance. She used this
tactic to force her remaining coworkers to go out of their way to
be supplicatory lest her victim's fate be theirs. This wasn't a
novel tactic; Cecil B. DeMille used to use it to great advantage.
If his star was getting out of line, DeMille would chew out the
actor's hairdresser or double, thus establishing just who was in
charge without offending the star directly. Sinatra was famous
for his tirades as well, though he would usually soften them
by giving the object of his wrath a new Cadillac the following
day. In each case, the tactic was purely calculated. In Lana's
case, I believe that she really *did* come to dislike the person as an individual.

On *Murder Among Friends* Lana's prey was the young
actor who played Ted, her lover. He was a competent player.
Typical of Lana's ploys was the way she used the first scene of
the play to humble him. The scene opened in Angie's darkened
Manhattan penthouse after she and Ted had just made love.
This scene was hopelessly contrived to begin with because
the actor did not have a muscular body, and Lana found it

difficult to play love scenes with anyone she would not have taken to bed in real life. Regardless, shortly after curtain it was necessary for Angie to go offstage for thirty-odd seconds to change, while Ted muttered under his breath, gulped down a drink, and crushed a cigarette. With each performance the half minute would grow longer. Each night, the actor would be forced to improvise more and more while the audience grew impatient. One night, Lana irrevocably lost the respect of each and every member of the cast and crew, not to mention myself. She kept the actor alone onstage for a full three minutes. I had been in the audience, and when Lana finally reappeared, I hurried over to ask the wardrobe girl what had happened. It seems that Lana had slipped into her gown and shoes in plenty of time, but checking herself in the mirror, she noticed a slight smudge of her lipstick from having kissed Ted. She snapped up a tissue and, after completely wiping her lips, took a lipstick from her kit and redid her makeup then and there.

"If I hadn't seen it, I'd never have believed it." The girl shook her head. "I finally said to her, 'Miss Turner, he's *dying* out there,' but all she said was 'Fuck him.'"

Nothing was ever the same after that incident. No one would have anything but the most necessary professional exchanges with Lana, and she honestly, incredibly, couldn't understand why. If Lana was aware that she was committing professional suicide, she seemed remarkably unconcerned. I approached her and said, with all the feeling I could still muster, "Lana, we all know that the most successful negotiators are those who bargain from a position of strength—even if that strength is an illusion, a front. So much of any profession is just game playing. But what you're doing here goes beyond that. You're really losing sight of just how much pull you actually have in this business."

Lana was quiet for a moment and then said, "Two o'clock."

"What?!"

"That's when I'd like you to wake me," she said. With that, Lana presented me with her back and retired.

Chicago was difficult, and our stay there holds but one genuinely fond memory for me. Not only do I recall the event itself with genuine fondness, but it was doubly pleasurable because I was able to use it with Lana as a sign of my resurging independence.

We had been in Chicago for several weeks when columnist Shirley Eder called. A loyal Lana advocate, whom I'd first met on the set of "The Survivors," Shirley was traveling with the musical play *On the Twentieth Century*, which had just arrived from Detroit. She wanted to come up to the suite and visit, and Lana agreed. While Shirley was there, Rock Hudson, who was starring in the musical, called to tell her where to meet him for dinner. I dutifully took the message, and Lana chatted with Rock on the phone.

A few days later, I happened not to feel like sitting around the suite. I went to a movie, and as it was too muggy to mix afterward with the crowds at some bar, I returned to the Ritz-Carlton. As I was heading toward the message desk, I noticed the six-foot-three Rock Hudson strolling across the lobby with a woman I recognized as a member of the local press. Rock's walk is rather Ivy League, proud but casual, and I found it difficult to believe that he was not to the footlights born. He had taken a bit of a pasting for his allegedly stiff portrayal of the hammy Oscar Jaffee in *On the Twentieth Century*, and it was said his singing voice was not up to the part. But, like Lana, I had to admire him for getting on the stage—and in a musical, no less!

The lobby of the hotel is twelve stories above the street, and while I was waiting for my messages, Rock came to ask the desk clerk which elevators would bring the lady to the street level. Before he could turn away, I introduced myself, and Rock smiled genially. In that wonderfully resonant voice, he invited me to join him for a drink once the columnist was safely on her way, and I wasted no time accepting. The three of us went down to the street, where Rock personally hailed a taxi and saw her off.

The lounge of the Ritz-Carlton was practically empty as we settled into a circular booth tucked in a far corner of the room. The young cocktail waitress recognized me from the several times I'd come down with Lana, and she was now *very* impressed to be serving Rock Hudson. We each ordered a tall double scotch and soda, then we fell to discussing the rigors of being on the road. I was impressed to discover that what bothered Rock the most was not the exhausting travel, redundant interviews, or luxurious, but ultimately anonymous, hotel suites. His concerns were purely craft oriented, such as not having a chance to rehearse thoroughly with the different musicians in each city, the disorienting change in acoustics from theater to theater, the fact that variance in stage sizes threw off his timing.

After bringing our second round of drinks, the waitress informed us that we should drink quickly since they were going to be closing in a few minutes.

"Go right ahead," Rock replied.

The girl hesitated before saying sheepishly, "You don't understand, Mr. Hudson. That means we'll have to take away your glasses."

Rock's reply showed me how a really classy individual is able to assert himself without being rude. "No, you don't," he said pleasantly. "When one registers at a hotel, that hotel becomes for a time his home. And in one's home, one does anything he wants. Isn't that true?"

"I—I suppose it is, sir," stammered the girl.

Rock grinned. "Of *course* you may close up the bar and go home. However, Mr. Pero and I will take our drinks into the lobby and finish them there. We'll see that the glasses are returned to you."

There was no arguing with the logic of what he had said or the way he'd said it, nor were there any hurt feelings. In fact, before leaving, the girl asked for Rock's autograph.

We sat in the rattling-huge lobby of the hotel for a half hour, by which time our glasses were empty. Since we were having a great time swapping Tales from the Road, I suggested we continue upstairs, where Rock could help me empty a bottle of scotch I kept for emergencies. He said he was game, and depositing our glasses by the door of the lounge, we retired to my room.

I was already very impressed with Rock, and becoming more so by the minute; I could see why he is so well-liked by everyone in the business. He's devoid of the insecurities that plague so many other actors, and he doesn't talk down to "common folk" the way many stars do. I felt befriended and secure as I filled our glasses. We both fell into overstuffed armchairs and talked for well over an hour. Much later, Rock stood up and announced that he had better go to his suite and get some sleep. He put on his jacket and went fishing for the key, but even after turning the pockets inside out, he was unable to find it. "No matter," he said, his speech slightly slurred. "I'll go to the front desk and get another." We promised to get together again if possible, after which he left.

Chapter Fourteen

I felt quite in control of matters when we reached Southern California, in particular of my resolution to work out the problems with Lana or to leave her. Though she was still swellheaded from her trouble-fraught but nonetheless successful Chicago engagement, being back at the Ivory Tower brought her closer to earth. Without the adoring masses, Lana was her old, enjoyable self once more. But there was a lot of turbulent water under the bridge, and I didn't think I'd be able to simply forget about it. Any thought of departing was put aside not because I presumed things would once again be the way they were but because I was waiting for a time when I would have her fullest attention so that I could read her my list of grievances. I didn't want to cut myself off from her entirely; we'd been through too much and still had a lot to offer one another. However, I was prepared to do so if things didn't improve.

Ironically, Lana forced me into broaching the subject sooner than I had planned—like the very first day I was back at my desk. I overheard her discussing Chicago with her manicurist, and I realized that although her lofty airs had subsided, she really *did* have a warped perception of her own guilt and innocence. I felt a creeping tide of nausea as Lana grandly recounted how the show had been sold out every performance and how she had been letter-perfect. I tried to get back to work, paging through the written and recorded notes I'd made in Chicago; fittingly, my first order of business was to talk to Lana's lawyers about the possibility that we might be sued by Tony De Santis through Actors Equity for the vast sums of money her lateness had cost him. I pushed the notebooks and tape cassettes aside and listened while Lana praised herself through a pedicure. The manicurist fortuitously left at the point where I could literally stand no more; deciding I'd best arrange for a time to discuss my grievances and my plans with Lana, I strode into the living room. She was still examining her newly polished nails when I said as discreetly as possible that sometime during the week I wanted to have a long talk with her. She raised her eyes until they met my own, arching a thin, penciled-in brow as a half smile played across her face. Lana loves a good fight and no doubt felt capable of handling anything I could dish out.

"Why wait?" she asked in a frosty tone. "Let's have it now."

I reluctantly agreed, and we retired to our usual places at the bar. I prepared us both a drink while reassuring Lana that I loved her deeply and always would, no matter what occurred between us. I went on to say that I had overheard her conversation with the manicurist and was surprised at how someone so devoted to honesty could exhibit such incredible disregard for the facts. I explained that although I would not make her look foolish and would publicly back her on any lie she happened to tell, Lana should never presume that she was putting one over on me as well.

I pressed on, reciting a very long, very specific list of complaints about how she had mistreated me, abused the cast, and taken advantage of Tony De Santis in Chicago. Through it all Lana stared directly into my eyes, though the wry smile quickly faded and her jaw hardened with defiance as she was made to hear facts that did not please her. When I had finished, there was a tense but not unexpected silence, but I made no effort to apologize or to soften anything I'd said.

Lana finally looked away and after lengthy consideration regarded me and softly asked, "You're going to leave me, aren't you?"

"I don't want to," I answered truthfully. "But my job is to deliver a product on time and to the customer's satisfaction. The product happens to be Lana Turner. Since it's obvious I can't do that, I've no choice but to find another product I *can* deliver. I'll stay as long as you like, in whatever capacity you like—but as long as you deny me the chance to do my job to the best of my ability, I will not even attempt that job."

Lana said that she understood what I was telling her, then she requested time to give it some thought. I agreed, of course, feeling very good about the way my impromptu speech had gone. I was confident we could orchestrate an orderly, amicable understanding. I clung to that hope. There was still enough love on which to build something rewarding and even exquisite as long as it was as equals.

In the meantime, there was business to attend to. Apart from defusing Tony De Santis's suit, we had to consider a proposal submitted by Phil Sinclair, the young man who had organized the fateful San Francisco junket during which Dante had left Lana. Phil had been packaging popular tributes to stars like Jane Russell in the Bay Area; and now his dream was to put together a touring show to honor Lana, in much the same format as the Town Hall gala assembled by John Springer. Phil had been biding his time, waiting until he had had enough of these things under his belt before contacting Lana.

Phil's a good fellow and was not looking for personal gain in any of this, the money beyond expenses being earmarked for various charities. His real motive, being a Lana Turner freak, was to get her name and face into national magazines such as *People* and *Newsweek,* to help boost her Broadway or film career. I was all for this, and enough time had passed since Town Hall that Lana might consider involving herself in lesser spectacles. Phil and I worked out a tentative schedule to present to Lana.

For two days following my talk with Lana, nothing was said about that conversation. She was polite and businesslike, though nothing more; I was neither disappointed nor offended, having been preoccupied with catching up on accumulated work and, frankly, having become somewhat inured by the way she had treated me in Chicago. It's analogous to taking small doses of arsenic until you become immune to the poison. Besides, there was a sense of inevitability: come what may, I reasoned that she might not change her stripes sufficiently to undo the damage that had been wrought. With my expectations so low, it was difficult for her to disappoint me.

Finally, on the third day, Lana stopped me beside the

bumper pool table. "I've been thinking about what you told me," she said in a neutral voice that hinted nothing of what was to come. "I want you to know, Taylor, that in all the years I've been in this business, *nobody* has ever spoken to me like that."

I was surprised at her latest display of tunnel vision but composed enough to say, "I'm sorry if you were offended by the truth."

I could literally *feel* the indignation as it rose from her gut and infused her voice. Lana all but demanded a retraction.

"I've no reason to apologize," I offered, "just as I've *every* reason to believe you when you say no one has ever said the things I did. If they had, you might not be in the position you are now. You've lost a producer, alienated a city, cost yourself Broadway, and disillusioned your manager to the point where he's on the verge of taking a hike. All of us can't be crazy."

Like Denver in the spring, the clouds blew at once from Lana's face. In classic schizophrenic fashion, she became a sunny little girl warming up to me with charm and pouty innocence. "Taylor," she cooed, "you *know* I need you if I decide to do this tour for Phil Sinclair. Won't you stay with me, at least through this, and then we can talk about your future?"

"And what about your future?" I asked. "If you accept this tour, and if you act up with all kinds of press in attendance, you're going to put your career in the ground once and for all."

It was as if Lana hadn't heard a word I'd said. "Yes, I know," she said peremptorily, tuned in to one goal and one goal only as if this were Monopoly and nothing existed on the board except for the deed she wanted. "That's why I *need* you. Do I have your promise that you'll stay with me through the tour? At *least* do that for me."

I told her I wanted carte blanche to do whatever might be necessary to ensure the success of the tour; she granted it, willingly. I told her that at the first sign of lateness I was leaving; she replied she'd pay for my ticket out of town. I told her that while I'd take the heat for her, the way I had in the past, I expected her to return the favor by at least *defending* my actions and preserving my fragile ego against the likes of the kept-man jokes she had found so amusing in recent months. Lana promised all this and more, and while I had grave doubts, I couldn't be a bastard for the sake of this important tour. I told Lana that after nearly a decade, I'd gamble on her one more time. I smiled down into her hazel eyes and then took her gently in my arms.

Phil Sinclair was delighted when I called with word that Lana had decided to go ahead with the project. I immediately presented to Lana the plans we had blocked out, and when she approved them, Phil began reserving the dates in question at the most prestigious halls he could book. The date for the opening tribute would be November 5 at the Warfield Theater in San Francisco; simultaneously, Phil petitioned the mayor's office to have that day proclaimed Lana Turner Day. Phil also informed us that his friend Lia Belli, the wife of attorney Melvin Belli, would be lending her time and contacts to the project, as well as traveling with us. Lana became suddenly *very* enthused with what was clearly going to be a first-class operation, and she had Mary Rose create a new wardrobe for the first six-city tour—a different gown for each stop.

Plans fell neatly into place, and Phil flew from San Francisco to personally discuss the tour with us. I knew he was concerned about how we had held him up ten years before, but I guaranteed over drinks at the Century Plaza Hotel that I had Lana's permission to throttle her if she were not pleasant, cooperative, and above all punctual. Phil was somewhat relieved, then proceeded to ask one of the strangest questions I'd heard in quite some time.

"Will Lana want to have someone lay her every night?"

It was several seconds before I could lift my lower jaw from the floor and blurt, "My God, *no!* Jesus, Phil, why would you even *think* that?"

"Because I had an actress insist on that once," he replied. "She refused to come to her own tribute unless I promised that she would get boffed by a different guy every night. I'm asking just because I don't like surprises."

I didn't give a goddamn about his surprises. I promised that that wouldn't be a problem with Lana, then I urged him to reveal who the horny lady had been. He refused to talk, and threats of physical violence failed to loosen his tongue. I begged him but my pleas, too, fell upon deaf ears.

It's a whopping understatement to say that Lana was thrilled when tickets to her event sold out within hours of having gone on sale and when San Francisco's Mayor Feinstein indeed declared the fifth of November as Lana Turner Day. Never in the history of that city had an actress been so honored. I'm sure that Lia Belli had a great deal to do with influencing Her Honor, but it was delightful all the same. Lana took it in stride, actually living up to her word by remaining demure and as kind as could be toward me during the gearing-up period.

I was thrilled for Lana's sake by the publicity windfall, though I admit being more intrigued by the fact that through the Bellis we'd be traveling in some rarified social circles. We'd be meeting dignitaries and members of the social upper crust wherever we went, contacts that could only do Lana a world of good.

The commencement of the tour was not an auspicious one, though for once it wasn't Lana's fault. When we were settled in San Francisco, I happened to pick up a copy of the local newspaper and, as is my custom, turned to the entertainment section. I was surprised to see a large photograph of Phil beside an article about the tribute. No one had called to interview Lana, and I found it difficult to believe that someone had bothered to do a front-page article based solely on ancient data gleaned from the morgue. The answer came swiftly and horribly as I read the piece, every syllable of which caused my hair to curl. I had known that Phil was enthusiastic, but in the interview he had overdone it. In his haste to create an exotic aura surrounding Lana—as if it were a quality not indigenous to the star—he said such things as, "Turner has several residences. You should see her at her mansion in Malibu. She's quite the star. She goes for a walk on the beach every day, and a ray of sunshine never touches her skin. She has these muscular Mexicans who look like Nubian slaves, and they walk alongside her with big umbrellas. Her figure is still sensational, and she walks with her bosoms out. She wears dark sunglasses studded with diamonds. She's a blond vision, like something out of a Fellini movie. She doesn't want anyone to recognize her, but everyone on the beach says, 'There goes Lana.'"

It was stuff that would be considered extreme even for Greta Garbo! I didn't show the article to Lana, of course, but as soon as I could get to a telephone out of earshot of Lana, I phoned Phil. We agreed to meet at a coffee shop, and leaving under the pretext of going to visit my mother, I hurried to our rendezvous. There, I gave Phil the severest verbal thrashing I'd ever laid on anyone. He tried to interrupt, but I wouldn't have it; I tore onward, concluding that if Lana ever found out about the rubbish he'd spun, she'd cancel the tour in a flash. He honestly couldn't understand why I was upset, and I realized that to Phil, Lana Turner lives a fantasy life; so *what* if some of the details were "off a bit," as he described them. There was no way that I could convince him not to continue giving out this kind of absurd information, and I demanded that we contact Lia Belli.

We phoned, and after Lia heard me out she graciously suggested that the two of us come right out to the house. I felt uncomfortable intruding on time reserved for Lia and her husband, but circumstance had left me no alternative. We drove to the ultrafashionable Pacific Heights section of town, and Lia herself answered the door of the mansion. A beautiful, young, statuesque woman, she ushered us into a grand living room that offered a view of all of San Francisco, including Alcatraz and the Golden Gate Bridge.

Melvin Belli has a reputation for being one of the most influential men in the United States, indeed in all the world. He is the only American attorney permitted to maintain an office in Moscow. Ironically, Belli was also the lawyer who represented Johnny Stompanato's young son in the suit brought against Lana after the murder. Naturally, I was prepared to meet a man of imposing if not frightening stature. Instead, Melvin Belli proved to be a cheerful, almost jolly man of imposing *girth*, who waved us over to the television, thrilled to have someone to whom he could recount the plot of *King Solomon's Mines*. He filled us in while we sat around and watched Stewart Granger and Deborah Kerr battling a wave of natives. After a minute or two, Lia suggested that it might be better if she, Phil, and I adjourned to the formal dining room for our exchange. As we rose, her husband, this earth-mover and man of extraordinary power, this figure who brings corporate giants and international potentates to their knees, said from behind a severely wounded expression, "Doesn't anyone want to stay and watch the Watusi?"

Lia was of immeasurable help getting my point across to

Phil. Her tack was to argue that there was certainly no need
to fabricate stories about one of the most colorful lives ever
chronicled and that it might just be better in any case to let
Lana do these interviews personally. Phil argued that he was
just giving the public what it wanted, and Lia counseled that
he would be wiser to give Lana what *she* wanted. As I was
her spokesperson, that meant giving me what *I* wanted. We
eventually agreed that I would desist ranting about the article
and somehow keep it from Lana and that Phil would give no
more interviews of *any* kind to anybody.

As Phil and I drove away, I tuned out his blather and
reminded myself how I used to think that nothing on earth
could be more objectionable than an overzealous publicist on
a film or play. They schedule interviews for press releases
with timing that is uniformly inconvenient, and they arrange
press functions, luncheons, and junkets that are more often
than not disorganized as hell; the one-on-one interviews are
often no better, set up with people who haven't bothered to
see the play or the film and as a result ask questions that are
unenthusiastic and ignorant. However, far worse than these
overpaid trucklers is an overzealous *fan*. I'd formerly criticized Lana for keeping at arm's length from her admirers, but
I understood now why that was necessary. If you encourage
them a little, they start up a correspondence. If you encourage them a lot, they try to arrange tributes for you. If you
encourage them more, they take that as a dispensation of
priesthood and begin canonizing their own versions of your
life.

Of the many difficulties we faced prior to the tour, the
most rewarding was the selection of a charity to benefit from
the money earned by the tributes. Phil said that Jane Russell
had had it easy, since she had founded the organization WAIF,
which provides food, clothing, and the like for orphans around
the world. Lana also wanted to do something for children;
our problem was that most children's organizations already
had celebrity spokespersons. That did not preclude others
signing up as well, though there are egos to consider
beyond the cause. Happily, there was "Bean Sprouts," a fledg-
ling television series about Chinese-American children. Produced by the Children's Television Project and cosponsored
by the Association of Chinese Teachers and Chinese for

Affirmative Action, "Bean Sprouts" seemed a worthwhile and prestigious program. Without bothering to watch the show, Lana had agreed to help it out, and Phil sent us all the available literature. After all, we wanted Lana to be able to speak intelligently about her "favorite charity." Many people openly supposed that Lana was simply capitalizing on the well-known fact that the public loves stars who lend their time and energy to children. That was not the case, however, Lana's motivation being that *no* child should be denied anything an adult has the power to give him or her. It's a pity the Chinese-American kids never made a nickel due to the absolute chaos that was about to be unleashed.

The itinerary for the tour was diverse and exciting. After the kickoff in San Francisco, we were off to New Orleans, Miami, Atlanta, Washington, D.C., and Honolulu— the latter in time to spend Thanksgiving with Cheryl, Josh, and Gran. Phil even managed to make slight amends for his earlier blunder by contacting a representative of Elizabeth Taylor, who was now the wife of Senator John Warner and the cream of Washington society. Though Elizabeth was presently off in the Orient, she said that she would try to cut short her visit by two days in order to host a Washington reception for her onetime MGM colleague. If due to some last-minute glitch she was unable to return, Vice-President Walter Mondale and his wife Joan would be thrilled to do the honors. The vice-president was even quoted as saying that, for inspiration during World War II, he had carried around a picture of Lana while fighting in the trenches.

Because of our tight schedule, the public relations firm handling our tour arranged for telephone interviews between the reporters in the next town and me. That way I could answer any superficial questions they might have. As Lana said in sanctioning this arrangement, "Hell, Taylor, you know more about my life than anybody." During these interviews I also managed to drop the information that we expected to be Broadway-bound within a year— I've always clung to dreams, even as they were evaporating right before my eyes—and I filled the reporters in on "Bean Sprouts," trying to sound as if Lana had been boosting the show for years. More importantly, while I spoke with each journalist, I would scribble notes for Lana's use during the subsequent personal interviews. These follow-up calls were necessary so that the reporter could accurately write that he had gotten the story from Lana's own lips. The terse profiles I gave to Lana worked wonders in her hands. Armed with such information as, "He speaks with a Southern drawl," she would be prepared to remark at once what a delightful accent he had, charming the pants off him to get a favorable story. Subtle bribery of this sort is not unique to Lana, though she is its nonpareil master.

On the night of November 5, Lana was slated to arrive at the Warfield Theater at eight. At 7:45, Phil called us at the Stanford Court Hotel to report that there was a mob of fans and photographers anxiously awaiting Lana's arrival, was I sure we'd be there in time? I looked at my watch. I stole a glance at Lana who, though a tad behind, seemed to be making good time. I told Phil that there was no way we'd make it on the hour but to keep the red carpet clean; we'd be no more than fifteen minutes late. I hung up the phone and gently reminded Lana about the time. She apologized sincerely for taking so long—and didn't increase her pace one iota. I told myself I was being paranoid, that Lana hadn't suckered me into going on this tour just so she could deliver a royal coup de grâce, lateness at every conceivable turn. She couldn't *possibly* be that calculating or mean.

I swore silently as 8:00 came and went, then 8:15, and finally 8:30. Lana seemed to be going *slower* with each passing minute, though I was sure that, too, was my imagination. With a sickening sense of déjà vu, I began to receive nervous telephone calls from Phil and then from Lia. They told me that several reporters had already departed, and that if we were any later, we wouldn't get the full spectrum of national coverage that the public relations people had so meticulously arranged and that formed the foundation of all the regional coverage to follow. I pointed all of this out to Lana, who said, "But I'm *hurrying*, Taylor dear." What I took that to mean was, "Punctuality is for trains and accountants. I'm not going to be bound by such restrictions."

By nine o'clock an exasperated Phil called to say that they were going to start the film clips without Lana. We had wanted her to make a brief but grand appearance *first* to juice up the audience, but that was not to be.

Calling upon my so-called powers of attorney, I informed Lana that if she weren't ready in ten minutes, I was going to dismiss the limousine and we'd have to go by cab. She said that I was free to cancel the car, but in that case she'd cancel her appearance. My bluff had been called, and I sincerely wanted to play out my hand. I knew that if I *didn't*, my credibility with Lana was going to be shot to hell; I recognized that if I *did*, it would take months for Lia to clean the egg off her face. Accordingly, I took a generous bite of crow and threw myself against the wall to brood and wait.

Lana and I finally arrived at the theater at fifteen minutes to ten; the hundreds of onlookers had dwindled to exactly six photographers and less than two dozen fans. Lana later blamed this embarrassing minithrong on the public relations people for not having properly publicized the event, never believing that there were *ever* any more onlookers than she herself saw. As we entered the Warfield, the unspooling of the film was abruptly halted to enable a spotlight to follow Queen Lana down the aisle to her seat. The audience served up a cheering, standing ovation while Lana beamed at her subjects, waving and blowing little kisses. Before turning to face the screen, she gave me a fulsome, I-told-you-so grin that set my blood boiling. I never told her, since she'd never have believed it, but Lia later confided that the audience had been so angry before the show, convinced that Lana wasn't going to appear, that she and Phil had actually feared for her safety. They were surprised but relieved when Lana was instantly forgiven the moment she entered the auditorium. What made the Catch-22 worse from my point of view was that Lana *knew* she could do that to an audience, and she was convinced that it actually added to her mystique: it takes time to descend from Olympus, you know.

The spotlight was doused when the divine derriere had snuggled into its seat, and we watched the remainder of the film clips. Afterward, Phil conducted a brief interview with Lana onstage. The show was followed by a reception at the Belli mansion, where several hundred people would have the privilege of enjoying a buffet dinner and a drink with Lana. They had paid twenty-five dollars apiece for the honor, and of course Her Highness wanted to give them their money's worth: before making her entrance, Lana scored a double play, making a *second* crowd wait in one evening while she used the master bedroom powder room to freshen her make-up. Meanwhile, Melvin Belli came up to congratulate Lana on the success of the evening. He seemed to harbor no bitterness, though I was sorely tempted to ask if he had taped *King Solomon's Mines*, since I'd rather have watched the film than been with Lana. Instead, the attorney took a moment to show us one of his proudest possessions, a massive four-poster bed that had belonged to Errol Flynn, one of the first beds ever to sport a mirrored canopy.

Melvin himself escorted Lana to the congregation below, and Lana spent several minutes at the bottom of the great curved staircase greeting people and shaking hands. After-ward, we retired to the living room, where Lana continued to dazzle the guests with her regal mien and satin-smooth voice. She seemed to be having a grand time, and when we finally left in the small hours of the morning, Lana invited several people back to the hotel for a post-party celebration. That proved to be the most enjoyable part of the evening, since Lana was by this time quite relaxed and had everyone in stitches with incredible anecdotes. I played the amenable cohost, though inside I was filled with red-hot anger. Helped along by alcohol, I reveled in thinking vile thoughts about Lana: Cliff Robertson telling me that she was often so drunk on the set of *Love Has Many Faces* that they could only shoot her close-ups for an hour each morning ("Why didn't you shoot her face?" Kirk Douglas asks Barry Sullivan in *The Bad and the Beautiful*. "She was too drunk," was the prophetic reply); Alex Singer confiding that this self-professed divinity was tremulous with doubt and in need of constant reassur-ance while making that film; one of her producers allowing that he'd sent a double to Maine for exterior scenes in *Peyton Place* because Lana indolently refused to go herself. I was angry with her and with myself for being pulled along by the nose yet again. I accepted the painful truth that she didn't give a shit about me, that she held onto me because I was efficient and because I was convenient. Of course she hadn't defended me when Jim Pappas and others had called me *kept*—she earnestly believed it. She relished it. Now she was rubbing my face in it.

I was going to get off this mad merry-go-round. For Lia's sake, I'd wait until the instant the last tribute had ended; I couldn't in all good conscience leave that good woman to the mercy of such a self-devoted dowager. But as soon as the tour was over, it would be cold turkey—so long, Lana. Right then and there I started counting the hours, like a kid looking forward to summer vacation.

Chapter Fifteen

We missed the plane to New Orleans by three minutes.

Lana had puttered us into lateness once again, and she sealed our fate by demanding a wheelchair at the terminal, even though we were pressed for time. Lana held American Airlines culpable when we reached the gate and found our plane halfway down the runway. By her reckoning, as we flew the airline whenever possible, they should have had the courtesy to hold the plane.

The airline attendants were as accommodating as possible, hurriedly placing us with another carrier. This would necessitate a stopover in Houston and a change of planes, but we might reach New Orleans in time for the press conference Lia had scheduled for early evening.

Because of the recent, tragic plane crash in Chicago, Lana had instructed me never again to book her on a DC-10. Naturally, the Houston-bound aircraft was a DC-10. Lia had flown ahead to make sure that all was in readiness; they had extended such superhuman effort that I was not about to have Lana miss tonight's press conference because of irrational fears. I decided to lie—telling Lana, when she asked upon boarding, that this was an L1011, then racing to our seats, plunging my hand into the seat pocket, and ripping away the card that tells you more than you care to know about the plane. Alas, once we were taxiing, some turkey across the aisle slipped the card from his seat and began reading along with the flight attendant. I'd never seen *anyone* do that, and just as naturally Lana happened to look in his direction and notice the big red letters that announced the pedigree of our airplane. She said nothing at the time, waiting until we had landed safely in Houston before assailing me. I was pushing her wheelchair to the gate for our connection when she looked back and said, "You lied to me."

I felt like saying, "So what? You lied to me," but instead played dumb. "Why Lana," asked I, "what do you mean?"

"Come *off* it, Taylor. You knew that plane was a DC-10. You *lied* to me."

"All right," I 'fessed up, "I lied." Not wanting to belabor the issue, I added, "Anyway, it's a little late for repercussions, and this is not the place to make a scene."

Scowling, Lana stepped from her wheelchair and walked the rest of the distance to the second plane, which, mercifully, was a Boeing. She refused to hold my hand as was our custom during takeoff, and she didn't speak to me during the entire trip. I couldn't have cared less, since in my present state of agitation a double scotch was all the company I required.

Our flight was late arriving, and the press conference had to be called off. However, Lia had managed to persuade a half dozen reporters to stop by the Hilton Hotel for an interview with Miss Turner in her suite. When we reached the hotel, Lia immediately apprised us of the change in plans. Lana was not thrilled to be having total strangers up to her sanctum sanctorum, but she went along for the good of the tribute. Unfortunately, while cataloguing the luggage that had gone before us, I discovered that one of Lana's larger suitcases was missing, the one with the furs and gowns. I tried to conceal this fact from her, but she overheard me asking one of the porters if this was everything that belonged to our room. Lana went absolutely berserk. While Lia, Phil, and I stood there, Lana began screeching at each of us in turn, yelling that she was canceling the remainder of the tour, starting with tonight's interview.

Lia, a sea of tranquillity, refused to be intimidated. She smiled benignly at Lana and, without saying a word, went to the phone and called the airline. No one had bothered to do that, and Lia discovered that the suitcase was there, being held for us under lock and key. Phil Sinclair hastened to our limousine and rode out to retrieve the luggage, while Lia explained how silly it had been for Lana to get upset over something that happens to travelers every day.

"Not to *me* it doesn't," was Lana's callow reply.

Lia managed to calm Lana sufficiently to agree to do the press conference, which came together on time only because Lana did not bother with eye makeup, choosing to hide behind dark glasses. As any journalist will tell you, there is nothing more irritating than not being able to see a subject's eyes. Remarkably, she was otherwise accommodating, and all the articles turned out quite favorably.

The turnout for the New Orleans tribute was disappointing. Though Lana had recovered from her bout of nastiness, her natural allure played to a house that was less than half full. After the tribute, we went to the French Quarter for a night on the town. It was the last time Lana and I would share an evening of fun and relaxation.

The next stop on our tour was Miami and the Frank Sinatra Suite at the Fountainbleau Hotel—a suite so named because it's Frank's abode whenever he's in town. The suite is really something to write home about. The lower level alone is awesome, white marble floors leading to a sprawling living room with a bar, all of it overlooking the Atlantic Ocean sixteen stories below. Off the living room is a study with a full-sized billiard table and giant projection television; adjacent is a formal dining area and, of course, a complete kitchen. To reach the upstairs bedrooms, of which there are five, one must climb a curved black marble staircase. Each room is appointed with the plushness one would expect of Frank Sinatra.

In spite of our bright, opulent surroundings, the day of the tribute proved to be the darkest of my life. Through her gossipy hairdresser, Lana learned that ticket sales were dismal, with less than a quarter of the seats sold. I can't say I was surprised. Our transportation and board were costing so much that there was very little money left over for advertising. San Francisco was the one exception, since it was the Bellis' home; the other cities were expected to generate interest via the interviews and word of mouth. That hadn't happened in New Orleans, and it sure wasn't happening here.

Lana's hairdresser was a lisping, sassy, mincing boy, the kind of tulip who gives hairdressers a bad name. That bothered me, but his penchant for whispering to Lana behind my back riled me even more. Hearing from him about the ticket sales, Lana called me into her dressing room while he fixed her snowy tresses.

"I'm told our box office is slow," she droned in a voice like poured concrete, thick enough to bury me.

I responded truthfully. "We expect a last-minute surge when the rest of the phone interviews you did appear in the afternoon papers."

"I hope so," the hairdresser put in. "It would be a shame for a star of Lana's stature to appear before anything less than a full house."

"We're doing our best to ensure that that *doesn't* happen," I answered through grinding teeth.

"You're *not*," Lana shot back. "If people knew I was here, those tickets would be sold!"

I don't think Lana actually believed that; I think she was daring me to respond otherwise. Reiterating that everything possible was being done, and pointing out that Lia's reputation was also on the line, I left the suite and burned off my indignation by padding up and down the hallway. Before long, the hairdresser emerged to go to the beach. His appearance, as they say, was just what the doctor ordered.

He grinned at me, and though I'm not by nature a violent man, I grabbed the prancing bean pole by his shirt collar and slammed him against the wall. "Listen, you son of a bitch. Your one and only function is to take care of Lana's hair. When it comes to publicity, strategy, box office, or for that matter ordering fucking *room service*, you're to keep your fat, goddamn mouth *shut!*"

"I only told her the truth," he simpered, "that there hasn't been enough publicity. I don't want her to be embarrassed by an empty house."

"No one does, asshole! But we're not talking ego, we're talking *obligation!*" My face inches from his, I had to check myself to keep from ripping out his throat with my teeth. "She made a promise, and she's going to live up to it. Which means, fuckhead, I'll trouble you not to ruin things with your flapping lips! Do we *understand* each other?"

The young man nodded nervously, scurrying away when I released him. I stood staring at the wall for several long minutes, huffing off residual anger. Though I felt better for having roughed up the little shit, the damage was done. I felt certain we were soon to see the pattern I'd witnessed so often when one of Lana's plays was not sold to near capacity.

Sure enough, when I returned to the suite, though Lana

was beginning to apply her makeup, she kept excusing herself to go to the bathroom. Each time Lana returned, she would complain of ever more severe stomach cramps. Her trips to the bathroom became more frequent, and after an hour I had to face the fact that Lana Turner Night in Miami was not to be. Oh, the audience arrived as scheduled, filling a quarter of the house, and the excerpt reel was duly begun. Lana didn't respond to my pleas about her fans or the organizers. Instead, she pleaded sickness and lay in bed while the evening fell apart. Nothing I could do or say convinced her to pull herself together and put in even a token appearance, just to wave at the audience and blow those fucking little kisses of hers and *forget* about the questions. Thus, as the film clips were nearing their conclusion and Lia called from the auditorium to inquire when the Grand Dame would be arriving, I had no option but to report, "She's not."

Cool under most circumstances, Lia was utterly dumbfounded. "You mean she's not going to be on time," Lia said hopefully.

"No, I mean that she's not coming."

"Taylor," Lia implored, "you've got to make her change her mind! Throw her fur coat on her and put dark glasses on her if you have to, but *get her here!*"

I explained that I'd tried every argument in my extensive Lana Turner repertoire, and that short of kidnapping her, what Lia had asked was impossible.

"Here's one you *haven't* tried," she said in dead earnest. "There are press people here who are claiming that the whole thing is a *fraud*. They don't even believe that Lana's in town!" I was not hurt by her wrath and was actually glad that she had somewhere to spew it. Lia had been working hard to make everything as smooth as possible and deserved better than this, just as Tony De Santis had deserved better than what he got.

"Well," she said, "we'll have to return everybody's money, and when we're through paying for the hall, I'm sure 'Bean Sprouts' will owe *us* money. Meanwhile, get a doctor up there and have him examine her. We'll need that when we make a statement to the press about how she was too ill to appear."

I promised Lia it would be taken care of. Lana, of course, steadfastly refused to have an unfamiliar medic examine her precious person. I snidely opined that Dr. Mac didn't make house calls east of the Rockies, adding that she might find a lawsuit slightly more oppressive than an examination by a local physician. Impressed by my logic, Lana grudgingly agreed to allow someone to look at her. A kindly old gentleman was sent up, and after taking Lana's pulse and checking her respiration, he did indeed prescribe something—Gatorade. He could find nothing wrong with her, save for a touch of exhaustion that was due to improper nutrition. Luckily, fudging the details of his "prescription," the doctor's visit was sufficient to get us off the hook with the press. Lana was actually pleased with the way things had developed. Instead of limiting herself to vodka and cranberry or papaya juice, she quickly discovered the joys of vodka and Gatorade.

The following morning, with the empress still abed, Phil, Lia, and I conferred over breakfast about the future of the tour. Foremost among our concerns was Washington and the embarrassment we'd all suffer if Lana canceled on Senator and Mrs. Warner or the vice-president. We decided to drop all but the Atlanta date where, thanks to an entertainment front-page newspaper story, ticket sales seemed brisk. As for Honolulu, I actually took sardonic joy in canning it. The only reason Phil had arranged it in the first place was as a courtesy to Lana. To hell with that.

When I informed Lana of our unanimous decision, she saved face by telling me that we had read her mind but that she would like to cancel Atlanta as well. Personally, I couldn't have cared less, though I pointed out that Lia had put considerable effort into a reception there. In the wake of the previous night's fiasco, keeping this one commitment was the least Lana could do. She promised to consider it during her bleach, then left with her hairdresser for a nearby salon—which I'd rented so she would not have to mingle with other ladies.

It was there that I received an urgent call from my ex-wife Sharon. She managed between sobs to tell me that our seventeen-year-old daughter Maylo had cleaned out her closets and run away from home. Sharon had no idea where she was, or with whom.

My first reaction was abject helplessness. I had known for some time that my daughter was unhappy, and I'd presumed it was due to the difficulty she was experiencing in launching her acting career. I didn't know then that it was Sharon's live-in boyfriend who drove my daughter away, demanding that she wait on him hand and foot even though she worked harder than he. Unaware of the whys and wherefores, here I was three thousand miles away catering to an ego-bloated peacock instead of being with someone who *really* needed me.

My second reaction was surprise that Maylo hadn't called me. She had always done so when trouble loomed; I could only presume that something truly awful was afoot. In a frenzy, I phoned the front desk and demanded they search for the message from Maylo that *must* be there. I always made a point of giving her my complete itinerary, and she never hesitated to avail herself of it even when I was in Europe or in the Orient with Johnny Mathis. But there was no message. I begged the clerk to look again.

My third reaction, and the most punishing of all, was that clearly I'd failed her. Maylo must have assumed that Lana Turner was more important than she was. That was a joke, obviously, but how could *she* know that? We hadn't had a good heart-to-heart in months. Travel had helped to ruin my marriage; maybe it had finally undermined what I thought was a solid, very honest relationship with my daughter as well.

I couldn't shut out the thought that perhaps if I'd been in LA, she might have come to me; not that it mattered, since I'd be on a plane soon enough.

I told Lana what had transpired, and her features clouded with concern; she genuinely liked my daughter.

I advised her that I wanted to leave at once for Los Angeles, to which she replied succinctly that I was out of my mind. "You don't even know where to look," she scolded.

I sniffled. "Maybe she just wants to know that I care enough to drop what I'm doing and—"

"Honey," Lana interrupted, "if she doesn't know by now that you care, nothing is going to change that." I began drinking scotch after scotch. Lana said she was going to call Sharon to get another reading of the situation. I began to

protest, but I was more loaded than I thought, and the words
came out garbled. Feeling dazed, and glad to have someone
else take charge of this mess, I mixed a vodka and Gatorade
for Lana and followed her up the staircase. I left her with the
drink and went to my room while she phoned.

A few minutes later, Lana and her hairdresser stormed
into my room. "All right," Lana began, "I've spoken to
Sharon, and I'm going to tell you *exactly* what happened to
your daughter."

Now I was bound to be unusually thin-skinned due to
the day's events and the amount of liquor with which I'd
embalmed myself. But there is no doubt in my mind that
Lana's voice had lost its gloss of concern.

"I know what goes through a young girl's mind," she
announced, "and I think your daughter has run away with her
boyfriend and he is going to turn her into a prostitute. Sharon
told me he's been trying to get Maylo to sleep with his
friends for a long time, and now she's going to *do* it."

Like a child, I stood miserably beside the bed and took
Lana's punishing remarks, burying my face in my hands as
she spat out her prophecy. I started to cry as images of my
baby flooded my brain, mingled with loathing of a faceless
boyfriend—and a very vivid, very clear picture of Lana.
Shivering, I began to howl, a long, continuous sound that
came from a part of me I'd never heard nor seen, a naked and
defenseless nerve that was the soul of me. I didn't care who
heard me or what they did to try and quiet me; I was
oblivious to everything except the picture that Lana had
painted, an awful portrait of my daughter being abused—
framed by Lana's vicious delivery, the way she seemed *glad*
to see me suffering so.

With tears streaming down my face, I began screaming
that I didn't want to live, wanted only peace at any cost. Just
then, my hand happened to come to rest on something at my
side. I didn't bother to see what it was, just threw it across
the bedroom with all the force I could muster. It shattered a
huge picture window, most of the pane falling in large chunks
to the carpet. In the same motion, I scooped up a heavy
ashtray, and while Lana and her hairdresser ran from the
room, I sent the ceramic piece flying out the window.

Still venting my fury, I stumbled over to the broken

window and began punching and scratching at the jagged fragments that remained upright. I saw blood on the glass, didn't realize I'd been cut, and didn't really care; my attention was riveted to the cement path seventeen stories below. I felt a near irresistible desire to hurl myself into the night, to smash myself completely on the pavement, to suffer the purging pain that would lead me to sweet oblivion. What prevented me from jumping seems silly now, but in my disturbed state it rang with authority and stayed me from releasing my grip on the frame. Echoes of a very strict Catholic upbringing jolted me with the reminder that someone who took his own life would spend an eternity in hell. As I thought about the nuns, about my youth, about less dismal times, that focus helped me to get a handle on my actions. I realized where I was, what I was prepared to do, and how excessive it all was. I stopped clawing at the window, stepped back, and stood in a pile of broken glass. I looked down, saw blood on the white carpet, held my hands before me, and examined the few cuts I'd sustained. As if reminded of my mortality, of the fact that as little help as I was to Maylo now, I'd be less help dead, I turned from the jagged window.

By this time I had expended all of my energy, and was possessed by a remarkable calm, I walked slowly into Lana's room. I remember thinking, oddly, that even sex had never relaxed me quite so much as my outburst. As I entered Lana's room I found her sitting on the bed with her hairdresser. He was trying to comfort her—*her*, for Christ's sake! I couldn't understand why Lana needed to be consoled. All she had done was to light the fuse and enjoy the fireworks.

"I'll have to pay for it," I said quietly. "I'll have to pay to replace the window." It sounded like a line from Steinbeck, worrying about a pie you left on the sill while your house is being destroyed by a duststorm; one of those human-focus lines, though I didn't feel like I was playing a scene.

Lana's eyes lowered to my hands, and noticing the blood, she went to get a washcloth. Numb, I sat on the bed and allowed her to minister to the gashes; it was the first time in a decade that Lana had ever tended to *me*. All it took was a nervous breakdown. I thanked the stone-quiet Lana for her concern, then wandered back to my room. Swallowing a Dalmane and a Valium and washing them down with more scotch, I switched off the light and left my misery behind.

I was dragged from a very deep sleep by the fresh ocean breeze gusting through the broken window. I lay in bed not wanting to move a muscle, wishing I could remain so blissfully peaceful forever. Instead, tiny fragments of the horrible night before began creeping into my mind like ants, festering until my thoughts were black with them. I opened my eyes. The brilliant Florida sun hit me like a hammer, and up for less than a minute and already in need of a pain-killer, I reached for the scotch. As I did so, I drank in, instead, the carnage inebriation had helped me to wreak the night before. I pushed the glass away and then allowed my head to flop back on the pillow.

I couldn't believe any of this had really happened and felt twice damned because of the shameful way I'd handled it. To say to me that I could have sold my soul and had my daughter safe and the wreckage undone would have been to offer me a bargain. I was no longer the terrified father of the previous evening, I was a frightened little boy. However, I knew that a child could not deal with the problems that lay ahead, so I swung my feet to the floor and tried to get a grip on myself. I had Lana to thank for the impetus to do so, since my first coherent thought was how she had pushed me into this and how I detested her for it—for last night and for the night before, for the months before that and the ten years previous. I realized that Lana had never loved me the way I loved her, that she was incapable of loving anyone except herself. It had taken ten years to recognize that deception, so skillful is she at her craft.

I shuddered when I considered next what Lia would think when she learned about my tantrum. But it was too late for remorse. If she gave a damn about me, as I prayed she did, she would understand and help me face the consequences. Somehow, I suspected she would.

I walked unsteadily toward the bathroom to brush my teeth, which seemed a good place to start the day. As I stood in the doorway and surveyed the damage, I realized that my shoulder bag was nowhere to be seen. My stomach churned with the dim recollection that it had been the first thing I threw out the window. I must admit finding it pretty damn amusing that my first wanton flourish had cost me not only emotionally but materially as well, since a great deal of cash, my checkbook, Lana's credit cards, and some of my diamond jewelry had been inside the bag.

Pulling on some clothes, I raced downstairs and searched the walkway and foliage directly beneath my window. Nothing. I kept looking for a quarter hour, after which I decided to hell with the bag. I'd let Lana worry about her fucking cards, and, as for my own possessions, they didn't seem to matter that much.

I arranged a phone call with Lia, and much to my relief, she was not only sympathetic to my plight but promised to smooth things over with the hotel, legally and financially. She asked if I planned to return to Los Angeles, and considering it now with a clear head, I decided to stay with the abbreviated tour. In her coldhearted bluntness, Lana had been right about one thing: there was nothing I could do for my daughter just then. In contrast, there *might* be something I could do for Lia pertinent to Atlanta.

Lana slept most of the day away, while the hairdresser went happily off to the beach. I called Lana's business office in Los Angeles and notified them of her "missing" credit cards. I spent most of the day waiting for word about Maylo, but with no results. As the afternoon was turning to early evening, Lana got up. She said very little about what had happened the night before, dismissing it as "drunkenness," though I could tell she didn't mean it. Even with my daughter missing, the most urgent line of conversation between us was about finishing the tour in Atlanta. She steadfastly refused to go, on the grounds that she was in poor health and didn't want to arrive in Los Angeles in a pine box. She said that she needed rest right where she was— Atlanta and Lia be damned.

The following morning under my bedroom door I found a note hastily scrawled in Lana's own hand. It read, "Taylor, dear . . . at 2:00 A.M. had diarrhea. I had been struggling with the thought that perhaps I could make it to Atlanta. Now, I know I *can not*, even more so because I am weak. I'm writing this note to you at 3:40 A.M., so you can tell Lia early that it is impossible, and don't anybody twist me around again. Please wake me at 3 P.M. this afternoon." The declaration bore the following postscript: "This is my last word on the damned project!!!"

Lia realized that nothing shy of a miracle could get Lana to Atlanta. However, she told me she was going ahead all the same and that I should try my damnedest to change Lana's mind. I informed Lia that I wouldn't let her down; was, in fact, prepared to lie my brains out, telling Lana that two of Hollywood's hottest young directors would be in the audience to talk to her after the show about a new film. Lia thanked me; I reciprocated *most* sincerely and hung up.

Madam was awakened precisely at 3:00, and I told her I'd made two plane reservations, one to Los Angeles, one to Atlanta. The choice was hers. She listened but was simply trying to appease me lest she trigger another outburst. This feeling of circumspection was reinforced when not once during the day did Lana allow herself to be alone with me. Most of the time she kept her fluff-brained hairdresser by her side, which was exactly the treatment I'd have ordained in any event.

Matter-of-factly bringing up the Atlanta tribute, I told Lana that in spite of her letter she should reconsider. Lana mechanically refused, but I forged ahead all the same. For one thing, I said, aside from her obligation to "Bean Sprouts" she owed the Belli Foundation at least a chance to break even through the box-office receipts in Atlanta. For another, a second no-show would encourage further talk of professional misconduct, gossip that was sure to endanger any future work in *any* medium. Of the two appeals, the second obviously had the greater impact on Lana. She heard me out, after which there was a long silence while she stared at the floor and considered her options.

"All right," she said at last, "I'll go to Atlanta."

What Lana meant, of course, was exactly what she had said. She would *go* to Atlanta. There, if ticket sales warranted, she would condescend to appear at the theater. Regardless, I viewed her concession as a battle won. The fact that I'd been able to put aside other distractions and string together a logical argument would have been victory enough, but the fact that Lana *agreed* with me was sheer glory.

Chapter Sixteen

Everyone was delighted that Lana had come to Atlanta, though we knew that this homestretch would be the most difficult part of the tour. We checked into the VIP Suite of the Hilton Hotel, where Lia used her own room as a command post, making last-minute arrangements for Lana's final tribute.

The flight from Miami had been darkened by the seamy presence of a reporter from the *National Enquirer*. The magazine was home-based in Florida, and having heard about Lana's no-show in Miami, they must have sensed there was muck to rake. Unknown to any of us, the reporter slyly placed a tape recorder beneath Lana's seat in an effort to capture her in-flight conversation.

I had not been sitting next to Lana—her choice, not my own—and it wasn't until the plane landed that we learned what had happened from a passenger who had been seated next to the reporter. We thought at first that the good fellow was joking, that sort of skulduggery having gone out with Richard Nixon. But a glance at the man in question revealed him busy packing up a typewriter and a tape recorder and looking as guilty as hell.

Lana saw red and, storming at the culprit, began assaulting him as he tried in haste to deplane. All I could think of was an unfortunate photo that had made front pages the world over when Rita Hayworth was in a similar situation. Seeking to avoid that kind of publicity, I convinced Lana to let the crew handle the matter. Still bubbling mad, she backed off while the captain was summoned by an obliging stewardess.

Our pilot was most understanding, though he explained that he could not do as Lana was insisting, that is confiscate the man's tape machine. This was a civil matter, and it would have to be pursued in court, not on a 727. Hearing that, the reporter squeezed past us and was gone. Lana swore to get even with him, twice as angry now for having been stymied. Even worse, upon arriving at the Hilton, we discovered that the selfsame journalist had finagled a room next to our suite. We notified the management and had him moved to another room, although they refused Lana's demand that he be exiled to another floor entirely. The reporter proved a fairly harmless annoyance after all, though he gave Lana something else to carp about in her unyielding efforts to make everyone's life miserable.

The tribute was held at the World Congress Center, and, against our hopes and expectations, only two hundred people showed up. We later learned that the small turnout was due to the fact that Lana had canceled an Atlanta play date once before. That, plus advance word of her exploits in Miami, caused most people to doubt she would actually show up. Ironically, we were early by Lana's standards. When I saw that we were running late, I phoned Lia and told her to pause for an intermission between each of the film reels. This gave us an extra twenty-odd minutes, enough time to reach the hall just as the last clip was ending.

Angry at Lana as I was, I surprised myself by instinctively laboring to preserve her goddess image, fawning like a eunuch in the service of the sultana. As she walked onstage, I noticed that the management had provided her with nothing more imposing than a cushionless Samsonite folding chair. Scooping up Lana's floor-length white mink, I quietly walked around the spotlight and draped her coat over the chair. As I was tiptoeing off, Lana turned and seemed puzzled to see me there; before her confusion could blossom to indignation, I smiled and said, "May you always sit on nothing but mink." Lana picked up on my meaning and was so pleased that she introduced me to the audience—as her secretary, of course. No matter. The photos taken during the question-and-answer session make Lana look like an angel perched on a cloud.

With the house lights turned as low as possible—Phil did not want Lana to see how small the turnout had been—Lana fielded a flurry of questions and exited to enthusiastic applause. Afterward, we made our way to a restaurant reception where a larger crowd had paid fifty dollars per person to partake of an unthinkably late supper with Miss Turner. We stayed only for an hour; the guests would have done better having bagged a sandwich and gone to the tribute.

We left the restaurant and, with our friends Tim and Ede Goodwin and Phil Sinclair made for our hotel's swinging disco. Lia did not join us, heading straight for her room to get ready for the following morning's departure. I'm sure she was quite glad to be done with this whole matter of Lana Turner tributes. Our party was shown to a booth enclosed in beveled glass where, once the small door was shut, I felt slightly claustrophobic. But it was worth being encapsulated, since we could actually hold a conversation in the midst of the musical tumult, and none of the other patrons was able to bother us. Lana commented that she didn't give a damn about the accommodations as long as she could get a strong drink and do some dancing.

In true Turner tradition we closed the disco, whereupon Lana was disappointed to learn that nothing else was open in all of Atlanta. We were forced to go back to the suite, where after a while the party dwindled to just Lana and me. Even her hairdresser had had the decency to retire.

Neither of us was totally drunk, but that didn't prevent us from giggling like schoolchildren. I cherished these minutes of abandon, time that allowed me to shake off the clinging nightmare of Miami and for a moment free my mind from recurrent fears about my daughter. I helped Lana out of her gown, and it was just like the old days, teasing and joking and having a great time. I fell onto the bed while Lana removed her jewelry, and I couldn't help telling her how gorgeous she looked. It was, God help me, the absolute truth. The Atlanta newspapers would describe her as "dazzling," but that's a stage presence. Here, under room light, she was simply a beautiful and desirable woman. I reminded myself that she was also the woman who had taken me on the maddest roller-coaster ride of my life. I couldn't understand why the very sight of her didn't fill me with shuddering and aversion—unless it was because I still loved her. Like any thrill ride, life with Lana had its peaks and chasms, with curves that caused intermittent laughter and sorrow. But beyond the harsh words and clash of wills, in the lulls, the quiet moments, there *was* love.

I'm sure that when I asked Lana to marry me she

thought that my proposal was inspired by scotch rather than by devotion, but she was very dear about it just the same. "No, Taylor," she said, "you and I will never marry. I never want to go through that again."

I was not about to give up and argued that I was different from the others, that I had already survived ten years with her. I suggested that if we could take that final step, become husband and wife, become *equals* again, we'd once more be the happy, fun-loving couple that had built such pleasant memories together. But Lana obviously didn't want equality, and I was gently rebuffed for a second time.

I was disappointed but undaunted; I was also dead in my shoes and decided to let the matter lay for now. It was four o'clock in the morning, and I excused myself to go upstairs to my room. Fearing that I was too tipsy and might break my neck on the steps, Lana told me that I should stay with her instead. Her concern seemed specious in light of how she had helped me get a leg up on suicide two nights before, and I suspect she simply didn't want me incapacitated before I could escort her back to the Ivory Tower. That wasn't the motivating force I felt at the time, however; having just been shot down in matrimonial flames, I was frankly too self-conscious to remain. I thanked her for the offer, but I continued toward the stairs. Lana began yelling that I was too drunk, and I snarled back that I was perfectly capable of ascending the single flight. Lana remarked that she hoped my disability was paid up, and, the battle lines drawn, the mood flew from romance to bitch-fight in nothing flat. Lana dredged up every oath and put-down at her command, and I fought her in kind; insults about our sex life and her professional talent, financial holdings, and spiritual assets filled the air like fan-blown confetti. Then Lana got onto the subject of Maylo, and though I responded with chapter and verse regarding Lana's own success in child rearing, my wound was too fresh to take the salt. Afraid now that I'd kill Lana, I realized the only way to prevent homicide was to get Lia in on this. I called her, and the poor woman raced to our suite. By this time, Lana was carrying on full steam about the havoc I'd caused in Miami, I was shouting back about how she had propelled me into that fracas, and Lia saw that she would need an extra body to restore order. Phil came right up and proposed that he find me a separate room, to which I readily consented. It so happened that the room directly across the hall was available, and after showing Lana that I could walk a straight line from one room to the next, I fell face down on the bed. My last conscious thought was to wonder whether I could, in fact, have made it up the stairs.

I awoke the following morning when Phil called to tell me that I'd best get up if we were going to catch our plane. I thanked him for the call and for his help the night before, and I began anticipating the return to Los Angeles.

I felt Lana would keep at arm's length from me, though I was not prepared for the reception I got as I ambled through the double door of my bedroom. Like some quaint family portrait, Lana was sitting in a large, cushioned chair surrounded by her hairdresser, Phil, and Phil's assistant. I could not help noticing the hairdresser's look of delight and Phil's contrastingly forlorn expression. I knew at once that Lana was going to play a scene for them, and I resolved that if I didn't care for the tone, she would play it alone.

Lana's voice was very steady but gentle, and she did not beat around the bush. "Taylor," she began, "I have already spoken to Jess Morgan, and he will be sending you a check in the mail."

That was it.

Short take, I thought. But then, Lana was seldom capable of sustaining a lengthy scene. What she was telling me, of course, was that I'd been fired. But Lana had made one mistake: there was no script. I'd play this drama the way *I* wanted.

My voice was almost jovial as I replied, "That's fine with me. Now if you'll excuse me, I have to relieve my bladder."

That obviously wasn't what I was supposed to have said, and Lana had no retort. She had probably wanted to lecture me about my behavior, about how I should learn respect for an employer, about how lax I'd *always* been in my responsibilities, about how she had kept me around only because of her compassion for underprivileged secretaries. I smiled because not only hadn't I given her a chance to say any of that but because I didn't have to listen to it even if she did.

When I returned, Phil and his aide were gone. I subsequently learned that Lana had fully expected me to go manic on her and had wanted them there for protection. Her hairdresser was still present, however, grinning behind her back like the Cheshire cat. It was a pleasure to ignore him as well.

"There are some items in your attaché case that I'll need," Lana continued, "those that you managed not to lose. May I have them, please?"

"Of course." Grinning, I wasted no time handing over her keys, plane ticket, and traveler's checks before going to change. As I did so, I realized that I'd actually been fired, relieved of my unwieldy responsibilities. Good God, I didn't have to *look* at her if I didn't want to! As the saying goes, there was nowhere to go but up, and I determined not to let anything spoil the delicious options that the future suddenly held for me. My love for her had held me from doing this long ago; her love for her had finally made it possible.

I sang as I packed my large suitcase, loud enough to drown out any audible signs of her presence. I was about ready to leave through the bedroom's private exit when I heard the hairdresser call to me from the foot of the stairs.

"Taylor?"

"Yes?"

"Lana would like to say something to you."

"Tell her to go right ahead."

"Would you come down, please?"

"Lana knows where I am," I replied.

I could hear the two of them gasp at my impudence, shock followed by hurried, whispered conversation between Rosencrantz and Guildenstern. I couldn't imagine what they were saying, nor could I have cared. As I slipped my fur coat over my shoulders and snapped my luggage shut, Lana broke from the huddle. "Taylor?" she chimed.

"Yes?"

With all the soppy melodrama she could summon Lana said, "I want you to know that I will always be praying for you."

Her words made my stomach turn. There was nothing intelligent to respond, and I wasn't even convinced that she merited a reply. After ten years, I'd earned better than a brief dialogue that had ranged from the disgusting to the silly. Gathering up my things, I opened the door. As I stepped into

the hallway, I heard her scream at the top of her lungs,
". . . And I don't think you're even *listening* to me!"

For once, Lana was one hundred percent correct.

I went directly to the hotel's VIP lobby, where I dialed
Lia and told her what had transpired. She informed me that
Lana had asked that she and her hairdresser be allowed
another day in Atlanta, which was fine with me. We decided
that I would drive to the airport with Lia, Phil, and Phil's
assistant. Not just travel but *drive* ourselves. Lana could have
the limousine: We'd rent a station wagon and have some fun.

I spent the intervening hour munching complimentary
sandwiches and feeling very good about myself. I also used
the time to phone Sharon, who told me that while there had
been no word about Maylo, the police were checking out my
daughter's haunts and would probably come up with a lead or
two. That reassured me somewhat, making my morning all
the brighter. Thus, when we had all assembled, we were a
happy little band indeed, eager to get home to our relatively
sane lives.

Phil seemed confident that Lana would want me to come
back to her. However, I explained that not only would she
never admit having made a mistake in firing me, but also *I*
had no desire to return to a servile place in anyone's life. Phil
would not be persuaded, remarking, "Leave her with that
bubblehead for a few days, and she'll be begging for you to
come back." I answered that their catty, complementary
natures had the makings of a long-term, successfully one-
sided relationship.

The instant I arrived at my modest but wonderfully
homey West Hollywood apartment, I called my ex-wife Sharon
for a progress report. It was less encouraging than I'd have
liked. Maylo hadn't contacted anyone, nor had the police
unearthed any leads. I resigned myself to shedding a few
more tears before this nightmare ended, but at least I was
there if and when my girl needed me.

The following day, I was rather surprised to receive a call
from Lana's hairdresser, informing me that they were back
from Atlanta. I could almost *see* Lana hovering nearby, and I
suspected that Phil was right after all—he was calling so that
Lana could try to squeeze a few extra months from me.

I hung up.

Shortly thereafter, Jess Morgan called to tell me that I could pick up my personal belongings whenever it was convenient at the reception desk of the Ivory Tower. When I made it over a few days later, I found a note attached to the top of the box. It was handwritten and read, "Nov. 19, 1979. Taylor—this box contains everything that Carmen and I could find belonging to you—I hope nothing is missing—if so write me a note—!" It was signed, "Lana." The same day I received a missive from Jess, which was no more endearing: "This letter serves as official notice that as of November 16, 1979, your services as secretary to Miss Lana Turner have been terminated as per her instructions and for cause." Enclosed was a check signed by Lana. My salary was by this time eight hundred dollars a week, but the pretax amount of this check was six hundred dollars. The actual net sum was $305.22, and when I told my mother, she had the perfect capper: "What was the twenty-two cents for?"

Now that I'd been officially and for cause "terminated," I decided I'd be as businesslike as the forces of Jess Morgan and Company. Going through my datebooks, I discovered that I had nine weeks of vacation back pay due to me. I hadn't taken this holiday time because we were either on the road or making a movie, and I explained all of this in a detailed letter to Jess. I didn't mention any dollar amount but suggested, "I understand that you will want to confer with Lana about this, and I'm sure that she will be fair." Jess's reply: "I have reviewed this matter with Lana Turner. Vacation time was available to you should you have chosen to take it. Therefore, I fell (sic) that no additional compensation is due you." Although the amount came to a few thousand dollars and I could have taken my claim to the State Labor Board for settlement, I considered the source and let it go.

Epilogue

Ten years.

I loved Lana, and I stayed through thick and thin for the same reason as Carmen had for thirty years, her former makeup man Del Armstrong for twenty-three, her onetime hairdresser Helen Young literally until her untimely death. We all stayed, not because we were particularly well paid for the awesome duties we performed but because Lana makes people believe that she's totally dependent on them. You feel like family. There's nothing wrong in that, and it's a benefit I wish every wage earner could enjoy. Yet, despite the girlish laugh, the flirtatious coquette, your self-described "best friend" and confidante, Lana Turner is the ultimate user and manipulator of people. Accordingly, she discards people, friends and husbands alike, when she has no further use for them. I remember what Jack Freeman had told me before I went on my first interview with Lana. *When she puts her trust in someone, she'd rather deal with a flawed "known" than an unknown.* Convenience, not love. That's all I, or anyone else, has ever meant to Lana. What she really doesn't understand, however, is that being done with Lana Turner is not the same as being done with life.

THE PRIVATE LIVES
BEHIND PUBLIC FACES

These biographies and autobiographies tell the
personal stories of well-known figures,
recounting the triumphs and tragedies of their
public and private lives.

☐	20805	**ALWAYS, LANA** Pero and Rovin	$3.50
☐	01712	**CONSEQUENCES** Margaret Trudeau	$3.50
☐	13592	**CHANGING** Liv Ullman	$2.75
☐	20563	**END OF THE RAINBOW** Mary Ann Crenshaw	$3.50
☐	14129	**ALL ABOUT ELVIS** Worth & Tamerius	$3.95
☐	20704	**BURIED ALIVE: The Biography of Janis Joplin** Myra Friedman	$3.95
☐	20416	**HAYWIRE** Brooke Hayward	$3.25
☐	22613	**ELIZABETH TAYLOR: HER LIFE, HER LOVES, HER FUTURE** R. Waterbury with G. Arceri	$3.50
☐	01334	**'SCUSE ME WHILE I KISS THE SKY** David Henderson	$8.95
☐	13824	**ELVIS: PORTRAIT OF A FRIEND** Lackers & Smith	$2.95
☐	14076	**JOAN CRAWFORD: A Biography** Bob Thomas	$3.50
☐	20756	**MONTGOMERY CLIFT: A Biography** Patricia Bosworth	$3.95
☐	01329	**COMPLETE BEATLES—** Deliah Communications	$39.95
☐	13030	**SOPHIA: Living and Loving: Her Own Story** A. E. Hotchner	$2.75
☐	20121	**STRAWBERRY FIELDS FOREVER John Lennon Remembered** Garbarine & Cullman	$2.95
☐	14038	**RAGING BULL** LaMotta with Carter	$2.50
☐	20857	**AN UNFINISHED WOMAN** Lillian Hellman	$3.50

Buy them at your local bookstore or use this handy coupon:

Bantam Books, Inc., Dept BG, 414 East Golf Road, Des Plaines, Ill. 60016

Please send me the books I have checked above. I am enclosing $_____
(please add $1.25 to cover postage and handling). Send check or money order
—no cash or C.O.D.'s please.

Mr/Mrs/Miss_____

Address_____

City_____ State/Zip_____

BG—11/82

Please allow four to six weeks for delivery. This offer expires 5/83.

THE LATEST BOOKS IN THE BANTAM BESTSELLING TRADITION

☐	22577	**EMPIRE** Patricia Matthews w/Clayton Matthews	$3.50
☐	22687	**THE TRUE BRIDE** Thomas Altman	$2.95
☐	22686	**THE PATRIOTS** Robert E. Wall	$3.50
☐	22582	**A BOOK OF RUTH** Syrell Rogovin Leahy	$2.95
☐	22704	**THE SISTERHOOD** Michael Palmer	$3.50
☐	20901	**TRADE WIND** M. M. Kaye	$3.95
☐	20833	**A WOMAN OF TWO CONTINENTS** Pixie Burger	$3.50
☐	01368	**EMBERS OF DAWN** Patricia Matthews (A Large Format book)	$6.95
☐	20921	**TANAMERA** Noel Baker	$3.95
☐	20029	**CIRCLE OF LOVE** Syrell Leahy	$2.50
☐	20559	**TOMAHAWK** Donald Clayton Porter	$3.50
☐	22613	**ELIZABETH TAYLOR: Her Life, Her Loves, Her Future** Ruth Waterbury w/Gene Arceri	$3.50
☐	20026	**COME POUR THE WINE** Cynthia Freeman	$3.95
☐	22775	**THE CLAN OF THE CAVE BEAR** Jean M. Auel	$3.95
☐	20664	**THE GLITTERING HARVEST** Maisie Mosco	$3.50
☐	05006	**ZEMINDAR** Valerie Fitzgerald (Hardcover)	$19.95
☐	14142	**A WOMAN'S AGE** Rachel Billington	$3.50
☐	22719	**FROM THE BITTERLAND** Maisie Mosco	$3.50
☐	20106	**SCATTERED SEED** Maisie Mosco	$2.95

Buy them at your local bookstore or use this handy coupon:

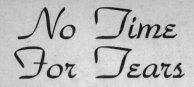

"I fell in love with these women's story . . . if you like family sagas, do yourself a favor and read *Traditions*."

—Cynthia Freeman, author of *No Time for Tears*

by Alan Ebert
with Janice Rotchstein

Through love and loss . . . through tragedy and triumph . . . through three remarkable generations . . . they were a proud family bound by *TRADITIONS*.

Read *TRADITIONS*, on sale December 15, 1982, wherever Bantam paperbacks are sold or use this handy coupon for ordering:

We Deliver!
And So Do These Bestsellers.